D1168222

To Vegas and Back

A Memoir by Suzanne R. Krauss

CHANGING LIVES PRESS

Changing Lives Press
50 Public Square #1600
Cleveland, OH 44113
www.changinglivespress.com

Library of Congress Cataloging-in-Publication Data is available through the Library of Congress.

ISBN-13: 978-0-9894529-3-9

Editor: Shari Johnson
Cover design: Asami Designs
Interior design: Gary A. Rosenberg

Printed in the United States of America

10   9   8   7   6   5   4   3   2   1

Contents

Part III

Part IV

To my family.

Do not go where the path may lead,
go instead where there is no path and leave a trail.

—RALPH WALDO EMERSON

Author's Note

In an effort to write this book as honestly and factually as possible, in addition to my own memories I relied on the memories of my mother, sister, and select family members. I have recreated the dialogue from my mother's showgirl days to bring those fascinating experiences to life. I used my personal journal for recapping and consolidating dialogue with my therapist. To ensure confidentiality, some names have been changed. If you see your likeness in a character and my mother, sister, or I don't know you, rest assured it is not you.

Our story is graphic—there was no way to sugarcoat it and retain the integrity. My hope is that by the time you finish this book, you will see the silver lining. If your story is like ours, or worse, I hope you will be encouraged to get the help you need to sort it out and leave it behind you—don't let the years that robbed you of your past rob you of your future.

Prologue

I was quietly playing in my bedroom with my rescue dog, Daisy, when the vicious screaming began. I picked her up and ran to the corner that was farthest from the door. I sat there and hugged my boney knees to my chest. My long, dark, straggly hair covered my face to protect me from whatever was happening outside my room. Daisy licked my hands, comforting me as I tightened into a human ball.

At church that Sunday I had learned that God was always listening. I called on every holy name I could remember, "Jesus, Lord, God, Holy One." Then I called on the names I remembered from my Jewish summer camp, "Adonai, Elohim, HaShem—whoever is listening, please make him stop." I rocked back and forth, wondering if I had confused the Gods by calling on them all at once. I listened to the hateful words echo off the hallway walls and make their way into my room. "You bitch! Whore! Bastard kike! I am going to kill you, Olivia!"

Each word felt like an assault. I had to see what was going on. I hesitantly got up and walked toward my doorway. Daisy followed, but I told her to sit and stay. I walked down the long cream-carpeted hallway that led to my older sister Rani's room. It was empty.

She slept at a friend's house most nights, so it was wishful thinking that she would be home. I hesitated for a moment to look at the mess of her favorite albums scattered on the floor: Ted Nugent, Elton John, Tommy. I then tiptoed toward the screaming and entered the spacious terra-cotta tiled front hall.

Thankfully, Rani was there. She was standing with her back to me, her six-foot-tall frame obstructing my view. I carefully came around to her side, staying as close to her as possible. I saw Paul sitting on top of Mom, straddling her long, thin torso—and then I saw a gun on the floor. I gasped, but no one heard me or even turned to look. I could see Mom's long, athletic legs kicking to break loose from his hold—her white stilettos kicking on the red tile floor. I moved to the other side of my sister to get a better look, my hands never leaving her waist as I crept around her. Paul had his large hands around Mom's neck.

"You mother-fucking whore! I am going to kill you!"

I looked down at my beautiful mom. Her always-stylish red hair was damp from tears and sweat. Her impeccably tailored white suit was now wrinkled and pulled open, exposing her large, braless bosom. Her flawless face was barely recognizable with blotchy red spots and tearstains. My breath hitched as our hazel eyes met—mine wide with fear, hers bulging and red. I saw the resignation etched in her face—she had finally been defeated. After six long years, our final fate would be to witness her death by this heinous monster.

I glanced at the large window adjacent from us and caught the reflection of my sister and me. It was the first time I had ever seen us side by side; I was less than half her size—a five-years-younger miniature. I tried to gain her attention with my eyes. I desperately willed her to look at me, but she was frozen erect with her fists clenched at her sides. My face contorted at the thought of the newspaper headline: "Vegas Showgirl Strangled to Death—Children by Her Side."

Part I

CHAPTER ONE

New York City,
October 1996—Suzanne

The ringing was intolerable. My heart raced in time with the relentless noise as I bolted upward in bed. I looked to the far bedside table and the angry-looking red numbers read 2:25. I nudged Bradley, my boyfriend, who was fast asleep.

"Bradley, get up. Turn off the alarm. I can't stand it!"

He groggily opened his eyes and said he didn't hear anything. He looked at the clock and reminded me that it was 2:25 in the morning. He was asleep seconds later. I put my hands over my ears. The ringing was excruciatingly loud—and only in my head?

I got out of bed and then froze as I felt my blood slowly drain from the top of my head to the tips of my fingers. I cautiously looked at my feet, confirming that I wasn't standing in a pool of my own blood. I felt cold and prickly, as though every nerve ending were exposed. I walked over to my half-open bedroom window and peered down. I opened the window a bit farther and stuck my head out to see fourteen floors down to the city street. I placed both of my hands on the windowsill and grasped it so tightly my knuckles turned white. I wanted to jump—I felt I had to jump, but instead stumbled backward, eyeing my window as if it were a mortal enemy. When I bumped into my bed, I quickly spun around, ran out of my room and headed for the bathroom. My legs were trembling, and I grasped the walls to keep my balance. Something was terribly wrong with me.

In my six-by-six-foot bathroom, I splashed water on my face and looked up at my reflection in the mirror. My tired eyes looked back at me, revealing nothing other than the traces of black kohl eyeliner I had worn for my brother's wedding in Vegas just thirty hours earlier. I couldn't tolerate the irritation of my long hair brushing against my back and arms. I grabbed a black elastic band and hastily threw the thick mass up on top of my head. I thought maybe I was simply dehydrated from the daylong Sunday flight. But then I pensively took another look at myself and watched as my face lost color and perspiration broke out on my forehead. I was not dehydrated. I was pretty certain that I was going mad.

I felt that the walls of my small bathroom were closing in on me. I was cold, but sweating; heart racing, but I wasn't moving. I collapsed on the closed toilet seat. I had to focus on a happy place. Happy place, happy place . . . the past weekend in Vegas, Todd's wedding, happy place . . .

My mom, my sister Rani, and I had not been in Vegas together since we fled in June of 1979. My entire east coast family had gathered at the Mirage Hotel and Casino for my brother's wedding.

During our visit, Rani had the brilliant idea to get our rental car and visit our former home. The handsome casino valet addressed my mom with a dazzling grin and bedroom eyes, "Do you need directions anywhere?" Rani grabbed the keys from him and said, "We got it. We used to live here."

I playfully punched my mom in the arm. "I mean, that guy was twenty years old and basically asked you to go to bed with him!" We all laughed as Rani drove the white compact Dodge down Las Vegas Boulevard. The farther away we got from the strip, the more unfamiliar the territory was. What we remembered as a one-stoplight town with an endless sea of desert and cactus was now an endless sea of stoplights, housing communities and strip malls. I sat quietly in the backseat, looking out the window while my sister and mother chatted breezily about how much had changed since we left.

Fifteen minutes later we were in front of Sierra Vista, our former gated community. I peered between the two front seats to get a better look. Instead of a simple sign and two stone pillars at the entry, there was now a gatekeeper. This very large gatekeeper sat inside a small white security booth. It was clear that no one could get in without getting past him. He looked pissed at the sight of us.

Rani pulled alongside Mr. Gatekeeper and explained that we had lived here seventeen years ago and wanted to drive by our former home. He looked at her, then at my mom and me, as if we were vagabonds who crawled out from Sin City's underground tunnels.

"Absolutely not." He informed Rani that we could only enter with the permission of a Sierra Vista homeowner.

"Pffft," my mom said as she leaned over, her head practically in Rani's lap. "Hi, sir, my name is Olivia and these are my daughters. I used to be a showgirl at the Tropicana when we lived here in 1975. We drove all the way out here from the strip. My son is getting married later today and we only have half an hour."

The man replied with a comparable, "Pffft!" I had to agree that this wasn't a valiant effort. What did he care that her son was getting married or that she was a former showgirl? He probably thought she was in some trashy, booby burlesque.

Mom continued, "We made this special trip just to see our former home. Please?"

Then Rani said, flashing her 1,000-watt smile, "With a cherry on top?"

He was clearly aggravated with us and scintillating humor was not going to work. My sister gently pushed Mom out of her lap and opened her wallet. She handed him her license and her Costco membership card. "Please, sir. We will be back in ten minutes."

He looked at the license and without making eye contact, handed her back her Costco card. "Ten minutes."

The gates parted and we were in.

It took less than a minute to get to our former cul-de-sac. Once Rani turned onto our street, I saw the A-frame house that Frank Sinatra built before we moved here, but never lived in. It sat at the far end of the street, just across from ours. Seconds later we pulled in front of our former house—the last Vegas home we lived in. It looked just like it had years ago. It was a sprawling, single-story ranch house, every inch of it still painted dark brown. The six-foot-tall wood fence still stood prominently, providing the ultimate in backyard privacy.

We sat looking at the house in silence.

We were ten feet from the carriage driveway where my sister and I had stood hand in hand seventeen years earlier. We were waiting for our mother to get home, and when she did, Rani yelled, "We are leaving today! With you or without you!"

As we lingered, I sat frozen, hugging my knees to my chest. The only audible noise was the sound of Rani chewing her thumbnail. We were all watching a different version of the same horror movie.

I felt myself lose my balance on the car seat and said louder than I intended, "Rani, let's go!"

———

I had dozed off, unconsciously hugging my knees. I fell from my perch on the toilet seat and hit the tiled floor with a painful thud. I narrowly missed hitting my head on the porcelain sink. I was literally knocked out of my "happy place."

I scrambled to my feet and walked through the short hallway to the den. The cold wood floor under my feet was a welcome respite from the heat that radiated from my body. My New York corner apartment's six sets of windows stared at me. *Arggh!* I gasped for air. *Damn windows!*

I tripped over the sofa as it dawned on me to look up "anxiety." I grabbed the dictionary:

anx-i-e-ty (ang-zi'i-te) n. 1. A state of uneasiness and apprehension. 2. A state of intense, often disabling apprehension.

Aha! I had successfully diagnosed myself! I was in "a state of uneasiness and apprehension." I just couldn't understand what caused it.

I had to get out of the apartment and down to ground level. I pulled on a pair of sweatpants, ran out into the hallway and down fourteen flights of stairs—at this point I was afraid of getting stuck in the elevator.

The lobby's glass doors were wide open and welcomed me with a cool breeze. I staggered for a moment, taking in the cool air, and then bolted forward, stopping within inches of my tall, grinning Colombian doorman. I let out a big "humph," stepped sideways and let myself fall onto one of the two oversized black leather sofas in our sparse, clean, wood-paneled lobby.

I said, a bit too enthusiastically for three a.m., "How's it going, Carmen?"

He replied with a laugh, "Not bad. You?"

I sighed.

"Wanna cookie? Mr. Jacobs on the fourth floor gave me a box of gag fortune cookies. Looks like you could use one."

Yes, that was just what I needed! A good Chinese proverb to give me a spiritual uplifting.

He tossed the cookie into my hands. I tore open the cellophane wrapping, broke the cookie and pulled out the small slip of paper: *I can't help you. I am just a little cookie.*

"What? You must be kidding!"

"But it's funny, right?"

I sank into the sofa and said flatly, "Funny on any night but tonight, Carmen."

I knew he thought I was a tenant gone mad, but I didn't care. Regardless of the heartless fortune, my little trip to the lobby helped me feel less manic. I was safe on ground level, far from high-up, open windows.

I headed back up to my apartment at six-thirty, just as the Wall Street guys streamed out of the elevators.

———

I pulled on my reliable, NYC outfit: snug-fitting black from head-to-toe, plus oversized black sunglasses. I raced out the door in a hurry to get to work and dial-a-therapist who could administer medication. I had a fear of taking pills, but I felt so desperate, I would have taken anything prescribed with a childproof cap.

I ran into my office, red-faced from the October chill, and closed the door in an effort to avoid Monday small talk. I tossed my ridiculously large sunglasses on the floor, as I manically flipped through the company's health benefits manual. I could not control what was going on with me physically, but I could certainly control whom I chose to fix me. I found a list of local providers who helped crazy. I selected a psychiatrist who had everything I wanted: a kind name, convenience, specialized in anxiety, and could prescribe medication.

I called immediately, keeping my index finger on Dr. Laura Tanner's name and number. It was 7:45 a.m. and, as luck would have it, she answered on the third ring. I told her my name, that I had almost died last night, and that I needed immediate treatment. Dr. Tanner complied without too many questions and said she would squeeze me in at 4:30 that afternoon. I said thank you three times before I let her hang up.

————

I scooted out of work at 3:30, making sure I had ample time to get to her office. I felt a wave of relief as I walked from my office to the subway, immersing myself in a crowd of unknowns. I had a skip in my step by the time I got to the front of her medical building. I felt as if I had arrived at the stoop of my savior. I would see her today, get fixed and be on my merry way.

I walked down the long corridor, as she had directed me earlier on the phone. I came to a white door numbered 216 and knocked.

Come in.

I entered and saw a pleasant, forty-something woman sitting on a black office chair. I quickly scanned the room. It was bright white with one high window, a brown desk, an oriental area rug, a brown leather loveseat, a matching armchair, a large box of tissues, which I found annoyingly predictable, and one wall clock with an exaggerated "tick" when the second hand moved.

I had never been to therapy. I was sure this would be a one-time occasion, and I wanted to maximize the experience. I stood in front of the loveseat, plopped down, placed both feet up on one arm and my head on the other, just as I had seen it done in the movies. I then cocked my head toward Dr. Tanner for my next cue. She said nothing. I assumed it was my time to talk, so I virtually regurgitated my story. I told her about my recent family trip to Vegas, my sleepless evening, how I felt like I wanted to jump out my window, how I may be on the brink of insanity, but think I self-diagnosed "anxiety" via the help of my dictionary and how I was quite certain I needed medication, but was incredibly anxious at the mere thought of taking prescription pills.

Once I stopped talking, she looked at me blankly. I could tell she wanted to make sure I was finished with the spewing. I nodded, assuring her I was.

She gently asked me about my current life, as if I were a fragile egg. I briefly told her about my happy workplace, great boyfriend, solid friends and family. She continued to probe with questions that did not seem to apply to the reason I was there.

How old are you?
Twenty-six.

Do you have any siblings?
Two. A brother, Todd, and a sister, Rani. They are four and five years older than I am, respectively.

Do you have a close relationship with them?
I talk to my sister more frequently, because we grew up together. My brother moved in with my father when he was eleven.

Dr. Tanner raised one eyebrow, tapped her fingers on her lap and said,

Are your parents still in your life?
They are both living. Divorced when I was three. I am close with my mother and speak to my father about once a year.

Where did you grow up?
I was born in Philadelphia. Then, when my parents divorced, we moved to Las Vegas.

Who moved to Las Vegas?
Me, my mom, my sister and brother.

Why Las Vegas?
My mom got a job as a showgirl.

Hmmm, okay.

Her face scrunched up, as though she didn't know where to go with that information. The answer sounded peculiar even to me, once I let it out there.

When did you move to New York City?
The week I graduated college. The summer of 1992.

What is your current occupation?
I'm the merchandising retail editor at a teen fashion magazine.

What are your responsibilities at work?
Varies day to day. But mostly I create incentives for advertisers to advertise in our magazine versus someone else's, and I host fashion shows. It is about as fun as it can get for something you call a job.

I then hesitated, looked at my watch and felt a rush of panic and frustration. Ten minutes had passed! I realized she hadn't begun fixing me within my allotted fifty minutes and time was ticking away on the darned wall clock. *Tick, tick, tick.* I felt broken, scared, in need of a quick fix, and here she was asking harebrained questions. If she didn't get to the point soon where she snapped her fingers and I got well, I was going to combust on her perfect leather loveseat.

She asked me about my childhood and my foot started to jiggle in frustration. I began to race through my childhood in Vegas, stealing glances at my watch.

I giggled as I told her my mom moved to Vegas with a Ponzi shyster, he died, she hooked up with a mobster, then a casino owner, became a showgirl at the Tropicana, then ended up with an anti-Semitic monster, named Paul, who almost killed us all.

Why are you laughing?
The whole thing is so ridiculous. I mean, how we got to Vegas and the reasons or sacrifices my mom made to keep us there. It's just so crazy. I don't know how else to react.

Ridiculous? From the little you just told me, it sounds anything but ridiculous, and it is certainly not humorous.

My face fell, and I felt embarrassed as she started jotting notes in her journal.

Have you spoken to anyone in your family about your experience in Vegas?
No.

You never once spoke about it to your siblings? Your sister?
We left Vegas and Paul when I was ten years old. I never even thought about it after that. I guess I just compartmentalized it. It's part of my past. It's all behind me now.

She started writing in her journal again.
What are you writing about?

I need to keep track of everything we talk about for our future sessions.
Oh. I was floored at the thought of having to come back again.

What is your first childhood memory of your mother and your stepfather, Paul?
Rani, Todd and I were disembarking a plane in Vegas when I was four years old. My mom was standing next to him on the tarmac, next to a white limousine.

Then what?
My mom said, "Say hello to your new daddy." Then she swung her hands his way, sort of like Vanna White does on Wheel of Fortune. I guess it was her showgirl thing; everything was slightly overdone, even introductions.

Dr. Tanner was scribbling in her notebook.

Taking in some of what you've told me, I would like to know how you feel about your mother today.
I love my mother. Why?

From the bits and pieces you are telling me, it would only be natural for you to have some resentment . . .

Huh? No. My foot began to jiggle again, as I did not like where the conversation was leading. She continued to look at me, waiting for more, and I gave it defensively.

This is not my mother's problem, it's mine. My mom is not waking up at night with an impulse to jump out her window. My mom is not seeking therapy because she thinks she is losing her mind. Blaming her for what is happening to me now is preposterous.

You seem to get very defensive when you talk about her. Why don't we move forward and see where this takes us. Let's start from your first Vegas childhood memory . . .

She glanced down at her book.

If I remember correctly, I think that was when you got off the plane.

If I'm going to tell you about my childhood, we logically have to start with my mom's story.

I would much rather focus on you. This is why you are here.

I sat stubbornly still.

Why do you feel it is important to tell your mother's story first? Do you think you two are very alike?

She glanced at the clock, playing me at my own game and reminding me that time was ticking away.

You will then understand why we ended up in the hell we did. To answer your second question, I am not my mother, but I do think we are all versions—bits and pieces—of our parents. With that being said, I am proud of who my mother is today. She is strong, loving and one hell of a survivor. I paused and felt the need to defend her more.

I mean, no matter how bad or ugly things got, she woke up every morning and got pretty, like nothing had ever happened. She was trying to make the best of a bad situation.

13

Well, this could explain why all of this has been pent up and has revealed itself almost two decades later. Not much of an example was set for you early on.

I tried to digest what she said without feeling malice. I knew she was not trying to hurt me; she was trying to help me.

Okay, let's start with your mother's story, Suzanne. If you feel this is important to understanding why you are here, I want to hear it. We'll pick up there at our next session.

She wrote me a prescription for Paxil. She told me it would take the edge off. She confirmed my self-diagnosis of anxiety and said it was most likely set off by my recent trip to Vegas. She also confirmed that I was not going crazy. She said we would need to meet two times a week and see how things progress from there. We agreed that since I feared an anxiety attack relapse, I should come in the next day.

As I got up to leave, I looked in her eyes and my voice cracked when I asked, *Dr. Tanner, do you think you can help me?*

Yes, we can do this. There is a frightened little girl inside of you that needs to work her way out.

I looked down at the floor, suddenly feeling pathetically sorry for myself. I gave her a weak smile and left the office. I saw her next patient waiting in the hallway. She gave me a dirty look, because my session had run over four whole minutes into her time. I felt the urge to scream "Boo!" in her face and punish the bitch for her sour look, but I didn't have it in me. I felt weary. I couldn't wrap my head around how Vegas could come back to haunt me now.

———

As I walked down the street, I thought about what Dr. Tanner had said over the past fifty-four minutes. This was not a quick fix. This was not something I could control. It was obvious that I was going to need a journal to keep track of this mess. The only relief I felt was from the prescription in my hand, and Dr. Tanner's use of the pronoun "we." That simple little word made my burden a little lighter. My problem was now hers also.

I went directly to the drugstore to fill my prescription. The pharmacist looked at the form without paying much attention to me and said he could fill it by the end of the day. I told him with as much passion as I could muster that it was an emergency and I would wait. He hesitated, took out his spectacles and inspected the script. I was tempted to say that I was picking this up for a friend, but this was not a box of condoms; this was my very own screwed-up-in-the-head prescription. He looked at me as if he knew I was on the verge of some cockamamie story and said, "I will have it ready in five minutes."

I glanced behind me and saw that a long line of people had formed behind me, holding on to their little script notes for dear life. I felt like a bus from Bellevue had dropped off their craziest and they were all staring at me impatiently. I stepped aside, grabbed an issue of *People* and buried my face in it.

I took my first Paxil pill at six that evening. I sat idle for an hour, waiting for it to kick in. During this time I fought the impulse to read the side effects, knowing full well that I would manifest them all. By seven o'clock I felt relaxed and convinced that the Paxil was working, so I crawled into bed and phoned my sister.

We spoke two times a month and usually late at night, but I felt an urgency to speak with her. She answered the phone in her usual, perky business voice.

"Hi! Rani speaking."

I didn't skip a beat, "It's me. I know this is going to sound off the wall, but have you ever thought about the stuff that happened in Vegas?"

15

She inhaled deeply and blurted out, "Hell yeah."

Pandora's Box had been smashed open. We shared an hours' worth of unfathomable stories in rushed, frantic sentences. We had never spoken for so long and about so much. We had lived parallel lives for six years and had never once mentioned it to one another.

We should have cried—but we laughed.

CHAPTER TWO

Olivia Sandy Berger

As I walked the three blocks to my therapist's office the next morning, I felt well rested, but my stomach was in knots. I was about to share my mom's story and, in turn, my childhood.

My shoes clacked on the linoleum floor of the now familiar corridor. I stood in front of Dr. Tanner's office. The door was slightly ajar.

Please enter.
This time I sat upright, pressed tightly against the left arm of the loveseat.

How did you sleep?
The Paxil definitely kicked in and I slept really well last night.

That is good to hear. Just to be clear, Suzanne, Paxil takes a couple of weeks to take effect. I am happy to hear you are well rested, though.
She jotted something in her journal. I was convinced she wrote, "Patient is delusional." I felt like an idiot.
Guess I'm a good candidate for a placebo, I said half-mocking myself. She didn't even look up. *I spoke to my sister. We shared some of our Vegas stories.*

How did that make you feel?
It was like the floodgates opened. I hesitated a few seconds. *And we laughed.*

You both laughed?
I suppose there is no other way that we know how to deal with it. Such strange circumstances.

It got very quiet. Her mood was palpable. She was not happy with me. I had to change the subject and quickly.
My mom, Olivia I should say, grew up in a working class neighborhood of Philadelphia. She was the second of four children in her family . . .

It was post World War II, late 1940s, and everyone in their neighborhood was financially strained, but Olivia and her sister, Betty, agreed they were the poorest of the poor. They were the only Jewish family on the block with two working parents, which the two girls found humiliating. Her mother was a seamstress and her father ran a newsstand.

Throughout her childhood, Olivia constantly dreamed of a better life. She wanted money and lots of it. She wanted nice clothes instead of her neighbor's hand-me-downs; fancy perfume instead of her mother's talcum powder; and jewels instead of faux pearls.

By her senior year of high school in 1957, she had blossomed into a beauty who spent all her time running around with boys and friends. In January of that year, Olivia's mother deemed her not suited for higher education. "Olivia," she told her, "you will make something of yourself, but not with further studies. You just don't have the book smarts your sister has. You will make it rich or marry rich. I pray it's the latter."

Olivia knew she was right. School was not for her. She wanted to make her own money, buy fabulous clothes and continue dating. She had plenty of street smarts to get by and planned to get out of her parents' home as soon as possible.

Two days after high school graduation, Olivia prepped herself for an unscheduled interview. She pulled her shoulder-length, scarlet hair back in a knot at the base of her neck, applied red lipstick on her full lips, mascara to enhance her hazel eyes, and borrowed a form-fitting yellow dress from a friend that showcased her statuesque, five-foot eleven figure. She went directly to the most upscale retailer she could reach by the city bus. An hour later, she was the new "cosmetic counter associate" at the department store. She flourished in her new position and with her small financial independence, began going out nightly with friends.

———

Without much effort, fortune arrived a few years later in the form of Don Dushon. Don was the son of the locally famous David Dushon, owner of the Latin Casino in New Jersey. The Latin Casino was a supper club and the hottest ticket in town, seating 2,200 people nightly. Diana Ross, Engelbert Humperdinck, David Brenner, Tom Jones and Sammy Davis Jr., were all regular performers.

Olivia was smitten. Don was everything she could have wished for in a man; handsome, taller than she was, physically fit, full head of hair, Jewish, affluent, and had a steady job. He was her Casanova. Best of all, she knew she could make him want to marry her.

Betty, their mom
(my grandmom),
and Olivia, 1949.

Olivia,
19 years old.

Donald Dushon, 24 years old.

David Dushon's Latin Casino

CHAPTER THREE

Philadelphia, 1960s— Olivia Berger Dushon

Don didn't talk much or make an effort to woo Olivia during their first few weeks of courtship. While most women would find this discouraging, she found it intriguing. Don was perfect *on paper,* and besides, she didn't need a man who spoke a lot. She had plenty to say and could fill the void created by his mysterious personality.

Olivia and Don dated for three months before he asked her to marry him. She was twenty-one and accepted without a doubt in her mind that she had landed her dream husband.

Upon learning of the engagement, David Dushon was not pleased. He found it disturbing that his son wanted to marry someone he had known for such a short time. He had never even heard Don mention this woman and assumed she must be pregnant. He insisted on meeting Olivia face-to-face. David's secretary called Olivia at work. She asked her to meet Mr. David Dushon in the lobby of the Bellevue Stratford Hotel the following day. Olivia agreed to meet him on her lunch hour. The hotel was only a few blocks from where she worked.

The next morning, Olivia made sure she looked impeccable.

She wanted to make the best possible first impression on Don's father. She reached the hotel early and waited for David in the lobby. She knew what he looked like from the society pages of the newspaper; short, stout, mass of thick gray hair and a lit cigarette perpetually held between the first two fingers of his right hand. When she saw him enter the revolving doors, she walked his way, showcasing her well-practiced, cosmetics-associate smile. He eyed her up and down as she moved toward him in a fitted, red, knee-length, sleeveless dress.

They shook hands and took a seat in two oversized chairs. Forgoing small talk, he pointedly asked her how she and Don met. She told him. He asked if she truly wanted to marry his son. She said yes. He said in a direct, no-nonsense manner, "You are marrying the wrong Dushon."

Olivia threw her head back and laughed nervously, knowing that Don was his only son. She stood up, firmly shook Mr. Dushon's hand and walked out of the lobby, feeling his eyes on her back.

———

Don and Olivia married in the fall of 1963. They bought a two-bedroom apartment and spent most of their time out of it. They worked during the day and met friends for dinner in Center City or at the Latin Casino.

They had an open invitation to come backstage and meet talent on any evening. They spent a lot of time with recurring talent—Engelbert Humperdinck and David Brenner. Both of these men were openly taken with Olivia. She loved the attention and flirted just enough to make herself desirable, but not available.

———

Late fall of 1963, Olivia learned she was pregnant. She quit her job and reveled in the fact that she was going to be a mother. David generously provided a twenty percent down payment to purchase a five thousand dollar, split-level home in a family-friendly neighborhood of Northeast Philadelphia.

The Dushon home was the only house in the neighborhood with a pool, and it became *the* party destination. They welcomed a continual stream of friends in and out every Friday, Saturday and Sunday. Olivia was the ultimate hostess, making sure glasses were full, bellies were satisfied and the radio's volume was full blast.

Between the parties, the Latin Casino and Don's work, Olivia began to notice that she and Don were drifting apart. He spoke to her less and less as her belly began to show signs of her pregnancy. She purposely made a great effort to engage him in conversation, but he was not interested. She knew her hormones were causing her to be sensitive, but she was only seeking some small kind of emotional support from him. She was so upset that she turned to her father-in-law several times for advice. He responded by palming her $500, as though it were a business transaction, patting her on the back and saying, "It will be okay. Just hang in there."

By the time Rani Lyn Dushon was born in July of 1964, Don was barely speaking to Olivia. While she needed to tend to her newborn, she knew she also had to please her husband. She swore she would do anything to gain back his lost interest.

She would wake early and apply her makeup so she could look perfect when Don got up. She made his favorite dinners, made sure Rani was asleep when he came home from work, and kept a tidy house—but he didn't take notice of her efforts. While it was painful and unadvised by her doctor, they had sex a week after Rani was born, only because she knew it would please him.

Olivia missed her next period. And the one after that.

Todd Marcus Dushon was born the summer of 1965. Rani and Todd were eleven months apart. Olivia was so sick of having a huge stomach that she stopped eating meals and slimmed down to 118 pounds. She thought this new, trim figure would excite Don. She walked around with celery and carrots in her pockets to curb hunger pains. She forbade herself to gain weight and swore off pregnancy for good.

She reached a point of feeling so neglected that she made it a full-time job to gain Don's interest back. He didn't like the bump on her nose, so she used the cash she had socked away from David to get her nose fixed. Months later, Don complained that her boobs were too small, so she went back to the same surgeon and increased her breast size by two cups. Neither surgery garnered a reaction. The few times he paid attention to her were at night. He would initiate sex, and then roll away from her as though she had the plague, pulling the covers over himself. She felt increasingly worthless—dehumanized. She knew her marriage was slipping through her fingers.

One fall afternoon, she was feeling considerably down, and wandered into a local beauty salon. She told the beautician to do something radical. She said she wanted to surprise her husband. An hour later, she was a strawberry blond. Everyone in the salon raved at how fantastic she looked and she got a standing ovation. "Bravo to you! Your husband is going to love this!" She went home beaming and could not wait for Don's reaction.

After the kids were tucked in bed, she sat on the sofa waiting for him. She wore a slinky black nightgown, with a cigarette in one hand and a cosmopolitan in the other as accessories. By the time Don got home, her cigarette was long extinguished, the glass empty and her eyes half-mast. When she heard the door shut, she sat up straight and poised herself. He looked at Olivia for an exaggerated moment, trying to make out if it was her or not, then turned away and walked off into their bedroom.

In early 1968, Don told Olivia that he was offered the opportunity to become a partner in a restaurant. He had not spoken to her directly in years, so she listened intently.

When he paused to hear her response she replied, "I like the idea under one condition; that I am included in the partnership." He stared at her blankly. "I refuse to stay home any longer while you run around having all the fun. I want to get dressed like a grownup and speak to adults other than other homemakers. We are hiring a nanny. End of conversation."

A week later, Olivia hired Delma. She was a short, skinny, spunky Spanish woman in her forties with crazy gray and black hair. The kids loved her instantly.

Olivia liked commuting to work with Don because it was the only way for her to keep an eye on him.

She enjoyed working as the restaurant's hostess and became friendly with many of the regulars. Her favorite patron was Joel White. He was a young, practicing lawyer in Philadelphia and always brightened her day with light conversation about his clients. She made a point of taking Joel's business card and placing it in her wallet, thinking she may need his help some day.

Against her will, after four years of neglect and in a final act of desperation to save their marriage, Olivia got pregnant. She hoped this would bring them closer.

Suzanne Rachel Dushon was born in April 1969. She was a bundle of joy to Olivia and the kids, but failed to create a stronger foundation for the marriage. Don drifted even further away. He left for work without her before the sun rose and came home after midnight. The distance between them became so strained that Olivia finally suggested they see a marriage counselor.

"This is your problem, Olivia, not mine. Go see one on your own. Leave me out of it."

She was determined to work out their problems, so she sought solo counseling.

———

Financial strain caused the restaurant to go under in late 1971. With a block of free time on their hands, Olivia suggested she and Don go to Acapulco with some friends—advice she had received from her marriage counselor months before. "Maybe you just need some time away from the home and kids."

She knew that Don was not interested in working on their relationship, but she saw this trip as an opportunity to spend time together. It was her last hope. This was going to be the trip that would either repair or end their marriage.

Olivia met with her marriage counselor the day before their vacation. She provided her with what she called the simple rules of a marriage: "You can live together in love or live together in hate. You decide."

Counter clockwise: Olivia, Donald, Betty, Betty's husband Barry, Olivia's father Joe sitting across from Barry, next to him is Olivia's mother Ida, across from Olivia is her youngest brother Ken.

Donald & Olivia.

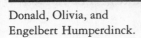

Donald, Olivia, and Engelbert Humperdinck.

Olivia on her front porch.

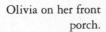

27

Mom and me.

Todd, Rani and me.

Family portrait about 7 months after I was born. Clockwise: Mom, Donald, Rani, Todd, and me.

Mom relaxing in her backyard pool.

CHAPTER FOUR

Acapulco, January 1972

Olivia and Don boarded the plane to Acapulco with several of their friends. For the first time in a long time, she felt that they were a genuinely happy, married couple. They talked harmoniously on the flight, and he seemed engaged. She felt this vacation was just what they needed.

When they arrived at the resort, Don and Olivia were shown to a luxurious suite overlooking the Pacific Ocean. Olivia looked from the view of the water to Don, who was feverishly unpacking his bags in a rush to get out of the room. She stared at this man and said a silent prayer that this vacation would save their marriage. She had made the decision that she was not going to live in hate.

On their first morning, Don was gone before sunrise. Olivia awoke to a note on his pillow: "Made an early tee time. See you at dinner." She sat up and phoned one of her friends to see if Don had gone to play with her husband. The resounding "no" echoed in her head, but she managed to brush off the heartache by planning to meet up with her friends at the beach. She was confident that everything was going to work out on this trip. She knew Don loved his golf game and concluded that he was being thoughtful by getting it out of the way bright and early on day one.

———

That night she saw Don briefly at dinner. She didn't give him grief about where he had been all day; she simply rewarded him with a dazzling smile. Don stood as dessert arrived and said he had a card game with some guys he played golf with that day. With a swift kiss on Olivia's cheek, he nonchalantly walked out of the restaurant and into the Acapulco darkness.

Olivia put on a brave face for her friends, but she was crushed. She could not believe he was doing this to her on their first day of vacation. However, she was determined not to badger him and to keep her doubts at bay.

Day after day, Don's solo plans and excuses continued . . . golf, tennis, cards, drinks. Olivia's heart sank each day as he disappeared without a trace. Her friends acted as though his behavior were nothing out of the ordinary and kept her busy at the beach, pool and meals.

———

By the fourth morning of waking alone, it was evident that Don was going to spend as much time away from her as possible. She hadn't heard him come back to the room the night before, but she hadn't heard him leave early that morning either. Her suspicion got the best of her. She was convinced he was sneaking around with another woman at the resort. At ten o'clock her phone rang, and she decided to let it go to the hotel message center. *Let him think I was out all night also!* When the light on her phone blinked, she grabbed the receiver, heart racing, and hit the message button.

"Good-morning-gorgeous! Just a reminder that we are all meeting at ten-fifteen for breakfast. Our flight is at one, so we'll be leaving here at eleven-fifteen. See you in a few."

Olivia felt sick to her stomach. It was the chipper voice of her girlfriend. She had forgotten that all her friends were leaving a couple of days earlier. She was feeling so melancholy, she couldn't bear to meet up with them. Olivia called her back and said she wasn't feeling well and couldn't meet them for breakfast. They said their goodbyes over the phone. She knew her friends had to know something was wrong, but no one dared to broach the subject.

Olivia sat on her bed, conjuring thoughts about Don's flying a mistress down to Acapulco. She imagined his spending time with her in some room at their very resort. She was between a state of fury and anguish when she realized the woman had probably been on their same flight. Feeling crushed and worthless, she curled up on the bed and began to sob.

It wasn't until one o'clock in the afternoon that she sat up, determined to get out of her room. She put on a bathing suit, a beach cover-up, a straw hat large enough to conceal her face and headed to the pool.

Olivia found a secluded area where no one could hear her cry. She sat down on a lounge chair and pulled her wide-brimmed hat down over her face. She wept for her dead-end marriage. She wept for the marriage she was trapped in with an awful, cheating husband. She wept for her three children who had a heartless father who didn't care about them.

After the sun moved from east to west, Olivia came to a conclusion. She was not certain of much, but she was certain that she could not be in this marriage any longer. She just had to figure a way to get out.

As she grabbed a handful of tissues to dry the tears on her face, she heard a male voice say, "Excuse me." She ignored it and started cursing Don under her breath.

"Excuse me." The voice was more persistent. She looked up,

squinting against the sun. A man stood above her, casting a large shadow along her legs. "I'm sorry to interrupt you." He extended his hand, "My name is George. You look so unhappy. I don't wish to bother you, but I wanted to come over and see if I could help."

It was that small hint of compassion that caused her to break down. She took his hand and said, "I'm Olivia," as a new wave of tears rolled down her cheeks. He released her hand and took it as an invitation to sit in the vacant chair next to her.

"Tell me what's wrong. I hate to see a beautiful woman cry." Olivia tried not to sob as she told this complete stranger about her cheating husband and how he had stranded her on this vacation. She told him Acapulco was supposed to save their marriage, but now it was over and she was completely devastated.

George listened intently, hanging on her every word. When Olivia paused to dry her tears again, he told her she was going to be all right and these things always have a way of working out. He said he could not let her cry any longer and wanted to cheer her up. He asked if he could introduce her to his travel companion.

Open to a diversion from her tears, Olivia nodded yes, and out of the blinding sunshine, a gorgeous young woman stepped into view. She softly introduced herself as Patty, sat down next to George and said, "Please, continue."

Patty and George listened while Olivia explained that she had tried to save their marriage so many times, but now she wanted out. She told them about her three children and that she didn't know how they were all going to survive if she left Don. She said she was trapped—she didn't have a job and couldn't support her family if she left him.

When Olivia seemed to have nothing more to say, George grabbed Patty's arm with one hand and slapped his knee with the other exclaiming, "We are going to cheer you up. As I said, I can't stand to see a beautiful woman cry . . . the whole damsel in distress thing gets to me. You must come spend the afternoon with Patty and me."

Olivia took a hard look at both of them for the first time, pulling back the floppy brim of her hat. George was not typically good looking, but he was polished. He was short and stocky with thinning white hair, nicely dressed and oozing with confidence. Patty was a foot taller, at least a couple of decades younger, and was so striking she looked like she may have been a model.

Olivia thought about her plans for the rest of the day. She had nothing to do other than feel sorry for herself. Don was probably not going to be returning any time soon. Sensing her reluctance, George stood up and held out his hand. She put her hand in his and he pulled her up. It surprised her that she felt instantly warmed by this stranger's touch and kindness.

Without further hesitation, she smiled and impulsively said, "I am happy to go wherever you want to take me." George and Patty were elated. They agreed to meet in the lobby in ten minutes.

————

Olivia went to the pool bathhouse to pull herself together. She felt a surge of excitement that she was doing something so uncharacteristic as to leave the safe compounds of the resort with two strangers. She trusted her instinct that they were good people. She knew the change of scenery was going to do her good. She put on her long white beach cover-up, freshened her makeup and met them in the lobby.

George had a chauffeur and sedan waiting for them. Olivia was relieved that there was a driver with them, just in case she wanted to turn back. George told them that he was taking them shopping. He said they could have anything they wanted. He continued to be upbeat and conversational during the ride, informing Olivia that he was a bicoastal businessman living in both New York City and Las Vegas. He said he had brought a group of friends down to Acapulco for a weekend of relaxation. While he spoke, Olivia sized him up. This was a man who spent a great deal of money caring for himself; he was incredibly well groomed, his hands were manicured, he smelled of expensive cologne and his face had the glow of a recent facial.

They drove into a quaint Mexican village not far from their hotel. George ushered them into the first shop. He implored them to buy anything they wanted. Olivia looked at Patty, linked arms with her, and like giggling schoolgirls, they took off down the narrow aisle of the store. If they looked at anything for more than a moment, George took out his wallet and said, "We'll take two of those."

After two hours of shopping, George insisted they get a cocktail before heading back. Olivia was having so much fun, she had almost forgotten her former state of mind . . . until George mentioned heading back to the hotel.

Once they got back into the car, George saw the sadness wash over Olivia's face. He smiled, touched her arm and invited her to join his group for dinner. He said his friends would love to meet her and he would not take no for an answer. Olivia thanked him, but said she should try to meet up with her husband.

Back in the hotel lobby, Olivia thanked George again and again for a wonderful afternoon and embraced Patty with a warm hug. She couldn't help but notice that George seemed genuinely pleased to see her smiling. He insisted that she should join them for dinner. He also invited her to spend the next day with them. She smiled and agreed to see them the following day, knowing that Don was probably going to be occupied elsewhere.

When Olivia got back to her room, there was a note from Don:

"Won't make it to dinner tonight. Playing cards. See you later." She fumed that he could be so callous as to leave her another note. He knew their friends had left already and she would be alone that evening. She picked up the phone to call George. She sighed with relief that he was in his room and told him she would be joining them for dinner. She took every measure to get ready that night. She wanted to look and feel fabulous—if not for her husband, for a group of strangers.

As expected, dinner was entertaining. George had a boisterous group of friends who knew how to have a good time. Throughout the evening, George was attentive and treated her like a goddess. This was the most enjoyable evening of her vacation and she was grateful to George for his kindness.

She stood up from the table and said her good-byes at twelve-thirty. She returned to her empty hotel room, finding it as she had left it earlier—void of her husband.

Don never returned to the room that night. Olivia couldn't fathom shedding another tear that evening. She would deal with Don the following day, the day before their departure.

———

The next morning Olivia met George, Patty and their friends for breakfast. Patty announced that she was ready to head back to New York, and George said he would see her there within the week. With a hug and a kiss to everyone, Patty went off to the airport. George then astounded Olivia by saying he would stay and keep her company in Acapulco until she left.

With Patty gone, George and Olivia were alone for the first time. They sat by the pool and Olivia told him that Don had not returned to their room the night before. George looked at her, his eyes sympathetic and said, "If you want out, I will help you end your marriage."

"I do want a divorce, George, but I don't see how it's possible. Financially, with my kids . . . it is just too difficult."

He hesitated for a moment and said, "I just told you I will help you with your divorce, Olivia. I'll take care of the financials, but under my conditions."

Olivia was stumped. Here was a man willing to help her, but how much was he willing to do? What kind of conditions? It was clear that George had a lot of money. He was staying in the penthouse and treating a number of people to a weekend in Acapulco. He had been flashing a wad of cash around from the time she had met him. He seemed like the kind of man who was capable of accomplishing many things, but could he do this? She was so desperate, she was open to anything he had to offer. "Let's discuss your conditions."

"Do you have an attorney?"

"Yes"

"Call him right after we have lunch. Tell him to start divorce proceedings today."

A lump rose in her throat from a mix of anticipation, fear and reality. She was actually doing this. She felt that George was sincere and was going to help her make this happen. She wanted to trust him. She had to trust him.

———

Back in her room, she took Joel White's card out of her wallet. He was not aware that he was her attorney yet, but she was hoping he would oblige. He had always been a friend to her, and she hoped she could rely on him. Joel's assistant put her right through to his personal line. Olivia was relieved to hear a familiar voice, an old friend. She told Joel what was going on with Don and how badly he was treating her. She told him about George and that he was willing to help her pay for a divorce. Joel voiced his concerns about this George character and the promise he was making her. Yet he couldn't deny the desperate tone of her voice. He said he would help her and that he would start the appropriate paperwork that week. After she hung up, she called George. She needed to know the next plan of action.

"Pack up all of your belongings. Act as if you are leaving on your scheduled flight with Don tomorrow. However, you are not to leave the resort with him. Do not go to the airport or get on that flight back to Philadelphia with him."

She felt empowered. George's support was making her strong. As long as he dictated her next move and she followed the plan, it was going to be okay.

———

Their flight was scheduled to leave at eleven that morning. Olivia packed her bags and left them by the door. She had not seen or heard from Don in over forty-eight hours. She slipped into a bathing suit and headed to the pool. She sat as casually as possible, reading a magazine with her heart banging in her chest. It felt like every hair on her body stood up on end as Don entered the pool area. He looked handsome as ever, wearing his crisp, blue, travel suit, and she knew he was looking for her. He eventually spotted her poolside and walked directly in front of her chair. Olivia winced and held her breath. He said, "You coming with me?"

She responded with a composed, "No."

He stood there for an exaggerated second and said, "See you around, kid."

He turned on his heels and walked out of the pool area, toward the hotel lobby. She exhaled, grasping onto the sides of her chair. She felt as if she were spinning downward, falling into a dark, bottomless abyss. The pain that shot through her body was excruciating. She tried to breathe between sobs, her chest heaving as though she couldn't get enough air. She heard someone calling her name, but she just wanted to put an end to the pain.

"Olivia. Olivia!" Someone shook her arm. She was being pulled back toward the light, where she did not want to go. She thought she was screaming, but there was no sound.

"Hey, it's George. I'm here. It's going to be okay. Olivia, it is going to be okay. I am going to take care of you."

She felt both of his hands now, on the sides of her face. She looked up to meet his eyes and said, "George . . . what . . . have . . . I . . . done?"

"He's gone Olivia. You are going to be just fine. You just took the biggest step forward. You are going to divorce that man. You will be happy again. I promise you that."

Incredulous, she looked at him and said, "How? What about my children? Oh my God! What have I done?" She began to tremble as she realized that she had put her entire life in the hands of a man she just met. "Did you see him leave? Did he really leave without me? Where were you?"

"I was sitting at the restaurant, over there, on the other side of the pool, watching the interaction between the two of you. I knew Don would come looking for you, and I walked over here as soon as I saw him leave. I will get you through this, Olivia. Trust me."

George insisted that she join him for lunch. Wearily, she allowed him to put his arm around her waist and guide her to the dining patio. Over lunch, she became more at ease as he assured her again that he was going to help her get through it. He said he had secured her room for the next couple of nights—and that they would need a few days to figure out what to do next. He stressed that she should not worry and everything would work out.

By the time their lunch plates were cleared, she was convinced that she did the right thing by putting all her faith in George. He was going to save her.

That evening, after a nice dinner and a bottle of wine to calm her nerves, George escorted Olivia back to her room. As they approached her doorway, her palms began to sweat. The familiar panic she felt when Don walked away washed over her again. It was clear that George was expecting to come into the room with her. She couldn't believe how naive she was. Of course he expected sex in return for helping her. All she wanted, in that moment, was to be in the safety of Don's arms. Now she was trapped with a stranger in a strange country.

She searched for her room key, feverishly digging in her evening bag as a distraction. Once she had it in her hands, she looked at George and said goodnight as she quickly opened the door. He leaned in to embrace her as the tears began to flow and her hands shook nervously.

"George, I can't do this."

He stood back and looked into her eyes, and said he understood. He then raised her hand to his lips, gently kissed it and walked down the hallway, out of sight.

With a sigh of relief she slumped down on the bed, relieved that he was out of her hair for the evening.

"What the hell am I doing here?" she cried out loud to her empty room.

She grabbed the phone and dialed the front desk. She asked to be placed on the first flight back to Philadelphia. She stressed that she needed to get out the very next day. The hotel desk told her it was impossible for them to process a ticket for the next day. They explained that there was red tape when one misses their scheduled flight out of Mexico, and it would take at least a week to get on another flight. She hung up the receiver, too exasperated to argue with the front desk. She knew she had made a colossal mistake. The room started to spin. The dark abyss from that morning beckoned her and she fell in—sinking into her own personal hell.

She awoke at eight a.m. to the sound of the phone ringing. She fumbled with the receiver, hoping it was the front desk with news of a flight home. It was Don. Her heart soared. She remained as calm as possible as she told him she could not get out of Mexico. He said he would pull some strings and get her home as soon as he could. He told her to stand by the phone and he would call her back shortly. It was a very business-like conversation, but it was the first act of kindness he had shown her in years. She felt a sense of calm come over her for the first time in twenty-four hours.

She waited anxiously by the phone. The call came an hour later. "My father and I pulled every string. The best we could do was get you on a flight out in two days."

"Thank you, Don. I will see you in two days."

"Your ticket will be delivered to the hotel tonight. I will pick you up at the airport in Philadelphia. See you soon."

Although very formal once again, she was grateful to hear his voice. She was relieved that he had taken the initiative to save her. In the back of her mind she knew that his father must have laid into him for leaving his wife alone in a foreign country. She smiled at the thought of his being reprimanded like a child.

With a safe escape only two days away, Olivia was able to take a deep breath and relax. She was going to spend the next forty-eight hours getting to know George. She called to let him know she had gotten a flight, and he said he would coordinate his flight out the same day.

They spent every waking moment together over the next two days. George behaved like a gentleman, paid for all of her expenses and made no advances. Olivia had felt defeated for so long—George's tenderness was slowly bringing her back to life. He was listening to her, making her laugh and making her feel like a desirable human being again.

Even though she wasn't sure of what she was going to do when she got home, they did work out her divorce plan-of-action. George told her to continue with the divorce proceedings, and he promised to be in touch as soon as he got situated in New York.

Over dinner, he said, "You should be a showgirl in Las Vegas, covered with rhinestones and feathers."

Olivia's face lit up. "I'm serious, Olivia. You are gorgeous. You have the body for it. I'm connected enough to make it happen for you. Come to Vegas. Bring your kids. Make a new start."

She listened to him, but could not seriously imagine such a life for herself. It would be so reckless, different—exhilarating.

He continued, "I built my empire by selling stocks in slot machines and many of my investors own casinos. Olivia, I can make anything happen for you in Vegas."

After an hour of his cajoling, she was sold. Nothing had ever seemed so thrilling to her in her entire life. The thought of independence, money and being in show business . . . she greedily devoured everything he said.

"Once your divorce is complete, I will set you and your children up in a home in Las Vegas. I give you my word; I will build a new life for you." He had made her a promise, and she knew he was going to keep to it.

———

On the morning of her departure, Olivia wore a black suit with a wide-brimmed hat and large black sunglasses. She wanted to keep to herself during the flight. This outfit screamed, "Don't dare talk to me." She was too nervous about seeing Don and needed the flight time to process reuniting with him.

George took one look at Olivia in the hotel lobby and exclaimed, "You look like a movie star." He could not take his eyes off her as they drove to the airport. When they arrived, he walked her to her gate and acknowledged her anxiety. He embraced her tightly and said, "Don't worry Olivia. This is all going to work out. I will be in touch soon."

She watched the man who now had her life in his hands as he ran to catch his flight to New York.

She had a tight, half-hour connection in Chicago. Once the plane landed, she dashed out of the plane, dodging people in the Jetway to catch her next flight. As she reached her gate, a man tightly grasped her arm.

"Airport security."

"What do you need? I'm catching my connecting flight to Philadelphia."

"We are just going to need to ask you a couple of questions. Please come with us."

"Did I do something wrong? I am going to miss my flight!" She told him that her husband would be waiting for her and pulled away, but the more she resisted, the more he restrained her. She finally relented as two men escorted her into a private room within the terminal. They told her to take a seat and began questioning her.

"Where are you coming from?"

"Acapulco."

"Why are you in such a rush?"

"To catch my connecting flight."

"Who were you with?"

"I am by myself."

They continued to fire off questions as she hastily rattled off the answers.

"You traveled alone in Mexico?"

"Not that it is any of your business, but I'm coming back from vacation. I was with my husband, who had to leave unexpectedly for work. I was rushing to catch my flight . . . that I have now missed." She was near tears when they said they needed to search her and her single carry-on bag.

Once they completed searching her bag, her purse, and humiliated her by patting down every part of her body, they explained why she was stopped. They said her eagerness to flee a plane arriving from Mexico and the way she was dressed fit the profile of a potential drug mule. She was repulsed by this and did not dignify it with a response. They said they had arranged a seat for her on the next flight to Philadelphia that was due to take off in two hours. She asked to use a phone so she could call her husband. No one was home to receive her call.

―――――――

Several hours later she landed in Philadelphia, emotionally exhausted. As soon as she exited the Jetway, she spotted Don running through crowds of people to reach her. It was clear that he thought she intentionally missed her flight. He was in a panic. She had never seen him in such a state to see her and feared how she would react once they were face-to-face. Within seconds he had her in his arms, leaving just an inch between them. He took her by the shoulders and planted a kiss on her lips.

That was her moment of clarity. She could not be with this man any longer. He disgusted her.

She let him take her bag and endured small talk about the traffic and her experience in Chicago. During the car ride home, she could not bear to look at him. When they arrived at the house, her heart sank. All the encouragement that George had given her over the past forty-eight hours was a distant memory. She was not even certain if George was going to pull through for her. She clutched her hands together, feeling once again that she was trapped in her hopeless union with Don.

CHAPTER FIVE

George

The day after her return from Acapulco, the phone rang mid-morning. Olivia picked up the receiver as she cleared breakfast from the table. It was George. She grabbed a chair for support when he said, "I'm coming to Philly to see you this weekend. Call your lawyer and make sure the divorce paperwork is in motion. Can't wait to see you again."

Olivia had occupied her morning with the kids, putting aside any thoughts of George. Hearing his voice invigorated her and helped her regain her confidence. He was really coming. This was really happening. He was going to save her. That night she began sleeping in Rani's room.

———

George arrived on Friday and boo[...]
nights. Olivia asked Delma to w[...]
telling her she had an important fr[...]
ing in the city. She also called her [...]
spend time with the kids, provid[...]
didn't have to give Don a reason; h[...]
was, it was only very late at night [...]
if he wondered where *she* was for a[...]

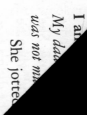

As soon as George saw Olivia in the hotel lobby, he swept her off her feet and promised her a weekend of extravagant fun and excitement. Olivia was again impressed by his impeccable appearance and commanding presence. His brown eyes were gleaming and radiated confidence. He was just what she needed; he was her security and salvation.

He told her he wanted to meet everyone in her life, including her parents, her sister and all of her friends. Olivia promised to introduce him to everyone. She was eager to show him off.

He reassured her that he was going to support her. He promised to visit two times a month until the divorce was complete. He let her know his work schedule was unpredictable, but he would call a day or two in advance to let her know he was coming.

Keeping his word, George continued to visit her twice a month on his way from New York to Vegas. Olivia kept her word and proudly introduced him to everyone in her social world; everyone except her children and Don.

————

You never met George?
No, we never met him. She didn't bring him around the house. I didn't even know this man existed until years later when my mom told me about him.

Did you or your siblings ever hear your parents fighting?
**I ask about your siblings here, because you were so young,
ʼm sure you may not remember.**
*ignored Mom for the most part. So from what I understand, there
ch bickering going on.*
notes in her notebook and asked me to continue.

————

Olivia told Delma she needed her full-time during the week and to be available on the weekends. She also asked her parents to come spend time at the house, since Don was never around. George's visits were unpredictable, and she wanted to make sure she was accessible whenever he was in town.

George made her feel alive again. Each week he surprised her with a lavish gift—from a fur coat, to a diamond bracelet and gold earrings, to bags filled with expensive designer clothes. Olivia had never been spoiled, and she relished the attention. She flaunted her fabulous new belongings in Don's face on their chance encounters. He was rarely home, and she no longer cared.

Olivia asked Don to move out of the house several times during the divorce proceedings. She could no longer stand to be under the same roof with him. He refused. After weeks of his defiance, Olivia rented a two-bedroom apartment twenty minutes from the house for herself and the kids.

One afternoon Don came home to find Olivia and Delma loading her car. She had packed up boxes of clothes, bags of toys and their wedding presents, which were still unwrapped in their original boxes.

"I'll move out," he stammered.

"I already got an apartment, Don!"

"I'll take it."

"Of course you want it now! I already put down a deposit and paid to turn on the phone. Once you pay me back for the phone, the deposit and put the apartment in your name, then you can have it."

That weekend Don moved out of the house and into the rented, two-bedroom apartment.

———

George took Olivia, her sister and parents out for lavish dinners.

They all fell under his spell. He was effervescent, vivacious and exciting. Olivia and George double dated with couples that she and Don used to go out with. They dined with Joel White so many times, he and George became good friends. It wasn't long before he became entrenched in her entire social circle.

When George went out with Olivia and her family or her friends, he insisted on paying for the entire bill. When they asked what he did for a living, he was happy to share every detail of his prosperous slot machine stocks. He offered everyone the opportunity to invest in his business, and promised that the return was one hundred percent guaranteed. He was undeniably successful and had more money than he knew what to do with. No one could resist investing. All her friends and family wanted to be a part of George's fabulous life. They gave him checks made out for five to fifteen thousand dollars with nothing more than a handshake on the deal. But the biggest investors were her parents.

Olivia's parents gave George their life savings of thirty thousand dollars. Her father even considered selling his taxicab medallion, which was worth several hundred dollars. But he decided at the last minute that he should hang on to his only source of income. He wanted a backup source of cash in case the check for the returns on the slot machine stock ran late.

———

Over the course of three months, George took Olivia on several extravagant trips, including New York City and a Hawaiian vacation. Olivia's parents gladly watched the children when Delma wasn't available. They saw how happy Olivia was and thought she had hit the lottery with George.

Olivia loved being treated like a queen. There was no denying their attraction, and they quickly became sexually involved. Olivia knew George was not the marrying kind, but she felt confident he would take care of her. On their last trip to New York City, in March of 1972, they made plans to move to Las Vegas.

Olivia told George the best time to move would be summer, while the kids were at sleep-away camp. This would give her a couple of weeks in Philadelphia to tie up loose ends and plenty of time to set up house in Las Vegas.

That May, the divorce papers arrived. George and Olivia spread the papers out on the desk in his hotel suite, and together they closely reviewed them.

George said, "Okay, these papers take care of my first condition. Here is the last one—in order for me to pay for the divorce in full . . ."

Olivia looked at him, aghast. She anticipated another condition, but the divorce papers granted her the children, child support of forty dollars per week per child, and the house. She couldn't fathom that he would want her nominal child support.

"I want you to put half of the house in my name."

Olivia drew in her breath sharply as he quickly responded, "This is the only monetary insurance I have for my investment in you."

She knew by the look on his face that he was not going to budge. He wanted to be sure she was committed to him in return for his paying for her divorce and moving her family out to Vegas. She had no option but to concede; however, figuring she could play at his game she said, "Okay, George. I agree to your condition with one addendum, which I will have Joel put in writing. In the event of your death, the house will be one hundred percent mine."

He grinned at her with an, *I'm-not-going-anywhere-baby* smile. "Agreed."

———

After breakfast one morning in May at George's hotel, he jumped up and said he wanted to buy her a celebratory divorce gift. His excitement was contagious and Olivia laughed. "What did you have in mind?"

"It will be something deserving of your beauty!"

He grabbed the phone and ordered a car service. When the car arrived, George whispered directions to the driver and instructed Olivia to close her eyes.

Fifteen minutes later, he had her open them. They were parked in front of a Cadillac showroom. Incredulous, Olivia jumped out and said, "Are you buying me a car?"

"Any car you want, my dear."

They walked around the dealership parking lot hand in hand. She couldn't contain her excitement. This was the most ostentatious gift she had ever received. She made a full assessment of the cars in the lot and set her eyes on the car featured inside the showroom. It was slowly moving around on a turntable. Without hesitation, George turned to the salesman, "We'll take that one."

The salesman said that was their luxury model. He began to explain all of the car's bells and whistles when George cut him off. "How much is it?"

The salesman told him. George pulled out his wallet and paid in cash. The man, now stunned and stuttering, asked them to come inside to fill out the paperwork. Once outside with the car, George handed Olivia the keys to her brand-new, 1973, metallic green Cadillac Brougham. "This is the car we will drive to Las Vegas."

In June of 1972, they embarked on their road trip out West.

Part II

CHAPTER SIX

Las Vegas, July 1972

George rented a spacious four-bedroom, furnished home for Olivia in the luxurious Desert Inn Country Club Estates. It overlooked the golf course and the International Hilton Hotel where Elvis was performing nightly. George set her up with groceries, spending cash and an envelope containing her children's airline tickets for their August arrival.

"You have thought of everything, George. I can't thank you enough."

"I don't want you to worry about anything. I am going to take care of you." He kissed her on the cheek and said he would be back in a couple of weeks.

Olivia had taken up much of his time during the past couple of months and knew that he must have plenty of work piled up. "When I get back, we are going to set you up with some auditions. Olivia, you are going to be the most fabulous showgirl this town has ever laid eyes on."

She felt exhilarated and free for the first time in years. She looked forward to her stress-free summer in which to make a home for the children and get familiar with her new city.

By the end of her second week in Vegas, it felt like home. She had preregistered the kids for school and had time to relax before they joined her. It was a lazy Wednesday morning when a knock came at the door. She was reading the paper and wasn't expecting any company. It had been two weeks since she heard from George and figured it had to be him. She jumped off the sofa and excitedly opened the door. Standing there was a woman who looked vaguely familiar.

"Hi, Olivia. I'm Loretta. Remember me—George's business partner?"

Olivia then remembered a brief introduction when she was in New York with George a couple of months earlier, but that was the only time she had seen her.

"Yes, of course. Please come in."

"I live a couple of houses down, and I would love for you to come to my place." Since Olivia had not been out of her house that much for two weeks, she welcomed the opportunity to get out and visit with a potential friend.

As they walked down the street Loretta seemed uneasy in her presence, but Olivia filled the awkward gaps in conversation by telling her about how much she loved her new home, about the children's school, and how she was looking forward to George's return.

When they arrived at Loretta's home, she invited her into her living room and motioned for her to have a seat. Olivia looked around briefly, taking in the white sofas, white pillows, white walls and white carpet. She concluded that Loretta didn't have children. No one in their right mind would decorate like this if there were little ones running around.

Loretta took a seat directly across from Olivia and said abruptly, "George is dead."

Olivia stared at her. "What are you talking about?"

"I don't know how or what happened, but he's gone. Dead, killed. His body has not been found, but I know for certain that he's dead. I thought you should know."

Loretta continued talking but Olivia only heard, "George is dead." Shocked, she sat there helplessly watching Loretta's lips move.

After some time passed, Loretta said, "Do you understand me, Olivia? George is dead. I just want you to know that there may be some problems."

"Uh-huh. I heard you." Olivia felt a crushing heaviness as she slid off the sofa onto Loretta's plush, white carpet. The enormity of what Loretta told her was too much for her. She had been to this dark place before and had hoped never to return. She hit her palms on the carpet and in a barely audible voice said, "No, no, no."

Loretta sat quietly, speaking only after Olivia became still. "Is there anything I can do for you?"

Olivia sat up cross-legged on the floor and shook her head side to side. The panic was overwhelming her, and she felt the need to get out of Loretta's home.

"I have to go back to my house. The house that George got for me."

Each step back to the house was like walking in quicksand. She wanted to fall and allow it to suck her in, but not until she got back into her house. She reached for the door handle and robotically entered her home. She went directly to her bedroom, collapsing on her bed and felt the weight of the world crashing down on her. Frantic thoughts ran through her head so quickly, she felt it would explode. She put her hands over her ears so she could think straight, *No job. No money. No George. No friends. No family. No husband. Stranded in Las Vegas. A house I can't afford. George is dead. The kids are coming.*

The emotional levees opened and her body shut down. There was no way out of this. She had a one-way ticket to nowhere.

Death was the only way to escape. She closed her eyes, welcoming the darkness and hoped never to wake again.

A full day passed before she opened her eyes. She thought of Rani, Todd and Suzanne. She shed fresh tears picturing her young, innocent children and knew death was not an option. Her children depended on her. She wearily sat up and grabbed the phone receiver. She dialed a number she now knew by heart. It was the one person she thought might be able to help her. Joel White.

————

She began to cry as the secretary patched her into Joel. "He's dead, Joel. George."

"Olivia? I can barely hear you. Are you okay?" Her sobbing was all he could hear. "Did you say George is dead?" He said with fatherly concern, "Who told you this?"

She told him about Loretta, George's business partner and how she had relayed the information to her.

Joel was stunned into silence. She told him she didn't know what to do or where to go. "George was going to take care of me. He was going to get me a job in a show, pay for this house . . . he was my lifeline, Joel. What am I going to do?"

There was a pause before Joel spoke again. He told her she was a fighter and it was going to be all right. She just needed to calm down and take a deep breath. He stammered, "Olivia, how can you be certain he's dead? There was no body found?"

"It is irrelevant at this point. I know what I know and he's dead. Loretta was certain. I don't need more evidence than that. I can't even think about it anymore. I need to think about what I'm going to do now. My kids are coming back in six weeks."

She paused to get her emotions under control, and then continued, "Joel I am in a city where I know no one. I don't have friends or family. I don't want to run back to Philadelphia. I put that life behind me. You are the only friend I feel that I can call. What should I do?"

Joel took a deep breath and suggested the unthinkable, "You have to call Don. You know he has connections all over Vegas through the Latin Casino. If you truly want to make a go of it out there, he is the only one who may be able to help you . . . and you know he will if he can."

Of course, and unfortunately, he was right, but calling Don for help *was* unthinkable. Yet she knew he had connections and the more she thought about it, he owed it to her after all the horrible years he had given her. She agreed that she would call him. She needed to get a job and sort her life out before the kids arrived.

———

As she dialed Don, she knew this was as desperate as she could get. Her stomach turned over with each ring. The thought of his knowing that she needed his help was agonizing. He picked up as soon as his secretary told him she was on the line. She maintained her composure as she calmly told him what had happened. She no longer cared if he felt satisfaction over her dire situation or even if he chastised her for leaving him and getting herself in this mess.

Don said, "Turns out I have a conference in Vegas next week. I will come out and see what I can do for you."

A sense of profound relief washed over her. She had hope that there was a ticket out of this mess.

Emotionally, she had to shut down her shock over George's death and focus on getting a job to support her family.

———

Don landed in Vegas five days later. He checked into a hotel and called Olivia to let her know he had arrived. Olivia was elated to have one person in Vegas that she knew, even if it was her ex-husband. He said he had several meetings with friends and business colleagues over the next few days. He told her he would see if he could help her get a job in one of the casino restaurants.

Olivia didn't hear anything from him, but didn't want to call his hotel and pressure him while he was collecting leads for her. She felt confident that he would reach out with a list of prospects before he left. As the date of his departure came, reality set in. Don was not going to help her. She felt depressed and lost. As she suspected, he left town without providing even one contact for her.

She could not believe what was happening with her life. Her kids were coming and she was stuck in this bad, dismal place. She had no time left for tears. She knew she had to do this on her own—she had to get motivated and find a job.

———

The day after Don left, her phone rang. It was the first call she had received since Don's call, days before. She knew he must be calling her with a lead. She dropped the want-ad section of the paper, grabbed the receiver and said, "Olivia."

"Is Don there?"

Disappointed, she said, "No he's not. He's gone back to Philadelphia."

The man was clearly rattled and said in a deep, coarse voice, "That's nice. I take him out on the town, set him up with shows, dinners and he doesn't have the fucking decency to call to say thank you or goodbye? Who are you?"

"I'm Don's ex-wife, Olivia. Did he give you this number? He wasn't staying here."

The caller said that Don gave it to him as a backup number if he couldn't be reached at his hotel. When he learned that Don had checked out, he couldn't believe it, so he tried the backup number.

Since she had someone with a pulse on the line, she decided to probe further. She knew he had to be somewhat connected in Vegas if he hooked Don up with shows and meals. She said, "I had asked Don to fly out here to help me get a job. Unfortunately, he didn't help me at all. He knows our children are moving out here soon and I need to find a job."

"My name is Tommy Vick. I work with the Vegas culinary union. That's how Don and I met." He hesitated for a moment and then said, "Listen, I live here and I know a lot of people. Let's meet. I can certainly try to help you out. By the way, your ex is an asshole."

She didn't want to discuss Don. She had already wasted too much time on him. Grasping firmly on the only rope that had been tossed her way she said, "That would be great, Tommy. I would be thrilled to meet with you."

He told her the address of where to meet him at nine o'clock that night. She hung up, hoping that she was going to meet someone who might actually be sincere enough to help her.

CHAPTER SEVEN

Tommy

Olivia dressed in a short, tight-fitting red dress and brushed her hair out of her face. She slipped on a pair of black pumps and headed out the door. She wanted to look like a knockout for Tommy—whoever Tommy was.

She glanced in her rearview mirror. *This is it. Things can only go up from here.*

She pulled into the lot across the street from the address Tommy gave her. She checked the numbers three times to confirm that she was in the right spot. She was in front of a strip club. She laughed out loud, "My god, it's a Monday for goodness sakes!"

She felt as though she had walked into a dark, noir thriller. She casually eyed the two topless women swinging around freestanding poles on stage as she approached the partially dressed hostess. "I'm looking for Tommy's table," she asked, per Tommy's instructions. The hostess pointed across the room to one of the booths. A man stood up as Olivia approached.

He was slightly shorter than she was and, although she had never seen one in person, she felt certain that Tommy was a gangster. Olivia's eyes quickly scanned his white pinstripe suit, burgundy shirt unbuttoned to the middle of his chest, and the mass of gold chains hanging around his neck. Her eyes slowly rose from the chains to his pockmarked face, and then met his eyes. Without even opening his mouth, she could tell this was a man without a conscience. She innately knew that if someone could make something happen for her in this town, this was her guy.

Olivia sat down, scooting close to Tommy in the plush, red booth. His breath quickened, making it clear to her that he was pleased with what he saw. He ordered her a drink without asking what she wanted, put his hand on her knee and said, "So, baby, what have you been doing since you got to Vegas?"

She smiled and put her hand on his. "Well, Tommy, it is a long and sordid story," she said flirtatiously while his rough, clammy hand rubbed her exposed knee.

"I want to know everything about you . . . Olivia." He seemed amused as he said her name, and with a sinister grin said, "I like how your name rolls off my tongue. Oliviaaaa."

She knew she had him under her spell, at least for the time being, and she metamorphosed from desperate divorcée to seductress. She laid out the details of her episode in Acapulco—meeting George, her divorce, and George's death. She told him that George promised to introduce her to everyone he knew and was going to get her into show business. She told Tommy that she now had nowhere to turn.

With much conviction, Tommy proclaimed, "Olivia, I am going to take you under my wing."

She smiled and took a deep breath, "I want to get into show business, as George promised."

Tommy said he knew everyone who made Las Vegas tick, and he would introduce her around. He told her this would be the best way to get a spot in a Vegas show.

They sat at the table for an hour, talking about Vegas. He invited her to parties.

"Come to Lake Mead this weekend. I'm having a small get together on my boat and I want you there. As a matter of fact, tomorrow night you will come to a Culinary Union party with me."

It was not so much a request as a matter-of-fact statement.

"I will go with you wherever you want to take me, Tommy." He had no idea just how desperate she was.

He wrote directions to both locations on a napkin and then kissed her on both cheeks. That was her signal to leave. She stood up and left the table without looking back.

Tommy was putty in her hands, and she knew that he was going to help her.

———————

The Culinary Union party was held in a large warehouse off the strip. From the way Tommy was received by attendees, there was no doubt that he was a major player, but it was also obvious that he did double duty as the eyes and ears of the joint—the if-you-fall-out-of-line-or-fuck-with-anyone-I-will-have-you-killed-or-kill-you-myself man.

His adrenaline was pumping when they left, and he announced that he was restless for some hard partying. They went to the strip club where Olivia had met him the day before and met up with an entourage of women. Toward midnight, and to Tommy's pleasure, the girls were sloppy drunk and getting out of hand. Olivia took the opportunity to excuse herself and slipped out the front door for home.

Tommy called her the next morning and said to meet him at a supper club that night. The rest of the week he continued to summon Olivia to his side from afternoon through the wee hours of the morning.

Tommy drank, tossed back random pills and fondled every woman that passed in front of him. Olivia played along, kept a smile on her face, and drank—but not too much—she wanted to keep her wits about her. She was mentally preparing herself for the party on Tommy's boat that Friday; if they set sail, she would not be able to leave on her own accord. Olivia had a feeling it was going to be an evening like no other.

———————

When Olivia pulled into the Lake Mead Marina, she could hear the music. She knew this was not going to be reminiscent of her suburban pool parties, where her friends sipped martinis and gaily chatted about the newest fashion trends. She took one last look in the rearview mirror. *I only have this face and this body, and I am going to have to use it to get what I want.*

Running her fingers through her shoulder-length, red hair and holding her shoulders back to gain full advantage of her five-eleven stature, she confidently walked toward the noise.

She quickly spotted Tommy's boat, and just as he had told her, it was the largest boat in the largest slip. It was the Las Vegas Culinary Union boat and he was part owner.

She was surprised to see that the party was already in full swing. She checked her watch to be sure that it was nine o'clock—the time he had told her to arrive. Olivia knew that Tommy wasn't a man who would tolerate tardiness.

As she walked down the boat's long slip, she saw dozens of half-dressed women dancing to a popular James Brown song. She looked up and down the boat, and spotted Tommy. He was wearing a white, button-down shirt that was completely unbuttoned, exposing the enormous belly that hung over his checked swim trunks. His layers of gold chains were impossible to miss under the bright dock lights.

Olivia caught his eye. He glanced at his watch, and then back to her. He was obviously anticipating her arrival. Tommy pushed his way through the girls and a handful of men, jumped onto the dock and announced, "Welcome, baby! This is my pride and fucking joy."

His pupils were huge, making his eyes seem darker than usual. He was repugnant and his mouth was pure filth, but this was her only friend in Vegas and he promised to make her a showgirl. She stood unwavering, took his hand in hers and said with an alluring smile, "Can't wait to get on board."

Tommy led her to the main party deck. The music was pounding, people sashayed, bumping into one another as Olivia and Tommy made their way to an empty seating area near the boat's steering wheel. As she sat, he looked down at her with a huge grin, letting her know that he was in his element and loving it.

Tommy reached into the pocket of his trunks and handed something to Olivia. They practically had to scream in each other's ears to hear one another. "Take one of these, baby. You will need it before the party *really* gets going."

"What is it?"

"It's just a Quaalude. It will make you feel great."

She had never taken drugs, but if she were going to immerse herself into Tommy's world, this was the moment. It wasn't that long ago that she was a housewife with three children, carpooling and baking brownies; now, here she was on a mobster's boat in Las Vegas with a strange pill in the palm of her hand. Once she took this pill, there was no turning back. Without hesitation, she leaned close enough to brush Tommy's ear with her lips and said, "Put it in my mouth."

Tommy grinned ear to ear. She was talking his language now.

An hour later, Tommy was undressing Olivia. She had hardly noticed that everyone else was already naked and an orgy was in full swing. She felt euphoric and more relaxed then she had in weeks. Tommy's touch sent shockwaves down her body as he lifted up her dress and pulled down her panties. She felt him slap her behind hard, but it didn't hurt. Her eyes were focused on the action going on around her. People were having sex in front of her, behind her and just steps from her feet. She had never seen any-

thing like it in her life. She was caught somewhere between reality and fantasy.

She faintly heard Tommy's voice. "Olivia! Hey, baby! I'm down
here. It's party time."

Through her haze, she looked down at Tommy, who was sitting
just below her. She had to blink twice before his image became
clear—he was sitting spread-eagled and naked on the white vinyl
seating area. "Your showgirl tits are going to look great with
rhinestone pasties."

Olivia cocked her head to the side and said, "Do you know
you're naked?"

"Yes, baby, and this naked body needs you to get to work."

"What do you want me to do?"

"You are going to suck my dick, while this one . . . " the girl
sitting next to him who was having sex with another man looked
up at her, " . . . is going to lick your ass while you do it."

Olivia looked around her. Bodies were intertwined. Girls on
girls; girls on boys; pills being tossed in the air from a woman
hysterically laughing from the boat's highest point. She knew this
was her hazing into Tommy Vicks' life. He promised to introduce
her to everyone he knew in Vegas. If this was her prelude to
becoming a showgirl—well then, she thought, the show must go
on. She slowly got down on all fours, took his penis into her hands
while the naked brunette fell down behind her and, as Tommy
instructed, licked her ass.

CHAPTER EIGHT

Dime Machine

Tommy took Olivia on his arm to every business meeting he had. She met casino owners, managers, chefs, bankers and CEOs.

In the middle of the week, he asked her to meet him at the Landmark Hotel. He said they were meeting with the food and beverage director. He suggested, in his most patronizing voice, "Wear that skirt with the zipper front. No underwear." She had become used to Tommy's directness, so she didn't bother questioning him. He was keeping his word and introducing her to everyone. She was certain she would soon have a job and be able to wean off her dependency on him.

Olivia and Tommy met in front of the Landmark Hotel glass elevators that led to the executive floor. Just as the elevator doors were about to close, a man jumped in with them.

"Whew, that was a close one!" he said, as he looked at Olivia and smiled. When the elevator started upward, Tommy slid next to Olivia and pulled down the zipper on her skirt. Olivia stood still, doing her best to look bored, yet completely humiliated. Tommy laughed as the man averted his eyes, looking everywhere but at her. He frantically pushed several buttons and got off on the next floor. Olivia yanked up her zipper and glared at Tommy.

"I told you, baby, you're going to have to get comfortable being naked if you want to be a showgirl."

"That doesn't mean I have to show every stranger in Vegas my vagina!"

He laughed and said, "Oh, yes you do! Think of it as beginner's practice. You are going to have to get used to showing off the goods, baby. Besides, nothing's wrong with showing a little pussy!"

After eight days of running around Vegas with Tommy, it finally paid off. He phoned Olivia and told her he got her an audition. "I told you that you could count on me. Go to the Aladdin Burlesque show rehearsal this afternoon. Be there at four. I spoke to the manager and set up a meeting for you."

"Tommy, that's fantastic! I will be there."

"Call me at my office right after. Good luck, baby!"

She couldn't believe it. Tommy had actually made it happen.

When she arrived at the Aladdin, she felt discouraged. It was one of the smaller casinos with none of the exciting luster of the larger outfits. She entered the unimpressive lobby, and she reminded herself that she had to start somewhere and had no business being particular at this point.

She approached the front desk to ask for directions to the Burlesque Theater. Without looking up, the desk clerk pointed and said, "It's down there. Take a seat in the audience and stay as long as you want."

The theater was intimate, yet surprisingly elaborate. The stage was hidden behind red velvet curtains trimmed in black ribbon. The walls were encrusted with gold-like trimmings that continued throughout the vaulted ceiling. She took a seat, sinking into the soft, red cushion. At exactly four o'clock, the curtains parted and jazzy music flooded the room. A dozen girls walked on stage, and

Olivia's mouth fell open. Just minutes into the rehearsal, she knew what kind of show this was. Girls were undressing, feather boa by feather boa. The first girl was naked by the time she stood up to leave.

Feeling humiliated and disappointed, she headed straight to the pay phones. She dug for change in the bottom of her purse. Plunking a dime into the phone, she dialed Tommy. He picked up on the first ring.

"Tommy. I can't do this kind of show! I have kids you know. Thank you for your efforts, but this is not the type of show I would or could do."

"Sorry, baby. I didn't know. Let me make it up to you." He told her to meet him at a specific address a couple of miles from the strip. "Meet me now. I have a surprise for you."

Discouraged about what he had in store for her she said, "No drugs or kinky shit, Tommy. I'm not up for it."

"Just meet me. You're going to fuckin' love this."

Deflated she said, "Okay. Ten minutes. See you there."

She parked in front of a warehouse in the middle of a deserted parking lot. Tommy was waiting for her at the entrance on the metal steps that led up to a red door.

"Wait until you see this." He opened the door, signed in with his ID and she followed him down a long, dimly lit hallway. He opened another door into a vast room filled with slot machines, thousands of them.

"Wow! What is this? It is unbelievable!" She was dumbfounded.

"I told you I knew Vegas, baby!" He told her this was a slot machine warehouse. If you needed machines for your casino, this is where you came. "Completely closed off to the fucking public. Pick one and it's yours; just for your own personal pleasure."

She walked up and down the aisles, marveling at the beauty of the machines.

"I want this one. A ten-cent machine. I like the smaller coins. This might bring me luck—I could certainly use some."

Tommy whistled and a guy about twenty-five years old came running with a hand-truck. "Take this one to my car. We'll pay at the front."

"I'm buying this with my own money, Tommy. This is my lady luck." She didn't want him buying her anything outright. Restaurant meals and cocktails were okay, but not gifts.

"If you insist, baby."

She handed the guy one hundred twenty-five dollars.

The dime machine. It resides at my sister's home in Philadelphia.

CHAPTER NINE

Feds

Tommy continued to take Olivia out for business lunches and dinners, but that didn't pay the rent. Money was so tight by the end of her fourth week in Vegas that she couldn't afford to pay it. She didn't want to ask Tommy for money, because she didn't want him to know how strapped she was. She also knew Tommy was not the type of guy who wanted to hear your problems—he just wanted to do business, kill people, pop drugs and fornicate.

Olivia approached her landlords and told them she couldn't pay the next month's rent. They knew George had left her in some kind of compromised position, and they suggested that she move into their two-bedroom carriage house above the garage. Fortunately, it was furnished as well. When she asked how much that would be, they told her to pay what she could. She thanked them for understanding and told them she would move that week.

It took Olivia the better part of two days to move from the large house to the carriage house above the garage. She took the smaller room and set up the larger bedroom for her daughters to share. Todd would sleep in the living area. They would have to make do until she could afford a better living situation.

While unpacking the last of her boxes, she thought about all the bad luck she had experienced over the past couple of months. The highs and the lows were extreme—too extreme. She thought of what moving back to Philadelphia would mean. She would have her parents and sister's support until she found a job, but the thought of moving back was more distressing than anything going on in her life at the moment. Going back would mean she failed. She was not about to give up on Vegas yet. She was determined to give it a year. If she couldn't make something of herself by then, she would head back to Philadelphia. Her train of thought was interrupted by a knock at the door.

"Who is it?"

"It's the FBI ma'am. Please open the door."

She assumed they had the wrong address. She opened the door to find two suited men flashing their federal badges. "Olivia Dushon?"

Dumbfounded, she looked at them and stammered, "Yes, I am Olivia."

"We have a few questions for you regarding your relationship with George Harris." Olivia's heart sank as she stood aside, letting them into the carriage house. They stood perfectly still just inside the front door as she closed it behind them. And then the interrogation began.

"How long did you know Mr. George Harris?"

"Has he ever been inside your home?"

"Did you know of Mr. Harris's business practices?"

"Did he ever ask you to hold any money for him?"

"Were you his girlfriend?"

"Did you know his friends?"

"Did you have any contact with him prior to his death?"

"Do you know where he keeps his money?"

"Do you know any of his family members?"

"Do you know if he has any children?"

"Did you know of his interstate money laundering and illegal activity?"

"Did you know he was running a Ponzi scheme?"

The questions came like a barrage of bullets one after the other. She didn't know the answers to any of their questions. She couldn't believe how much she didn't know about George and how foolish she had been to put her entire life in his hands.

She saw them eye her brand-new, ten-cent slot machine, sitting on a pedestal in the far corner of the main room.

"Did you know he was a crook? That he stole people's money by lying about investing in his fictional slot machine fund?"

This was the final blow, and she fell to the floor. She lay there on her side, crumpled up like a ball of paper. Her mouth was open, but her scream was only in her head as she pictured her family and friends' faces. George had not only died, he had taken their money with him. She couldn't believe that no one warned her. Then she faintly recalled Loretta's words, "I just want you to know there are going to be some problems."

Her life was over. The agent's words repeatedly ran through her mind, "He stole people's money by lying about investing in his fictional slot machine fund." She squeezed her eyes shut; the pain was unbearable as she recalled how she encouraged her parents to give George their life savings of thirty thousand dollars, and remembered her friends' putting their trust in George and handing him big checks on the sole basis of her association with him. Her anguish silenced the federal agents. They stood awkwardly in the doorway for several minutes, and then quietly let themselves out.

Olivia remained on the floor, eyes closed.

George had ruined her in every way possible. There was no way she could ever go back to Philadelphia and face her friends and family. They would all think she was his frontman, his shill. Knowing she could never go back left her feeling suffocated. Philadelphia was her last resort—a place where she had always been welcome—but never again. She returned to the horrible, dark place that had become all too familiar.

When she finally woke, she wasn't sure if hours or days had passed. She yearned for aspirin and a shower. She felt an urgency to wash away the filth that George had left on her.

She then called the only person she knew she could call, Joel White. When he came on the line she said, "Joel, I don't have the strength to tell you anything other than George was a thief. The FBI was just here."

Joel was appalled. He urged Olivia to tell him everything that had happened with the FBI. He couldn't believe that George had deceived them all.

"Listen, Olivia, the federal agents finding you in a rental home in Vegas is not to be taken lightly. It would be like finding a needle in a haystack. A law school friend of mine is just starting a law practice out there. I want you to call him. His name is Oscar Goodman and he's brilliant." He told her he would call Oscar and make sure he took her on pro bono, as a favor to him.

"I don't know what to say. I am so in over my head, Joel."

"I know. I understand. It will be okay. I want you to call Oscar in about thirty minutes. I just want to make sure I talk with him before your call."

Olivia was trembling as she pulled into Mr. Goodman's office complex lot. He had asked her to park in a specific spot, on a specific side of the building. After locating it she got out of the car, took a deep breath to calm her nerves, and then entered the nondescript, stucco building.

Mr. Goodman's office was on the second floor. He had a brass nameplate beside his door. She gently knocked as she peered into his office. Mr. Goodman stood up, walked around his dark wood, lawyerly-looking desk to shake her hand. He looked out the window, down to the only car in the lot—her shiny Cadillac—the one that George bought her just weeks earlier.

"Is that your car?"

"Yes." She hesitated to say more. Now she knew why he asked her to park where she did. He was going to take the only thing of monetary value that she owned. Her throat tightened as she thought, *I just can't take any more punishment.*

He looked at her, as if reading her mind. "Don't worry. I'm not going to take it. I'm going to help you." Relief washed over her. At least she had one less thing to stress about.

Oscar eased her anxiety by asking her to sit down, guiding her to a chair with his hand on the small of her back.

He took a seat across from her at his desk and said he wanted to know everything she knew about George, from the day she met him until the day she learned that he had died. Keeping her composure, she relived the small highs and the great lows of the past months. Oscar listened intently. When she was finished and emotionally drained, he looked at her, handed her his business card and said, "If the feds come back, you tell them to come see me."

That was it. They shook hands, she thanked him and walked out the door. She didn't dare look up to see if he was watching her get into her car.

When she got home, she laid on her bed, completely exhausted. She needed to get out. It was time to call Tommy. She had not been in touch with him in over two days.

"Olivia! Where the fuck have you been? I have been calling you." Even as crass as he was, her heart was warmed by the sound of his voice. She did have someone who cared about her in this town. She told him about the visit from the federal agents and what she had heard about George.

"Well, I'm glad that this George guy is dead, because if he was alive, I'd kill him with my own two hands."

She knew he meant it.

———

That evening she decided to stay in. She told Tommy she would see him the next afternoon. As much as she needed to get out, her body was unwilling.

The phone rang as she got out of the shower. She halfway smiled, thinking it would be Tommy, encouraging her to come party.

"Hi, Olivia. Good news! Your home has sold! I need to know where I should send your check."

For a moment, Olivia couldn't grasp what she was hearing. It was her realtor in Philadelphia. "Sheryl! Oh my gosh, thank you!"

"After my commission, you'll get sixty thousand. I thought you would be happy with the selling price. It did very well. I will be able to send you the check in two weeks."

Olivia couldn't believe how timely the call was. The only upside of George's dying was that the money was all hers.

She grabbed the newspaper from her bedside table and mapped out what to do with the money. She wrote "$60,000" in the corner, then subtracted 30,000 and wrote next to that *"pay back parents."* Next to the 30,000 left, she wrote, *"Rent, food, gas and children's expenses."*

With the news of this newfound money, the feeling of desperation eased. She had some finances to boost her confidence. She felt this was just the beginning of the good luck that would get her back on her feet.

CHAPTER TEN

Audition

Tommy encouraged Olivia to come out the next night. He told her this was to be the most important introduction he had for her yet. He was introducing her to the president of Valley Bank. "This is it, baby! Look your most gorgeous. Meet us at the Tropicana. This guy is a real, fucking investor. Casino bar. We'll see you at eight."

Olivia made sure she looked elegant, yet sexy, before she walked out the door. She was getting used to this. She put on a white pencil skirt and a white chiffon, low-cut, sleeveless top. If she was meeting someone with any sort of financial power in Vegas, she had to make this man want to help her.

She found Tropicana's main bar in the middle of the casino floor. From a distance, it looked like one unified party of high rollers, but everyone was paired off in little groups, having intimate conversations. The area was a dimly lit, smoky, circular area that allowed the patrons to see the action on the casino floor around them. The handsome bartender seemed to be standing in the center of this particular universe with a dark wood bar surrounding him. Beautiful waitresses dressed in rhinestone brassieres, full-cut panties and high heels ran to and from the bar with trays of designer drinks.

Olivia spotted Tommy and walked up to the table as both men

stood up. Tommy grinned as if he were introducing his firstborn to the president of Valley Bank.

"Larry, I would like you to meet Olivia."

Larry's eyes combed every inch of her. "Looking at you, I agree with Tommy. YOU should be a showgirl."

Olivia thanked him with a confident and lingering handshake and said, "Nice to meet you too."

Larry wore a dark, finely tailored suit and had the bearing of a man with great financial power. He was slim, taller than she was, and wore black spectacles that fit tightly against his full head of salt and pepper hair. When he smiled at her, the deep-set wrinkles around his mouth seemed to fit into place and his eyes lit up.

"How long have you been in Las Vegas, Olivia? And what brought you out here to our great city?"

His confident voice reminded her of her former father-in-law, and that familiarity allowed her to warm up to him immediately. She told him about George and that he had brought her across the country, away from everything she knew, and then disappeared. She didn't want to sour the mood by informing him that George was dead and the feds were after her.

After twenty minutes of acting like she was hanging on Larry's every word, he promised to get her an audition with the Tropicana's Les Folies Bergere. She was ecstatic—it was one of the most respected and glamorous shows on the Vegas strip, but she didn't want to appear desperate. In an appreciative, yet moderated voice she said, "Thank you so much, Larry. That would be wonderful. I would be forever grateful."

When the conversation began to dwindle, Larry turned to Olivia and invited her to dinner. Tommy excused himself for the evening, knowing time alone with Larry would guarantee her a place in Les Folies Bergere—the show, of which, he was indirectly an owner.

Olivia was so thankful for Tommy's introduction, she wanted

to squeeze him as he got up to leave, but offered him a simple peck on the cheek. Without using words, she communicated to him how much she appreciated this introduction. As Tommy left, Larry took Olivia's hand and led her through the Tropicana.

She beamed as it dawned on her that she was having her first real dinner date in Las Vegas with a gentleman—one who didn't use the work "fuck" as a noun and a verb. She tightened her hand around Larry's arm as they entered one of the casino's spectacular restaurants.

———

The call came the next morning. Not only did Larry connect her with the show's director, he got her an audition for that very week.

Tommy was jubilant when Olivia called him with the news. He told her he was certain she would get the job, especially since Larry had set it up for her. Tommy stressed that more than ever, she had to get comfortable with being naked. He explained that the Les Folies Bergere was not a strip show, but that she would be scantily clad on stage.

"We have to rid you of any inhibitions, baby. I want to make sure you fucking nail this audition."

She knew he already had something in mind, but wanted to make sure it didn't require her streaking down the Vegas strip. "I hope you're not thinking of anything twisted, Tommy."

"No. Nothing like you're thinking," he laughed. "The next two afternoons I want us to go out on my boat. Meet me there this afternoon at three—and bring a G-string."

At three o'clock sharp, Olivia was at the Lake Mead Marina. She was relieved to find Tommy alone on the boat, prepping to go out. This was an anomaly; he was never without a harem of women on his boat. He turned when he saw her coming aboard.

"Just you and me today. When we get out on the lake, you will take off every inch of clothing—except for a G-string, if you want to wear that. We will spend the entire day just hanging out, but you will be butt naked. You have to get used to that, baby."

They spent their time on the boat playing cards, reading, gossiping, sunbathing and drinking. They attempted to have sex several times, but Tommy could not get an erection.

"You know it excites me when people are fucking around me. It's not you. I need the tits and ass around. Baby, you know I can get it up when I see the fucking going on."

Olivia laughed off his excuses, but she was relieved that she didn't have to have sex with him—even though she knew there would be more attempts throughout the day.

After a late afternoon swim on the second day, Tommy stood on the bow of the boat and proclaimed that he was "ready to fuck." Olivia sighed and lazily straddled him on the same white vinyl sofa she serviced him on weeks earlier. Just before he climaxed, he popped open a small pill.

"Breathe this in! Quick, baby! Your orgasm will be fucking amazzziiiinnngg!" Their faces came close as they both inhaled the small amount of dry-ice-like vapor that was released from the pill. Their orgasm lasted for what seemed like hours. It was a sensation Olivia never experienced before.

She breathlessly rolled off his lap. "What the hell was that?"

"It's some kind of nitrate they use to revive heart attack patients. Crazy shit."

"What?" She was dizzy and weary. "Tommy, I think I need to get home. You are completely nuts and I'm exhausted. I'm confident I'm ready to audition."

She had nothing left to be self-conscious about. Tommy had achieved what he set out to do . . . rid her of any inhibitions.

––––––

Olivia stood in her closet for an hour, contemplating what to wear. Nothing seemed quite right. With minimal time left before the audition, she left the house wearing a white bikini and a trench coat.

She pulled up to the Tropicana and felt the *rush* of show business when the nattily dressed valet took her car. She stared at the flashing, bright bulbs of the grand entrance hall as if she were seeing them through new eyes. She knew she desperately wanted this job.

She walked into the theater and found the show director at the front of the stage. She introduced herself. He glanced at her and said, "Get up on stage, lose the coat and let's see what you got."

She walked up the steps to the middle of the stage.

She looked at him for a cue, but he just stared blankly back at her. She shrugged and took off her trench coat, allowing it to fall behind her. He looked at her, up and down, and instructed her to walk back and forth. She held her head high, shoulders back, radiating as much confidence as she could muster and took twenty steps to the right. She stopped, turned, and repeated her steps to the left. She then stood in the middle of the stage where she had dropped her trench coat.

"That's all. Go backstage to the left. See Flora, our stage manager. She will tell you what to do next."

She didn't know if that was a good or bad sign. She picked up her coat, smiled briefly and said, "Thank you."

She went back stage and found Flora taking notes just behind the curtains. She was a short, stocky, white-haired woman with a pad of paper in one hand and a pack of cigarettes in the other. They made introductions.

Flora informed her that they had two dancer spots to fill in the show. She took Olivia's contact information and told her she would be in touch the next morning if she had made the callback.

At nine, Olivia was pacing the floor of the carriage house waiting for the call. At eleven-thirty, the phone rang. It was Flora. She had gotten the callback. She told her to come in at one that afternoon for the final audition for a showgirl spot in Les Folies Bergere.

Olivia met Flora backstage promptly at one o'clock. She handed her a short, black piece of material she called a dress and said, "You are going to learn a routine with another girl named Josie, who is also auditioning. I need to see you both at center stage in five minutes."

Olivia's competition was warming up. Josie was a head shorter and flat chested, but looked like she had dance training. Not intimidated by the fact that she had no idea what she was doing, Olivia stood in the middle of the stage with her shoulders back, dwarfing her competition, and awaited instruction.

A frightfully thin dance instructor ran on stage clapping her hands loudly. She wore tight black leggings, pink leg warmers and a pink, half t-shirt that read "Vegas" in bold, black letters. Without any introduction she said, "I am going to teach you two a fast, two-minute number. You either get it or you don't."

Olivia didn't have time to think it over. She noticed the show director sitting in one of the empty rows in the back of the theater, swinging his glasses around and looking bored. She knew there was no second chance, and she had to nail this.

They practiced three times before the music started and the dance coordinator screamed, "Hit it." After the music stopped, Olivia stood in the middle of the stage looking around for their next direction. Flora appeared from backstage and told both girls to get dressed.

When Olivia got back to the dressing room, Flora told her she had been selected for the number-one showgirl spot. The good news had not sunk in before Flora introduced her to Risa.

Risa had tried out earlier in the week. She was five-ten, had a sweet face, an incredible figure and she was to be in the number-two spot. Flora said, "Clear your schedules for the next week. I need you both here tomorrow for private dance training. Olivia, you need to sign up for ballet lessons at UNLV. Pronto! In one week, you will both officially start in the Les Folies Bergere."

Olivia walked out of the theater with Risa. Once they were in the hotel lobby Olivia exclaimed, "Oh my gosh! We did it!" They held hands like old friends as they walked out of the Tropicana.

She called Tommy when she got home to let him know the good news, and thanked him for everything he had done for her. She also let him know that her children were coming back soon, and between her responsibilities at home and at work, she wouldn't be able to see him anymore. She wanted to politely wash her hands of him and start her new life with a clean slate. He said he was very happy for her, wished her luck and said to call him when she could come out and party. She knew she never would.

CHAPTER ELEVEN

Les Folies Bergere

Olivia and Risa became chummy in just two days. Their first day of training was from ten in the morning straight through to three in the afternoon, in front of the director. He sat among the empty audience, directing the girls to walk from one side to the other, from the back of the stage to the front. "Slower. Faster. Shoulders back. Head up. Eyes toward the audience. Graceful."

At two o'clock, he had the other fifteen showgirls come out to practice lining up across the stage. He placed Risa and Olivia in the procession where he thought their bodies and height would fit best. Risa was fifth in line and would be stationed to the left of the stage. Olivia was last to walk out and would be front and center—closest to the audience. Olivia felt exhilarated at the beginning, and by three p.m., exhausted. She still had to get to UNLV by five for an hour-long ballet class.

As she and Risa were packing their bags up to leave and were meeting some of the other girls, Flora ran in. "Tomorrow—here at ten a.m. sharp. You will get fitted for costumes and learn about show makeup. Your first show is in six days. And remember, girls, there are two shows a night—eight and eleven. We need you to be ready."

Risa and Olivia nodded in unison, smiling at their good fortune to be part of the most fabulous show in Vegas.

At five p.m. Olivia was standing in a room with eight other girls in a ballet class at the University of Nevada, Las Vegas. It was an hour of pure torture. She needed to learn discipline of the body and she was far from graceful. Her arms and legs had to move elegantly, gliding toe to heel with every step. Because she was given the coveted stage position of front and center, she knew the show director would be merciless if every move wasn't perfect.

––––––––

The next day Olivia was assigned a makeup station. Each station was equipped with a large round mirror surrounded with bright light bulbs, three drawers, and a white-cushioned stool. There were six stations arranged in pods of four, and Olivia was thankful that Risa was assigned to her pod. The other two women in their station were Maggie and Linda. They would be their "behind the scenes" instructors for the week and were in charge of teaching Olivia and Risa the art of stage makeup.

"We have to start with pasties," Maggie said. "They are a bitch, but the most important part of our costume. It's all about the way our breasts are perceived on stage, ladies."

Maggie had been with the show for three years and was a veteran. She had an exquisite face and was five-eleven, but had small breasts. She taught Olivia and Risa how she worked around her inadequacies.

"Unfortunately, I have small tits, but no one can tell under the bright pink lights on stage. You can disguise anything up there." Maggie proceeded to put layers of thick, beige foundation on her nipples. She then placed a heavy, rhinestone, nipple cover called "pasties" on the upper part of her breast. "See, by placing my pasties up here, it has the appearance of a larger, pear-shaped breast. No one can see my nipple placement from the audience. Great, right?"

The girls laughed, and Olivia asked how the pasties adhere to the breast.

"My tits are used to the torture. We line the inside of it with surgical tape. It is a bitch to take them off, so you will want to just keep them on between the two nightly shows."

Olivia worked the circular disks in her hands and grinned as she said that they should probably wait to try it out the following day. She gently placed the pasties back on the makeup station and glanced at Risa, who agreed that tomorrow would be the day to torture their nipples.

Maggie walked them into a large closet where Jezebel, the show's costume designer, worked. Jezebel was a dark-haired, heavy-set woman who was busy gluing bright yellow feathers onto a large headdress.

"Jezebel, introducing Olivia and Risa. New girls." Jezebel was prepared for their arrival and provided them with three different outfits. Olivia saw that there was a set of hanging racks labeled "OLIVIA."

Jezebel shook their hands as she handed an elaborate feather headdress to Risa. "You're going to have to stuff the tops of these to keep them standing upright on your heads. Use stockings, tulle, cotton balls, socks, whatever you can get your hands on."

Jezebel placed the yellow headdress she had just completed on Olivia's head. She held it in place like a child walking with a book on her head and tried taking a few steps.

"It will take some getting used to," Risa chuckled.

Jezebel then eagerly fitted them for rhinestone sarongs that felt like they weighed ten pounds each. Her movements were quick and frantic, as if they were actually in a pinch for time between shows. She said, "Gotta' be quick you know. Rush, rush, rush when you get off stage."

In an effort to slow her down, Olivia said, "These are the most beautiful, intricately designed sarongs. I think we're going to have to wear them just to get used to the weight."

Jezebel stopped working, enchanted by Olivia's compliment. She slowly and carefully ran her hand over the sarong and told them that each one was hand-sewn with the greatest of care and the best stones available. "Don't worry—you will have helpers changing you between acts—it won't be me be with my cold, rushed hands."

Jezebel handed Risa size-eight shoes and told her that they wear the same shoes for the entire show.

"And Olivia, you are going to have to get into a size nine. That's all we've got left."

Olivia squeezed into the one-size-too-small shoe and tried not to wince, thinking there would be no problem stretching them out over time. She asked, "How much time is there from when we get off stage until we go back on again?"

Jezebel asked them if they were aware that there would be dancers performing in the center of the stage while they were walking the perimeter of the stage "in my glamorous costumes." Risa and Olivia acknowledged they did not know that bit of information and were eager to hear more. She told them the dancers would be fully dressed, but the audience would only be looking at them, the *real* stars of the show. She hesitated for a second, realizing she hadn't answered Olivia's question. "Oh, I'm sorry, dear. I got lost in my own head . . . there are twenty minutes between each act, so that is when you change." She told them other performers, such as magicians and comedians, entertain the audience while they are changing. "After the show, you have an hour and a half break before the eleven o'clock show. You need to be dressed and ready to go at ten-thirty."

Risa asked where the other performers got ready.

Jezebel pointed out toward the hallway. "They have rooms out there." She told them they could check it out, but the other performers were forbidden to come into their space. "No one is allowed in the showgirl dressing room other than the director, producer, Flora and me. Someone even tries to sneak in here, they're fired."

Olivia smiled as she digested just how big of a deal her place in this show was.

When they got back to their pod, Linda was setting out pairs of fake eyelashes. "Glad you're back. I have to run through makeup with you. The long and short of it is, you need tons of it. Whatever you need, Flora will order it for you, but don't run out."

Then Linda said in a sweet, but distressed southern drawl, "Oh no—I'm one pair of eyelashes short for tonight," Her long brunette hair was gathered into a tight bun, allowing the girls to see her face flush as she looked around her area, careful not to step on them in case they had fallen to the floor. "I don't have time to get another pair for tonight!"

She was such a gentle soul, and the girls felt sorry for her missing eyelash set as though it were a national emergency.

Olivia pulled her stool up next to Linda's makeup station and counted four sets of eyelashes. "How many do you go through in an evening? I thought we went on stage three times during one show, so one set should last you."

Linda smiled sweetly at her and then Risa. "My dears, we wear five at one time."

Olivia threw her head back as she laughed and said she needed to see how that trick was done.

Linda placed one, two, three, four layers of eyelashes on her makeup table and glued them together. She then applied the entire mass just above her left, upper eyelash. It looked outrageous to Olivia and Risa, but she explained that everything needed to be overdone on stage.

Olivia sat at her mirror and, like a good pupil, put three layers of foundation makeup on her face.

"Blank slate. That's perfect Olivia, now you just paint on eyes, cheeks and lips." Linda told them to put on *at least* four coats of bright red lipstick, "If you aren't wearing enough lipstick, you will hear about it from the director or Flora. You can never have enough lipstick on."

After a day in makeup and wardrobe, Olivia ran out the door at 4:30 to her ballet class.

The rest of the week was a blur between fittings with Jezebel, dance rehearsals, and gluing on pasties, which tore at her nipples so painfully, she couldn't help but wince and tear up. On Friday she was handed her first, official, Tropicana paycheck. With that in hand and a free Saturday, she went to find a place to live. Even though she was comfortable in the carriage house, she needed a fresh start. She wanted to get out of the place George had gotten for her.

Olivia settled on a clean, spacious, three-bedroom apartment in Children's Village. It was an all-inclusive family community with daily activities and daycare. She could afford the rent with her weekly paycheck, plus have money left over to pay for the other necessities of life. She had banked the twenty thousand left from the sale of her home after paying her parents back and planned to buy a house the following year.

She telephoned Delma in Philadelphia to see if she had found another nanny position. She had not. Olivia asked and then begged her to fly out West and live with them for at least one school year. Delma was hesitant to leave her older parents for so long, but wanted to come for the kids. She agreed to come out for the school year. It was agreed that she would come a couple of days after the children arrived. Olivia then called Don to let him know he would be paying for Delma's flight and her year's salary.

With a large apartment and childcare in place, Olivia was fully prepared for her kids' arrival. But in the meantime, she was embarking on the experience of a lifetime—as a Las Vegas Showgirl at the Tropicana.

CHAPTER TWELVE

Showtime!

Her first night in the show was one she would never forget. The girls were weighed in promptly at five p.m. The show's director and three producers stood on either side of the medical scale while Flora moved the weighted pointer back and forth. They were weighed in order of their appearance on stage, with Olivia last in line. As she waited her turn she heard, "Good. Next." "You're Good. Next" "Too fat. Next." "Up a pound, lose it by tomorrow. Next." "Good. Next." One by one, the girls dropped off line until they got to her.

"Welcome, Olivia," said her director with a smug look on his face. He was proud of his latest recruit. "I would like you to meet our show's producers, Mr. Allen, Mr. Scott and Mr. Engle."

"Pleased to meet you," she said as she firmly placed her hand in theirs to shake each one. She was going to have to get used to the male mentality while she was in this business—they looked right past her face to her breasts.

She gracefully stepped onto the scale—126 pounds. Flora flushed with pride. "At five-eleven, good . . . very good." As the oldest girl in the show at thirty-two, Olivia knew that keeping to this first weigh-in weight would be critical.

The girls lined up backstage at 7:45. Nothing could prepare Olivia for what to expect when she walked out on stage. The curtain went up and the line of girls in front of her dwindled until it was her turn. She took a deep breath and walked out into the harsh, blinding, lights. She was tempted to giggle as she glanced into the audience, seeing nothing but the outline of a large crowd. When the music started, she and the other girls began to delicately move their arms and sway their hips. They walked past each other on stage around a professional dance team of two. Her mind was racing to remember everything she had learned that week: "Move like you are swimming." "Never *ever* move your hands above your head." "Move your arms from your elbow ever so slowly and grace-fully." "Remember who your partner is when you crisscross the stage." "Keep your space." "Do not run into one another." "Grace-ful." "Sexy." "Slow." "Smile." "Shoulders back." "Breasts out."

The girls winked at one another other in support as they passed on stage. They were a team, rooting everyone onward.

After the first twenty-minute act, they slowly walked off stage and, once out of sight, ran for a wardrobe change. By the time they reached wardrobe, they had fifteen minutes before they had to go back out for the next act. Each girl was assigned a *dresser* and Flora was Olivia's—yellow for the first act, blue for the second. With her new headdress on (stuffed with twelve pairs of stockings) and a fresh coat of red lipstick, she was in line for act number two.

By act number three, she felt more exhilarated than she had ever felt in her life. There was a standing ovation as the girls strut-ted in a line across the stage one last time. Olivia felt like a star. She had found her dream job—on stage as a Vegas showgirl.

There was an hour and a half between shows. She sat down with Linda and Risa, excitedly rehashing her first experience in the show, "What a rush that is to go out there like this." Olivia looked down at her pasties and gemmed sarong, "This is incredible."

Risa was just as exuberant. "What can or should we do between the shows?"

Linda pulled out a knitting kit and told them she knit

sweaters. "I would be happy to share and have you sit with me. I like to just take it down a notch after all that."

She told them they could take a tap-dancing class backstage, or if they wanted to, they could go out to the main casino bar. She said the show's producers encouraged the girls to go out and fraternize with the high rollers. She also mentioned that most of the time, men made requests to see girls after the show.

Just as Linda finished telling them this, Flora ran in with an armful of roses. "Girls, got roses for ya." She rattled off five names and the last one was "Olivia."

Flora tossed a dozen red roses on her makeup counter and told her that a Texan "would be honored" if she would meet him for a drink.

Linda nodded, encouraging her to go. She said it would be fun for her first time, but dared her not to go back to his room.

Olivia snickered as though it were the most ridiculous thing she had ever heard. "I am a mother of three kids. I am not about to go to anyone's room."

Maggie yelled as she wiggled into a short dress, ready to run out the door, "Well, if you do, make it a star fuck!"

Perplexed, Olivia looked at Linda.

"Sweetie, that's what we call safe sex. Anal sex."

Olivia snickered at her newfound advice. She grabbed Risa by the arm to get her to join her and the Texan. They kept on their heavy stage makeup, pasties, changed into cocktail dresses and headed out the door.

They walked through the casino to meet the six-foot-five Texan in the bar area. Every man's head turned in their direction as they walked by. It was their first experience on the casino floor as showgirls. Not a person walked up to them; they just stared with their mouths agape, as if Olivia and Risa were untouchable creatures that could only be gawked at. The feeling was incredible—and Olivia felt empowered.

To the Texan's delight, he got two girls for the price of one bouquet. He had a wide grin that displayed his horse-like teeth, and his stiff, dark hair blended into muttonchops that came down to his chin. He offered them drinks with a smile so big it looked dumb-ass silly.

"I don't drink, but I play twenty-one," Olivia said.

He replied in a deep Texas drawl, "Well alllrightty then, let's play twenty-one!"

An hour later and five hundred dollars richer, she handed the Texan back the hundred he gave her to start with and said they had to run to their next performance.

At their makeup pod, Olivia reported to Linda that she could handle the men and tossed four hundred dollars on the makeup table. Linda smiled and told her she was going to do just fine.

After the show, at midnight, some girls would go to the casino bar to meet men; others snuck out the back door and went for a girl's night. Olivia decided that was just what she needed. She had not spent a night out with the girls since she left Philadelphia.

Six girls, including Linda, Maggie, Risa and a redheaded busty girl named Monica, went to Maggie's favorite local watering hole, far away from the strip. She said if she was going to meet a man, it was going to be a local one—not some tourist from out of town who wanted to screw her because she was a showgirl. After three years of the show, she told them that the drooling men were the only part that "got old."

Olivia had the best time she had had in years. She made new friends, roared with laughter and felt cemented in her new life.

She walked into her Children's Village apartment at four a.m.

CHAPTER THIRTEEN

Philadelphia, August 1972— Suzanne

While my siblings were away at overnight camp, I spent the summer with my grandparents, Ida and Joe. They lived in a two-bedroom, first-floor apartment where all the old people in the world lived. I went to day camp during the weekday and swam all afternoon in the apartment complex's pool. I had a dedicated cheering section of silver-haired folks in plastic chairs. I was the official post-*One Life to Live* entertainment.

Grandpop drove a taxi and we spent every Saturday in it going from store to store. He drove us to Kmart in the morning where Grandmom would buy bags of nonperishables.

Lunch was a twenty-minute fiasco at a local fried chicken chain that had a satisfaction guarantee. *"If you are dissatisfied with your meal for any reason, get your money back."* There were three of these restaurants on our Saturday route, so we'd rotate each week. I would order the two-dollar kid's meal and Grandmom would order a three-dollar lunch meal. When we finished, she would summon the manager. It was impossible to hide my shame—I would be red-faced from the moment she stood up with our bare chicken bones on a tray. The dispute would always be the same.

Manager: How can I help you?

Grandmom: I was not satisfied with my meal.

Manager: (Looking at our plates) But ma'am, you ate your meal.

Grandmom: I did not like it.

The manager was no match for Grandmom—she would never back down. Thankfully, he would pause for only a moment, and then direct her to the register for her refund. Grandmom would righteously leave the restaurant with the same five dollars she entered with.

In the afternoon, Grandpop would drive us to Pathmark for double coupon day. I pushed the cart as Grandmom loaded it with everything redeemable with fifty-cent-off or more coupons.

When we'd reach the register at the checkout line, it was always a complete disaster. Grandmom had to sort out coupons for each item. If she couldn't find the coupon or learned it was a product not redeemable on double coupon day, she would stare at the item for an ungodly amount of time, deciding if it was worth it. The shoppers behind us would sigh loudly enough to humiliate me more than one would think possible for a toddler. By the time we got home, I was drained.

Sunday was return day. Grandpop would drive us back to Pathmark and Kmart so Grandmom could return 70% of what she bought on Saturday.

It amazed me that Grandpop never complained about these shopping rituals. He just drove Grandmom wherever she wanted to go, without a fuss. He would sit in the car, smoking his funny-smelling, self-rolled cigarettes while listening to National Public Radio. By the time we got back to the car, hours later, he was all smiles, asking where we would like to go next.

Several times a week, Grandmom would take me for long walks around the apartment building. She would pick up some broad, flat leaf that had fallen to the ground, hand it to me, and then tell me to focus on removing the fleshy green part, but leaving the veins intact. I suspect this was a project to prevent my mind from wandering while she lectured me about the importance of working hard and making money. She stressed the following life lessons during our summer walks and every summer thereafter:

Make your own money.

Save money.

Buy penny stocks.

Put the rest of your money in the bank.

Shop thriftily.

Use coupons.

Alphabetize your coupons.

Buy one, get one free.

If you don't need it, return it.

Polyester is best—cheap, practical, doesn't wrinkle.

Makeup is wasteful.

Plastic shoes are as good and as durable as leather.

Always be informed. Read the newspaper headlines. Watch the news.

Diabetic cookies are just like the real thing.

Freeze fruit just as it goes bad—healthy sweet treat, no waste.

Never waste food or clothes. Repurpose.

Keep yourself clean. Bathe daily with a washcloth.

Sleep is important.

Be very proud of your roots and being Jewish.

After dozens of shopping trips and Grandmom's life lessons, Rani and Todd returned from eight weeks of overnight camp. It was mid-August and we had two weeks before we headed to our new home in Las Vegas to be with our mom.

When all three of us were staying with our grandparents, we were assigned chores. Rani was on coupon-organizing assignment. She had to alphabetize coupons "by product, not brand" and place them in alphabetical order in Grandmom's Rolodex. My job was to water the half-dead plants and freeze the near-rotten fruit. I had to reuse the plastic bags that were used for last week's frozen fruit . . . even though there were rotted, brown fruit particles remaining in each bag. Todd's job was to take out the trash, get the mail and turn down the TV volume whenever there were commercials. Grandpop despised listening to commercials.

We spent some of our final days of summer at Aunt Betty and Uncle Barry's house. We had three older cousins that we adored. They had a huge basement where we could entertain ourselves for hours.

Uncle Barry took turns tickling us until we cried, and we'd spend the afternoons playing hide-and-seek or watching our cousins play street hockey. Uncle Barry would take us crabbing each summer, and Aunt Betty would cook the crabs in her oversized red crab pot. We'd top off the meal with Aunt Betty's famous chocolate cake, which I dreamed about sinking my teeth into from the moment we walked in the door.

Our last two days in Philly were spent uneventfully with our father. The most exciting news he had to share with us was that he was dating someone new and planning to marry her.

After forty-eight hours at his apartment, he dropped us at the airport in the care of a pretty TWA "stewardess." This was our first plane ride, and Rani was in charge because she was the oldest. We were excited about seeing our mom and our new home in Las Vegas.

CHAPTER FOURTEEN

September 1972–June 1973

The flight was bumpy and I became nauseated. When I turned green and clammy, Rani grabbed the throw-up bag from the seat pocket, and I used it to capacity. My brother moved as far from me as he could. My vomiting was making him queasy, and he could no longer deal with my close proximity. After the second bag was full, I put my head between my knees for the rest of the flight, while taking forced sips of ginger ale from Rani.

We finally landed in what looked like the middle of the Sahara Desert. I was sweaty and uneasy. The flight attendant's voice echoed over the speakers, "Please stay in your seat until the aircraft's engine has come to a complete stop. We will then open the cabin doors in the front and back of the plane for you to disembark. Thank you for flying with TWA."

The minute the roar of the engine came to a complete stop, Rani stood up, grabbed my damp hand and pulled my limp body toward the exit with Todd close behind. I peeked out the window and saw the tiny building that was McCarran Airport. Rani was still holding on to me as we got to the top of the steps, just outside the plane door. I breathed in the not-so-refreshing, dry, hot air and felt better. We used our hands to shield us from the blinding sun, which was doubly intense as it reflected off the silver, metal plane. We followed the line of people down the steps onto the steaming black tarmac.

We saw Mom as soon as we stepped foot on the ground. She was much taller than anyone else standing on the tarmac. We ran up to her and she knelt down, greeting us with a great big mom-hug. She ushered us to her green Cadillac, and we drove out of the airport, excitedly talking over one another about our new adventures-to-come in Las Vegas.

I sat between Rani and Todd in the backseat. They pushed me back and forth between them while Mom jubilantly told us about our new apartment and new life.

All I could see from my low vantage point in the car was some distant cactus, blowing tumbleweeds and a strip of road with very few cars on it. We didn't pass one stoplight on our way to our new home. While I was thinking about where our home could possibly be out here in the middle of the desert, Mom rambled on about her new job as a showgirl at the Tropicana. None of us knew what her new occupation meant, nor did we care, but we agreed that it sounded very cool.

After about twenty minutes in the car, signs of life started to emerge. Low buildings and a single strip mall appeared to our left. Mom announced, "Here we are!" as we pulled into the apartment complex with a sign that read, "Children's Village."

She explained to us that this was a community exclusively for families, and they had lots of fun activities. She told me I would spend most of my days at the community daycare while Rani and Todd went to the nearby elementary school. She also informed us that Delma would be living with us for the next school year because she worked at night. All of us were excited about seeing Delma and having her live with us.

Our new home was a ground-level condo. Once in the door, you could see that the kitchen, dining area and living room were all one common area. There was tan, wall-to-wall shag carpeting with matching tan-colored walls throughout. The apartment had three bedrooms and two baths. Mom gave Rani and me the master bedroom to share with Delma, Todd got the smallest one next to ours, and Mom's room was down a short hallway. We dropped our things and went directly outside to see the pool. It was only 200 feet from our doorway. Next to the pool was an activity center and daycare where I would be spending most of my time.

———

Life moved along on a regular routine our first year in Las Vegas. I went to daycare and played with kids my own age; Rani and Todd attended public elementary school. Delma spent the day cooking and cleaning while my mother slept. Mom was home when we woke up. She helped Delma get us out the door, and she was there when we got home late in the afternoon. We would all have dinner together, and then she would leave for work at 5:30. She came home sometime around dawn.

Mom worked every night but Monday and Tuesday. Monday nights were Mom's date night. She would sit with us for dinner and then head out the door at seven o'clock. No one ever came to pick her up—she always met her dates someplace else. Rani said Mom was trying to find us a new dad. Mom said she was determined to get us a house with a pool within the next year. My sister guessed that she was trying to find the right man to execute that for her.

Tuesdays were reserved for Taco Tuesdays at Taco Factory. We made a production of piling into the car to go to Taco Factory. We'd pull up to the takeout window and order twelve tacos for two dollars. It was the highlight of our week.

———

One morning, after about five months in our new home, Delma stopped Mom in the kitchen as she was headed back to bed after getting the three of us off to school and daycare.

"Olivia, I want to pray for you." She reached into the bottom kitchen cabinet and pulled out a tray of candles.

"Where did those come from?" Mom was surprised, because she hadn't brought them into the apartment.

Delma put her fingers to her lips. "Shh, Olivia. You have to stay quiet." She lit the candles, waved her hands close to the top of the flames, and said, "Help this woman and her children. Her life too hard. She work too hard. She need a man who will take care of her." She then mumbled an undecipherable prayer under her breath.

Chagrined, Mom stood beside her for a few minutes, then, yearning for her bed, she gently put her hand on Delma's shoulder.

"While you're at it, make that a handsome, nice, rich man who can buy us a house with a pool." She laughed and started back to her room. Then she added, "And if you can cast a spell to clean up that mess in the kitchen before I get up later, that would be great."

———

After months of our pleading to see her show, Mom eventually relented. We had never been to the Vegas strip, so we were looking forward to seeing what all the hype was about. It was going to be a late night for us, so Delma made sure we rested all afternoon. Mom said the show director had set aside special seats for us. She informed us that children were not allowed in casinos or the shows, so we had to be on our best behavior. Mom instructed us not to say anything when we saw her on stage. She made us promise that we would be very quiet. We were told not to point at her, say her name or speak at any time during the show.

"You must be invisible. Children are not even allowed in the casinos, let alone the shows, so you must be very quiet."

Mom reminded us a zillion times that night before she left, "Remember, you are not to say anything while you are in the theater. You must remain very quiet. It is important that no one knows that you are there so we don't get in any trouble."

We all repeated, "Okay! Okay!"

She looked at Delma to make certain that she understood as well.

———

The show director provided a car service to and from the Tropicana. We all hopped into the back of the black sedan, squealing with excitement while Delma mumbled prayers to herself.

When we pulled onto the Vegas strip, there were some hotels with signs lit up in bright, flashing bulbs: Sands, Golden Nugget, Circus Circus. There were more, but I couldn't make out the names because when we got close, all I could see were bright, flashing bulbs.

The driver pulled up to the Tropicana entrance, and we were in awe of all the blinking lights and the colossal entryway. Our heads jerked in every direction trying to take it all in. It was the most awesome display of lights we had ever seen. There were hundreds of fancy-dressed, smiling people coming in and out of a large set of glass doors.

We got out of the car, and Delma made us hold hands. She held my hand so tightly, my fingers went numb. We couldn't help but stop and "ooh and ahh" every couple of steps, but Delma continued to tug at our hands repeating, "Hush children. Keep walking. Stay close." We knew she was scared that one of us might get lost in the mass of fancy people.

As soon as we entered the lobby, a man in a suit walked up to us. Since we were the only children in the entire place and were being led by a crazy-haired, stressed-out nanny, we were easy to locate. He said he was a friend of our mom's and would be taking us to our seats.

He whisked us through a black, almost invisible door that looked like part of the wall. We followed him down a short hallway and entered an enormous theater. It was filled with more fancy people. We didn't have time to look around since the man was goading us to hurry and was herding us like cattle. We followed him down a zillion little stairs and finally reached our seats. We were in the first row and sat just as the lights began to dim.

His parting words were to be very quiet and try to sit still until the show was over. My sister rolled her eyes—as if he knew our mom had told us twenty times and we were that stupid to need to be reminded again. I glanced behind us and saw a sea of people. I felt a jolt of excitement knowing they must have all been there to see my mom.

The curtains parted and loud music exploded from an area below us where people were playing instruments. Rani and Todd were on the edge of their seats looking like they were ready to leap out of them any minute. Delma began to sweat as she kept pushing them back with her left arm like a bouncer at a bar deflecting a crowd. One woman walked out from inside the curtains wearing a dress of long feathers that flowed behind her. A few more women came out and that was when we saw her.

Mom was wearing a tall hat of yellow feathers on her head, a load of makeup, a long skirt that was way down under her belly button and two shimmery buttons covering her boobies. Rani and Todd jumped up, screaming over the orchestra music, "Mom! Mom! Over here!"

Delma was so startled that it took her a second to react. She held me down with one hand and tried to pull Rani and Todd back with the other as she hissed, "Sit down. Hushhhhhhh!"

Mom gave us an acknowledging glance that was enough to calm us down. Rani and Todd happily sat back in their seats, watching in awe as our mom walked right up to the front of the stage, half-naked, in front of hundreds of people.

Halfway through the show, there was an intermission, and it was time for us to leave.

Delma clutched the cross around her neck, looked up and thanked Jesus a dozen times that we were leaving. The same man who ushered us in was there to escort us out. Strung together by our hands, we followed one another out the same invisible black door we entered. We went out the main entrance and found the same car waiting to take us home.

The following morning, Rani found a pair of men's black dress socks on the floor. She asked Mom whose socks they were when she sleepily walked into the living room at eight o'clock. "Those are my friend's socks. He is an old friend of Pop Pop Dushon. His name is David Brenner. He was in town doing a show and just came by after the show last night to make sure I got home safely."

"Why did he leave his socks?"

"I just don't recall. Maybe his feet were hot. It is hot out there. Give them to me, and I'll return them." With that, she threw them in the trash.

Rani thought this Brenner person must have been in some kind of rush to leave without his socks.

———

By December, Mom's stories about her work at the Tropicana became more exciting, simply because she presented them that way. Her gestures were animated, her details colorful, and she seemed more alive than ever.

At the dinner table one night she said, "I met an old friend from Pop Pop Dushon's Latin Casino last night. His name is Alan

King. I know that might not mean much to you, but he is a very famous, talented and funny man." She made a silly face that set us all to giggling.

"I also met a man about this tall," she said, jumping up on her tippy toes. "He had the most gorgeous deep, blue eyes that looked like an ocean that went on forever and ever." Her hands moved in every direction like an octopus while her ceramic, bangle bracelets clanked against one another. "His name was Joe Namathhhhh."

Todd's eyes popped open. "What was he like? Was he wearing a JETS uniform?"

"Now that would be silly, my silly little one," she said as she tousled his hair. "That is only for the field." She paused, thinking about who was with him and where she saw him. "He was having a drink with a man named Steve Wynn. I was on a break with some of my friends from the show and they called us over to say hi."

"Did you get an autograph?"

"Sorry, buddy. It just didn't seem right at the time. If I see him again, how about I tackle him, bring him home and you can talk to him yourself."

"That is a great idea. Do that next time!"

———

Twice a month Delma had time off from three p.m. to six p.m., and Mom would take us to eat at a local watering hole she liked. Taking us to a bar seemed like a good way to kill two birds with one stone; we kids got a free meal while she got to socialize.

When we'd enter the Dust & Rusty Bar, every second and last Tuesday of the month, it seemed like "Copa Cabana" was always playing on the jukebox. This is where Mom would come after the show on most nights until four in the morning. The bartender would greet us as we walked in, while patrons eyed us strangely and smiled, probably thinking it was precious to see kids in a bar.

Little did they know that we were regulars, and the "no one under 18" sign did not apply to us.

Mom would sit us in a corner booth and instruct us to stay close to it. She'd point us in the direction of the happy hour buffet. While Mom talked to people at the bar, we ate our complimentary buffet of wings, pigs in a blanket and popovers. After an hour, we would go home stuffed and ready to go to bed. Delma would be back in time to take over so Mom could leave for a date night.

———

One evening at the Tropicana after the first act, Flora said she *had to* introduce Olivia to one of the owners. It was not the usual procedure to meet someone during their fifteen-minute breaks, but these were special circumstances; you did not deny an owner. She was one of the most sought-after showgirls, and this type of meeting had become the norm. Mr. Dale Gustafson had seen her in the show and wanted to meet her; it was as simple as that.

Dale was a banker from Minnesota. He was Olivia's height, had thinning brown hair and green eyes. He wore a gray suit that complemented his fair complexion. Olivia greeted him with a genuine smile, as she would any casino owner, while he gently kissed her hand. One cocktail and twenty minutes later, he told her he was crazy about her. They went on several dates over the following weeks whenever he was in town. She knew having a relationship with an owner allowed her to have certain privileges at the casino, so she made herself available to him whenever he called.

In May, Dale asked her to join him for Hubert Humphrey's birthday party in Minnesota. She was hesitant at first. She wasn't ready to leave her comfort zone of Vegas and be stuck with a man out of town. He quickly supported his invitation by saying it would be a quick twenty-four-hour trip and she would not have to miss any shows. She was amused that he assumed her hesitation was about missing work. He promised her he would get her back the very next day. She agreed, knowing he was a gentleman who would stick to his word.

They took off to Minnesota the following week. They checked into their hotel suite as a couple and, with limited time, began changing for the party. Olivia was not sure what to wear out of the several dresses she brought with her. She wanted to be the girl she thought Dale expected her to be for the night, so she opted for a skimpy, blue, low-cut, elaborately sequined dress. She applied her show makeup and met Dale by the hotel door of their room. His mouth fell open, which eventually made its way into a pleasing grin. She took that as compliment, and they were out the door.

When they entered the party venue, she realized she was completely out of her element. She was in Minnesota, not Vegas. She was either extremely overdressed or underdressed; she couldn't be sure by the looks she was receiving. It didn't help matters that it was extraordinarily cold for a May evening and all the other women were wearing floor-length gowns.

The conservative crowd followed her with their eyes all night. She held her head high. She made the assumption that they were looking at her because she was with a very important man, rather than some flashy, outrageous showgirl he flew in from his casino. Dale claimed ownership by keeping his hand on her back for the entire evening.

Disembarking plane in Vegas.
I am holding hands with stewardess,
Todd behind me and Rani veering
off to the right.

Olivia standing behind dancers.

Center stage.

Walking on stage for finale.

Showgirls during finale.

CHAPTER FIFTEEN

Philadelphia, Summer 1973

After an uncomplicated nine and a half months in Vegas, summer was upon us. It was time to head back east to see our relatives and go to summer camp. Delma was going to fly back with us, as she was moving back to Philadelphia. She missed her family and had promised Mom only one school year in Vegas to help us adjust to our new lives.

The night before we left, Rani overheard Mom on the phone talking about sleep-away camp. Her voice was high and tense as she spoke to a camp director. She was pleading with him to take her four-year-old daughter for the summer. Rani and Todd were old enough for overnight camp, but at four years old, I was still three years too young. From what Rani heard, he must have said he would not consider taking a child under six years old. Mom continued to plead, telling him that she was a single mother and needed the summer to make a proper home for her children. In a final act of desperation, she offered to pay extra. The camp director caved. He agreed to place me in a room with one counselor to look after me.

When we got to the airport, we got our big mom-hug. Her famous last words were, "I promise to find us a home with a pool by the time you come back at the end of the summer."

Delma huddled us together and guided us along the tarmac, up the stairs and into the plane.

————

When we arrived in Philadelphia, Delma was met by her father. She hugged each of us and whispered some sort of religious prayer in our ears before she left with him, carrying her single bag.

Grandmom and Grandpop were waving frantically to us as we walked down the airport hallway with our TWA agent. Grandmom gave us smothering hugs as I smiled, breathing in the familiar scent of her Ben-Gay and mothball-infused clothing. We piled into the back of the car, loaded with diabetic treats for us in plastic Pathmark bags and headed to their apartment.

When we got to their place we swam, alphabetized coupons and played bingo. They bought a state-of-the-art video camera and filmed us constantly. There was no audio, so we spent hours walking along the parking lot in silent-movie-mode, waving like fools into Grandpop's handheld camera.

In the evenings, Grandpop would sit with us in their parlor and tell us hilarious taxicab stories from the past year. He was a passionate storyteller. We felt like we were in the front seat of his cab, experiencing that ride with him. Inevitably, Grandmom would interrupt at some point, because she was frustrated that her coupons were out of order in the Rolodex. Rani would be assigned to correct the mistakes.

After four days, Grandpop dropped us off at Aunt Betty and Uncle Barry's home for a visit. The day before camp, we stayed with our father in his new home. His new wife was not fond of us. She had two children prior to marrying him, and our visits were a nuisance to her. My sister hated going there most of all because our father would just watch TV in his room, biding time until we left.

———

Did you have a relationship with your father? And what is the state of your relationship today?

When my folks got divorced, he was pretty much out of our lives, with the exception of the few days we saw him each summer. Once he was remarried, he was just as dismissive toward us as he had always been—as was his new wife. I didn't care much. I only knew him from those few times we visited him. Even when we moved back East years later, he made little effort to see Rani and me.

Do you wish you had a stronger relationship with him?

The term dad *had very little meaning to me personally. Between him and Paul, there was no upside to a dad. Today I feel no animosity toward my birth father; no anger. Frankly, I feel nothing. I was so young when my parents split, and he has never been part of my life. It's honestly okay with me.*

Uh-huh.

She started jotting in her journal and motioned for me to continue.

———

I was welcomed to summer camp as the youngest overnight camper (ever). As agreed, I bunked with one counselor. Rani and Todd checked in on me daily. On visiting day, our grandparents came to see us. They would walk down the dusty parking lot path, smiling and carrying treats for us in overflowing shopping bags from Pathmark.

Todd, Rani, cousin Tori, me and Grandmom Ida
outside her apartment building.

Aunt Betty and me.

CHAPTER SIXTEEN

Summer 1973—Olivia

While the kids were away at camp, Olivia's life in Vegas accelerated to warp speed. She was now a seasoned member of the Les Folies Bergere. She partied into the morning hours, went out with countless men, and embraced being showcased at the helm of the stage.

In the beginning act, she was now positioned as the first girl to walk slowly up a set of stairs of a Grecian-style stage set. She wore a flowing white robe, exposing her front; a sequined skirt; and matching pasties on her breasts. It was during one of these performances that she made her first and only on-stage blunder. She was walking up the stairs, elegantly swinging her arms at her sides, when the heel of her shoe got caught in her robe. She immediately remembered the director's harsh words from months ago, "If you *ever* trip or misstep, hold onto your goddam headdress and get right back into it."

She stumbled forward and grabbed her headdress, which was nearly tipping over, then bumped into a white column prop that was next to the stairs. She got herself upright in seconds, figuring no one would notice her trembling hands for the duration of the show. When she got backstage, the show director said, "It was the two pounds you put on this week that made you falter." He didn't have to say anything else. She didn't eat for the next two days.

During the final act of the show, Olivia was selected to be one of the girls who were suspended from the theater ceiling in a basket similar to one attached to a hot air balloon. It was an incredible sensation when the audience looked up at her in awe, as she gracefully tossed inflated balloons down over them.

She had built a strong kinship with the other girls and the casino became a second home to her. She was sitting at the same vanity with the same girls for over a year, and they now knew almost everything about each other.

For months, the girls good-naturedly teased Olivia about how meticulous she was in keeping her space tidy; she said it was the "mother" in her. However, after a year, her vanity was on par with the others; scattered makeup, fake eyelashes, surgical tape, hair sprays and gels. She had become far too busy with dinner dates between or after shows.

Following every show, Flora would have several bouquets of roses for Olivia from men who were back in town to see her, or ones who wanted to meet her for the first time. Either way, the roses always meant the same thing—an invitation, which turned into an obligation to meet the sender. If she was too tired, she had learned a trick . . . sneak out the back door of the casino and call out to Flora just before the door closed, "Tell him I fell ill!" She would then go on a prearranged date or hang out with her colleagues at a local watering hole.

On several occasions, Olivia was asked by the show director to escort a high roller to dinner. He would flatter her by saying she was singled out *just for a dinner date,* but she knew better. She knew exactly what the men were expecting when they got the Les Folies Bergere show director to summon her. These were men who dropped thousands of dollars at the casino and picked one show-girl they wanted, and expected, to sleep with.

The evenings with the high rollers were exhausting and inevitably turned into all-nighters. The man would begin with asking her for a drink, simply wanting a showgirl on his arm for the night . . . and expect to bed her later. She'd always deflect their insincere attempt at chivalry with her coin phrase, "I don't drink, but I play twenty-one."

As she and her "date" walked the casino floor to the twenty-one tables, she would wink at her friends who were casino-hired shills. They were the gorgeous men and women wearing brightly colored outfits and having the most fun at various gambling tables. They were gregarious, winning, flirting—and making wherever they were the table where everyone wanted to play.

Once Olivia had selected a twenty-one table and proved that she was "Lady Luck," the man nearly always provided her with the winnings. She would, in turn, give him back what he started her out with initially. She made a conscientious practice of that, because she didn't want to feel like she was being bought or owed any man anything.

Olivia became known backstage as the girl who consistently won at twenty-one. One night between shows, Maggie turned to Olivia and called out with a chuckle, "Olivia, I'm going to challenge you! Let's see who has better luck out there."

Olivia laughed and said, "What do you have up your sleeve, Maggie?"

"Whatever high roller asks us out tomorrow, we go. We'll do it between shows. Let's see who wins the most money on craps or twenty-one . . . whichever you fancy."

Olivia accepted the challenge. "Okay, I'm in!" The girls started to rally around their pod in excitement. It was a given that Maggie and Olivia would be invited out between the shows, so it was no question that they could challenge each other the next night.

Maggie made the rules and said each red lipstick line on their individual mirrors equaled one hundred dollars. The room went crazy with hoots and bets on who would win.

The competition went on for one full week, with Olivia top-ping Maggie's winnings every night. Her largest winnings of twelve lipstick lines in one night doused Maggie's competitive spirit.

————

David Brenner was coming into town to perform again. Olivia had not seen him in a couple of months, or at least not since Rani found his socks in the apartment. He got in touch with her shortly after he arrived, and they got together several times. It was very comfortable being with David. He had become an old friend, and they had a blast together. They would have dinner, experiment with drugs and end up passed out on the floor of Olivia's apartment.

Once David left town for his next gig, they would not be in touch until the next time he came around. This suited her. She knew she wasn't going to settle down with him, or he with her, but he was great fun and a friendly face from back east.

Throughout the summer, several men came to Vegas just to see Olivia at the Tropicana. She began casually dating many of these men—and each of them thought she was their exclusive girl. She filled their hearts with desire and their ears with what they wanted to hear. She got a kick out of spending time with them and playing the role of their fantasy showgirl. She kept her private life vague, never lying, but never telling the full truth. She was a showgirl in their eyes, not a divorced mother with three children. No man wanted to hear about her real life; they wanted what they saw on stage—the mirage of the perfect woman with three layers of foundation, five sets of false eyelashes and pasties on her nipples.

Yet after almost a year, it became tiresome when *new* men wanted to meet her. She didn't mind having dinners and gambling with her regulars, but she was reaching a point where she didn't want to meet new tourists and have them gawk at her. Toward the end of July, she found herself just wanting to find someone who would be a good provider and father to her children.

————

A prosperous Jewish deli owner from New York flew in to see her many times over the course of three months. He proclaimed his love for her in the Tropicana casino bar while she was wearing a simple black sheath that exposed her pasties from underneath, making her nipples look preternaturally erect. She felt bad for the redheaded, freckle-faced, five-foot seven-inch man and his illusion of their life together. She knew he would be crushed to learn that her life outside of the show was based in Children's Village with three children. She broke his heart when she told him not to come see her anymore. She knew this man needed a reality check, and she had to put a stop to his visits.

Like Maggie, Olivia had begun dating local men. She wanted a man from outside of the casino—hopefully, where her occupation would come second. No chance. Once she told a man she was a showgirl, his eyes would light up and he desired her even more for that reason. This was the first kiss of death, and the second was revealing she had three kids. No matter how much a man liked her, once she told him she was divorced with three children, she never heard from him again.

Olivia realized she could only expose her personal life to her backstage confidants. These were her true friends. The information they shared was sacred, and they all understood each other without judgment. After weeks of unsuccessful dates with local men, she decided to stop putting so much pressure on herself to find the right man and just have fun for the remainder of the summer.

————

It was announced that Engelbert Humperdinck was coming to perform at the Rivera. Olivia wanted to see him. She knew he would remember her from the Latin Casino. She called his manager and within minutes, Engelbert called her back. They made plans to meet up at his rental home after their shows that night.

She was greeted warmly at the door by Engelbert himself. He had rented a spacious home on a golf course not far from the Vegas strip. He poured them both a cocktail, and they chatted about old times at the Latin Casino. He then led her to the piano to play her some of his legendary songs. After several tunes, he offered her a tour of the house. He took her up the stairs and they ended up in his bedroom. Of course, once they got there, she knew what he wanted.

He looked at her knowingly, stripped off his clothes and got into the bed. Olivia stood there for a moment staring at him, perplexed. She was certain she was not going to go to bed with him and didn't know what to say other than, "I'm sorry. I can't do this. I have to get home."

She briskly walked out of his room, down the stairs, grabbed her bag, and ran out the door without looking back. The feeling of being used as a sex object had finally taken its toll. She went directly home, and for the first time in weeks, before midnight.

———

There were many celebrities in and out of town that attended the Les Folies Bergere show. Most of them came off movie sets filming locally. After one of Olivia's shows, Flora insisted that she greet a man who was very eager to meet her. He was an up and coming actor who was filming a western in town.

He was a handsome man, just twenty-four years old, and Olivia ended up dating him for a couple of weeks. She didn't tell him her age, where she lived, that she was divorced, or that she had children. They dated like a couple of teenagers, and she enjoyed their time without regard. When the filming of his western came to a close, so did the relationship. He was going back to California and asked her to come. She declined his offer.

When he came to town again a month later, she didn't return his calls.

———

Olivia's show director introduced her to John Fried. He was investing in the building of the Sammy Davis, Jr. Stardust Theater, which was going to be adjacent to the Tropicana. John recognized Olivia from the show and said he liked her looks, as though she were artwork. He invited her to the groundbreaking ceremony of the theater that week. He said the press photos would include her standing with Mr. Davis; Mario Puzo, author of *The Godfather;* and others involved in the project. This was one of the perks of being a seasoned showgirl—people recognized her as someone they wanted to be seen with, even if it was just a photo opportunity as a pretty face.

———

The Alan King Tennis Classic was kicking off and Vegas was bursting with celebrities. Olivia's friend Donna Gold was in town to see the Classic. She phoned Olivia to come celebrity-watch at her hotel pool, Caesar's Palace. Caesar's was where all of the hot shots stayed and they had the most spectacular pool on the strip. Olivia had not taken a day in the sun for a couple of weeks and knew that celebrity-spotting with an old friend would be an enjoyable way to spend the afternoon.

They were sipping cocktails in lounge chairs at the pool when something obstructed their sun. They both looked up to see a large, square man standing above them.

"I'm Rick, Mister Universe's manager." He looked directly at Olivia and said in a deep, resonant voice, "Mister Universe would like to meet you."

Being cocky, she replied, "Then Mister U can come over here and meet me."

The manager tilted his head to the side, miffed by her response, then turned around and walked away. He sat down next to Mr. Universe and apparently relayed her response. He didn't return, but the women kept their eyes on them.

About an hour later they spotted Rick and his muscle-endowed employer leaving the pool area. The women hustled from their seats, curious about where the situation could lead and caught up with them just inside the casino.

Mr. Universe turned to Olivia and said in a heavy Austrian accent, "I would like to see you tonight."

Olivia looked up at him, smiled and agreed to dinner. She said she would meet him in the lobby at seven o'clock. He then spontaneously hoisted her up above his head in the middle of the casino floor.

Olivia half screamed, half laughed, "What are you doing! Put me down." He set her down like a piece of delicate glass.

"My goodness! Just give me a heads-up if you are going to do that again," she said with a sly smile; then glancing at Rick she said, "Bring your friend here . . . we'll double date."

He smiled, revealing a gap-toothed grin and said, "See you later."

The women agreed to meet in Caesar's lobby at six forty-five. Olivia had two hours to drive home, pick up a dress, get back to the Tropicana to put on her show makeup for Mr. U, and return to Caesar's.

Donna walked Olivia to the valet and squealed with delight, "Can you believe you are going out with Mister Universe?"

"He's just another man, Donna. He just happens to come with a manager." She then got her car to head home.

She chose to wear a short, slinky black dress, no underwear or bra, lots of pearls draping from her neck and her stage makeup. Without a care in the world and a dash of confidence, she set off to meet Donna in the Caesar's hotel lobby.

They could hear the commotion as they made their way from the front of the lobby to the back. Mr. U's head was above the sea of people that had surrounded him for photos and autographs. Wearing a white suit jacket, he stood out like a football field.

When Mr. U spotted Olivia, he parted the crowd gently with his arms and met her halfway between the lobby and front entrance. The people followed, but he began to wave them away. Olivia said, "Please don't do that. These are your fans. Sign autographs. Shake hands. It's okay."

He smiled and began to shake hands with those around him. Shortly after, the crowd died down, and he took Olivia by the arm. Ten minutes later, Donna, Rick, Olivia and Mr. U were through valet and driving off in her car.

They dined at Paul Anka's Supper Club. The conversation varied from recent shows coming to Vegas to the tennis classic. During dinner, Olivia excused herself for a bathroom break. When she came back, they were all laughing and pointing at a pair of pink panties hanging out of Mr. U's lapel.

Mr. U said, "Look at this!"

Olivia replied, "What about it?" as she sat down without looking at them again. She focused her attention on the crowded restaurant.

He pulled the panties out of his lapel and tossed them to Donna. Their humor was lost on Olivia. Donna pulled her panties up under the table and said, "We thought you would think that was so funny."

Olivia ignored them and sipped her drink while continuing to size up the crowd. She didn't care that much about her date or who he was, so it would not have made her jealous even if Donna's panties were hanging out of his mouth. She just wanted to have a fun evening with her friend and this hot shot, for kicks.

After dinner, and a few drinks to shake off her dour mood, they caught Donna Summer's show at the MGM. A crush of people surrounded them after the show, snapping photos and shoving paper in Mr. U's chest for autographs. Olivia and Donna were giddy on liquor and laughed at all of the attention while posing in photos with him. When the crowd dwindled, it was nearly one o'clock.

Donna whispered to her, "Are you going to go back to his room to bed him?"

Olivia looked at her in disbelief. "I didn't sleep with Engelbert Humperdinck, why would I sleep with this one?"

"It's Mister Universe! Don't you want to check out his *stuff?*"

"Good point," she winked.

Olivia walked Mr. U back to his hotel room. Since he didn't drink, he didn't offer her one. It would have helped with the uneasy energy between them. They were clearly both uncomfortable and just stood there looking at one another. After a long hesitation, he walked in front of her and put his hands on her shoulders, then down to her breasts. Olivia found this to be even more awkward than staring at each other, since he was so strangely large and emotionless.

He clumsily attempted to take off her dress, his massive hands fumbling with the zipper that was hidden under her many strands of pearls. She finally stepped back and unzipped it herself. When it successfully fell to the floor, he took off his jacket, dress shirt, unzipped his pants and dropped them, along with his underwear, to the floor. This was her chance to look at the entire, bare, mass of Mr. U. Her eyes moved slowly down his body. He had muscles on every inch of his incredible being. She hesitated for a second at his waist, anticipating the enormity, but then exhaled and smiled—relieved that he was not shockingly enormous.

He seemed amused by what he considered admiration and walked up to her. She turned her back to him, bent over the bed with her backside to him. He grabbed her by the hips and she had her first official "star fuck."

Once the act was complete, Olivia put on her dress without saying a word. *There,* she thought, *I did it. He got a little bit of show-girl; I got a little bit of Mister Universe.*

She grabbed her bag and headed out the door, just glancing behind long enough to give him a simple wave of her hand.

As she walked down the long corridor, she heard a door open. She looked over her shoulder to see Mr. U standing in the middle of the hallway, stark naked. She turned around and yelled, "Flex for me."

He arched his arms, contorted his body and flexed every muscle he had.

She laughed, turned around, and disappeared into the bank of elevators.

———

How do you know these stories in such detail?
When I moved to New York City, my mom's story began to intrigue me. It's a mad, crazy, series of events that not many could live to tell. I heard bits and pieces of the Mister Universe story over the years, but never the whole story. I mean, if your mom slept with someone like that, you want to know about it.

She just came out and told you?
Not all the details at one time, but a whole lot of it. It was last summer after a dinner party at her beach house when she told me. Everyone else had left and she just opened up to my friend and me. I must have said some-

thing to provoke the conversation, and truth be told, she was totally ham-mered, so that's why we got so many of the gritty details. She put her hands up and said, "He was about this big, like the size of a big Polish sausage!" My friend and I were on the edge of our seats saying "And then . . . and then?"

Dr. Tanner shook her head back and forth as though passing judgment and said:

Okay, get it. Let's move on.

I looked at her, wondering what I said wrong or if I should be embarrassed by sharing the assumed size of a grown man's penis. She looked at me blankly, and I took that as my cue, thankfully, to continue.

Don called to say he was coming to Vegas. Olivia knew this was his first business trip out west since he had gotten married. He told her he was staying at a hotel on the strip and they agreed to meet for a drink. Olivia had an agenda.

Dressed to impress in a sexy, black, strapless cocktail dress, Olivia entered the hotel bar looking for Don. She found him already seated at the bar. After two drinks, and mindless banter about her life in Vegas, they ended up walking back to his room. As soon as they got in the door, they began kissing. Olivia abruptly took off his clothes, then her own. They moved to the bed and had quick and efficient sex. The instant they were done, Olivia got up and slipped on her dress. She looked at Don's bewildered face, still naked in the bed.

"I just wanted to see if a leopard changes his spots. Apparently not." She slammed the door behind her. The feeling of redemption and closure was incredible. She walked down the hall, 100 percent confident that she had lost nothing by leaving him. He would always be a cheater.

————

How did you feel about this story when your mother told you?
I was in my twenties when she told me. My first reaction was, "Wow. That was super slutty, Mom!" Then I thought about it and said, "But, good for you!" If someone cheated on me, I wish I would have enough gumption to do such a thing. I don't blame her for one second; she did what she had to do to vindicate herself and get closure.

Okay then. I was just curious how you would respond to that.
She then jotted in her journal and I continued onward.

————

By early August, Olivia became anxious about her children returning. She told her colleagues before each show that she had promised them a single-family home and a pool when they got back. Night after night, she counted one day closer to their arrival.

"I promised the kids a home with a pool. I can't have them come back to the same apartment. I don't even know where or how to start looking."

For days, the girls tried to comfort her. They told her where she lived was still great for her kids, but Olivia didn't want to disappoint them. A promise was a promise.

After a week of listening to Olivia moan and groan, Linda piped up as she completed knitting her zillionth sweater that year, "Listen, Olivia, I have a friend who recently told me his friend owns a real estate company. Why don't I hook you two up? He will find you something. I'm sure he can find a house with a pool, for goodness sakes."

The next morning Olivia contacted the realtor. His name was Paul Wagner.

Olivia (left) and her showgirl colleagues
having fun backstage between shows.

Backstage during costume changes.

Descending from theater ceiling,
overlooking audience.

On a date between shows
wearing stage makeup.

Photo during dinner
at the Tropicana
after the shows.

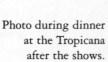

Photo shoot for groundbreaking of
Tropicana's Superstar Theater. Olivia
is far right, next to her is Mario Puzo
(author of *The Godfather*), Sammy
Davis, Jr., and developer

Olivia is far right with fellow showgirls and Sammy Davis, Jr.
Same photo shoot, but changed clothes to see what looked
best for print promotions.

Part III

CHAPTER SEVENTEEN

Paul

Olivia and Paul spent ten minutes on the phone before he suggested they meet at his residence. He wanted her to see his house, since it seemed to have everything she was seeking, "the perfect single-family home with a pool." She was eager to start the process, so agreed to meet him that afternoon.

Paul was tall and slender, wearing a white polyester suit and was impeccably groomed from head to toe. Olivia thought he might be in his early forties. He had a large, impressive home set on the corner of a busy street.

He was wide-eyed when he met Olivia, but by this time she was used to this reaction from men. She brushed it off and avoided looking at him directly. This was business, and she had no time for male hormonal nonsense.

Paul showed her around his home while he told her about himself. He was a former New York City fashion photographer with a part-time passion for boxing, and he had become enamored with Vegas during a photo shoot. He said that he knew everything about the real estate market in Vegas, and that there were a lot of potential homes for her currently available. After half an hour of small talk, they left in his pea-green Mercedes sedan to look at houses. She didn't like anything she saw in her price range, so they agreed to meet up the following morning to look at more properties.

At the end of the second day, Olivia fell in love with the last home Paul showed her. She stood curbside, admiring it—looking beyond Paul, who couldn't take his eyes off her.

"This is the perfect one. I want to make a bid."

She offered the asking price. She didn't want to lose the house by playing games. Twenty minutes later, Paul called her at home from his office and told her the offer was accepted. Olivia was elated. She thanked Paul for his help and agreed to meet him at his office the following day to start the paperwork.

A couple of hours later, Paul called her to tell her that the deal fell through.

Olivia was crushed. She didn't know much about the real estate market, but she knew that a deal was a deal. Something didn't seem right. She had a strange feeling that Paul had sabotaged it.

Paul called her later that evening. He expressed how badly he felt about things not working out and said he would like to make it up to her by taking her to Brian Head, Utah, for the weekend. He said the mountains and fresh air had a magical way of lifting one's spirits.

Even though she had known him for less than two days and didn't like the idea of being out of town at the mercy of any man, she figured she had nothing to lose. It was clear that he was crazy about her. She thought that he surely didn't whisk all of his clients away for the weekend. And perhaps he felt that he owed her something for killing the deal—which she felt quite certain he had.

Once they were in Utah and settled into a two-bedroom suite overlooking the mountains, Paul suggested they go down to the bar for drinks. Halfway through their first cocktail, Paul invited Olivia and her three children to move in with him.

"I'm divorced and only have my eighteen-year-old son under my roof. I have an empty room with twin beds that your girls can have, and your son can share a room with my son."

Olivia stared at him, allowing the words sink in. Without

emotion she said, "My children and I can't live under the same roof with a man I'm not married to."

"Marry me."

She looked into his light blue eyes. She knew this would be preposterous. She'd be making the ultimate sacrifice by marrying a man whom she didn't know, love or care about, simply to secure a proper home with a pool for her children. She looked from him to the windows just beyond his head and thought, *Here is a man willing to marry me and take in my three children. He has a house and a pool. The kids will be back soon.* It would be the craziest, most impulsive decision she had ever made.

"Yes. I'll marry you."

———

She told you that this was how she was asked and accepted the proposal?
That's the whole story—nothing more to it. She only told me when I was interested in hearing about it years later. I guess I was not so much interested as I was intrigued by the insanity of the short courtship.

Did this shock you? I mean, not even knowing what kind of man she was bringing into the lives of her children.
It is shocking; it's sad . . . it was desperate. But it was also a sign of the times; it was the early seventies—I guess a woman felt that she needed a man to take care of her? I'm not defending her, but what is there to say about it now? What was done was done. I'm just telling you what happened.

I started to sound defensive, and she backed off. I picked up quickly where I left off.

———

Two days later, Paul and Olivia were married in his home. His son, Junior, served as a witness and a Justice of the Peace officiated.

After the ceremony Olivia didn't feel particularly happy; she just felt relieved. The burden of raising a family on her single income was lifted. She had had the time of her life the past year, but she was tired of dating and being on her own. She had gotten too used to feeling fearless, yet desperate at the same time. This union afforded her the security she needed so she would never have to move back to Philadelphia. She was finally making a solid, proper life in Vegas for her family.

Olivia Sandra Berger Dushon Wagner took four days off from work to honeymoon in Hawaii.

———————

About a week before the kids were to arrive, Paul and Olivia had an intimate dinner at a supper club. As they ordered, Olivia conversed briefly with their handsome waiter about the dry summer weather. Paul seemed uneasy and guzzled drink after drink. Olivia tried to keep up with him, but he just consumed too much, too fast.

When they got into the car, Paul put the keys in his lap and just stared at her. She turned her head to look at him, not seeing his left fist coming her way. He punched her in the face with such force it left her breathless. She held her hands to her face, astonished by the shock of the hit. He started the car and yelled at her for flirting with their waiter.

Olivia was disoriented as they drove home. She held her hands over her throbbing cheek and nose, while staring out the window into the unlit streets. As they pulled into the driveway, she had already begun to open the car door. Paul slammed on the brakes, got out of the car and walked into the house.

She felt a familiar wave of emotion crash over her. She sat with her legs outside the car door, feet planted on the driveway, hardly aware of the oven-like summer heat that engulfed her.

There was now no doubt that something was wrong with him. She continued to sit as the tears came. The all-consuming anguish far outweighed the physical pain. She bent over, holding her stomach, realizing she had made a colossal mistake . . . again. She knew she didn't need to fall into the depths of hell, because she had married into it. If Paul was her new beginning, she feared that he would also be her end.

———

You think this may have been a sign to walk away? Of all of the impulsive decisions she made . . .

I shrugged my shoulders.

I guess you have to surrender to your bad luck at some point. She just crossed her fingers and hoped for the best. She could never imagine it would get as bad as it did. No one could have ever—

You're defending her bad decisions as if they were okay. This should have been the one alarming, huge, fire-engine-red flag that she should walk away. Putting her children into the home of a man with this kind of mental state was clearly a mistake.

My mom "trapezed" from man to man. She was always looking for someone to save her. Men with money were a draw because she needed a provider for her children. It is a different era now—most women today wouldn't stand for this shit.

Anyhow, I don't know if it was due to my childhood or just the mind-set of women today, but I am very independent and self-motivated. Money has never moved the needle for me; happiness and normality are far more important. I would fear having to depend on someone else to survive . . . the thought of that is actually crippling to me.

I was in a fragile state, but would not let myself crack under her pressure and blame my mother. Dr. Tanner saw my reaction and held back on saying anything further.

Olivia's nose and cheek had been badly bruised, but not broken. She successfully concealed the discoloration with several layers of show makeup. Paul never addressed the incident, and she feared bringing it up. He was kind to her the following morning and wanted sex. She was dealing with a Jekyll and Hyde.

Olivia walked on eggshells in an effort not to upset him that week, completely unsure of what would set him off. Each afternoon she slipped out to go to work. The Tropicana was her safe haven—both back stage and on stage. She didn't mention to her colleagues what had happened with Paul; she only spoke about how excited she was for her kids to come home.

She was on a roller coaster of emotion and hoped the tension would be alleviated when the kids arrived.

On the day of the kids' homecoming, Paul ordered a white stretch limousine to welcome them at the airport. He told Olivia he wanted to make a big impression. She was apprehensive, but semi-pleased with his efforts to impress them. In that moment, all she cared about was seeing the loving, beautiful faces of her children.

Olivia nervously twisted her new wedding band around her finger on the way to the airport. She was going to introduce her children to a new father, a new home, and a new life.

The driver pulled onto the tarmac, and they waited for the plane to arrive.

Olivia and Paul's wedding
in his home.

CHAPTER EIGHTEEN

Fall 1973–Spring 1974

The plane finally landed. I had filled up two throw-up bags that were sitting on the floor, waiting for the unfortunate stewardess. I needed fresh air and was thankful I didn't have to fly again for nine months.

The plane screeched to a halt just outside the airport terminal. I saw the stairway roll up to the airplane's exit door. I jumped up, eager to get out. Rani pulled me back down and pointed to a white stretch limousine a few hundred feet from the plane. We had never seen a car on the tarmac before and wondered how it got there. We finally got up and struggled with our backpacks along the narrow aisle to the front exit of the plane. Todd and I followed Rani down the flight of stairs into the familiar, stinging, Vegas heat.

When we walked onto the tarmac, squinting into the sun, we saw Mom step out of the limo with a man we had never seen before. As we got past the small mass of people, Mom ran up to us with a radiant smile. She stooped down to our level, put her arms around all of us and ushered us toward the man. She then stood next to him, swung both her arms in his direction and said, "Say hello to your new daddy." We stared at him blankly as he came over to hug us one by one.

Our new dad was as tall and thin as Mom was. He had a dark, leathery tan and light blue eyes. His big, round face was framed with large sideburns and topped with sparse, orange-blond hair that swept over to one side. He wore a white polyester shirt unbuttoned to the middle of his somewhat hairy chest and wore a heavy gold medallion necklace. The shirt was neatly tucked into his checked polyester pants that fell neatly down to his white patent leather shoes. He didn't look like any other father I had met before, but he seemed fond of polyester, and I knew Grandmom would approve.

————

Our new home sat on the corner of a busy street and the entrance to a private road. There was a vacant lot next to our house that was not green and lush like our lawns back east, but parched, cracked earth with scatterings of cactus and tumbleweed. We entered the front of the house via a long path that led to an enclosed courtyard. To the right was a cactus garden and to the left were two oversized dark wood doors.

Paul proudly opened one of the wood doors and led us into the front entryway. The foyer had a sky-high ceiling, the walls were all white and there was a grand, carpeted staircase that led to an upstairs area. The floors were covered with large squares of terracotta tile. To the left was a sunken living room with white plush carpeting, more white walls, and two white sofas. Straight ahead, beyond the staircase, was an open area dining room with a white Formica table that had six high-backed chairs neatly placed around it.

I was the first to start exploring. I went from the foyer into the dining room area and through an open doorway into a spacious, dark wood kitchen. I walked around a large island that jutted out into the middle of the floor and I ended up in front of a unique looking kitchen table. I slid my hand across the table's smooth, glossy finish. Then, eager to see more, I walked through another doorway into a den that had an L-shaped, brown sofa and large TV. From the den, I walked back into the foyer where my family and new dad were still standing.

Paul leaned down and gently whispered to me, "Your room is up the stairs to the left. Go check it out."

As I ran up the stairs, I heard him tell my sister and brother that all of our rooms were upstairs, while his and my mom's bedroom was on the first floor.

I found a room with twin beds. I knew one was for Rani and one for me. Each bed was covered with a yellow flannel Mickey Mouse–print blanket and pale pink striped sheets. I flopped down on the bed farthest from the door and declared it as my own. There was a bathroom next to our room, which we would share with Todd. We learned he would be sharing a room with Paul's eighteen-year-old son, Junior, who went to a local community college.

Mom and Paul's room was downstairs at the end of a long stretch of hallway. All of their walls were painted beige with the exception of one floor-to-ceiling mirrored wall at the foot of their bed. Their bathroom was huge with at least six feet of counter space between two spacious sinks. There was a four-person, sunken Jacuzzi next to a floor-to-ceiling window. The window looked out onto an enclosed garden. Paul told us the garden grew one particular kind of plant named marijuana. He instructed us that the garden was not for us. The only access to it was from the outside via a tall, locked, wooden door. I thought it was neat that we had a home with a secret garden. At this point, secrets were fun and exciting.

Next, I was introduced to our new nanny, who had just come by for a quick visit. Regina was a robust black woman who wore a red bandana on her head—just like the Aunt Jemima Syrup bottle. She told me she would come every day, and I would see her the next morning. I chatted with her for a couple of minutes to be polite, but I was eager to explore more of the house. After she left,

I darted in and out of each room like a mouse looking for scraps of food.

I went back into the kitchen to get a better look at the large, unusual table. On my way there, I opened and closed some of the dark brown cabinets and everything looked impeccably neat and orderly—even the pots and pans. I walked around the island and stared at the large table. I sensed someone behind me and turned to see Paul.

"I made the table with my own two hands. Come take a closer look."

The dark wood top had a thick, shiny, clear coating. Under the coating were various coins stacked on top of each other. He told me how he drilled deep holes into the wood, filled them with his collection of spare change and then covered it with thick coats of polyurethane. He said that the table was very important to him, because he spent so much time making it.

———

Did you call Paul "Dad?"
I called him "Dad" because my mother told me to when we got off the plane. I just can't refer to him as "Dad" as I talk about him.

Of course.
She jotted a note in her book, and I picked up where I left off.

———

The first evening in the new house, Mom helped us unpack and get settled in our rooms. Paul was downstairs, giving us private time with Mom. Sometime after dark, Paul asked Mom to come downstairs. She replied that she would be down shortly. There was a brief pause, and then a scream. "Olivia! Get down here!"

Mom repeated more sternly, "Wait a minute. I'm helping the kids unpack!"

Her reply was ignored, and he began screaming her name louder and louder. It came to the point where we all finally went to see what the commotion was about. Rani, Mom and I peered downstairs over the railing. Paul stood at the bottom of the stairs holding a cocktail in one hand, and his other hand was flailing in the air. He repeatedly slurred some words we couldn't make out. Mom screamed down, "What are you saying? I can't understand you."

He bellowed at the top of his lungs, "Kike bitch! Get down here!"

At only nine years old, Rani understood that this was not a nice thing to say, and she screamed back, "Don't ever speak to my mom that way, you asshole!"

My sister looked at my mom, then at me and mumbled, "Well, we're off to a great start."

————

The first couple of months in our new home, I made some interesting observations:

1. When someone consumes enough alcohol, they act differently.

2. Paul drank a lot.

3. Drinking made Paul angry.

4. Mom began drinking. When she didn't, she was agitated and chain-smoked.

5. Paul having sex with my mom.

It was early October, and we were hanging out with Mom in

her room. Snacks in hand, I sat on the bed with Mom, while Todd and Rani sat on the floor in front of me. They were *Irish twins,* born eleven months apart, so they looked almost identical from the back; the only telling sign of "who was who" was Rani's long hair. We were watching *Gilligan's Island* and laughing along with the canned laughter. We had not realized Paul was home until he briskly walked into the bedroom. He didn't acknowledge us kids; he just walked directly to Mom on the far side of the bed. She was lying braless, in a short T-shirt and underwear.

I saw Paul in the floor-to-ceiling mirror at the end of their bed as he aggressively took off his belt, dropped his pants, and then pulled down Mom's underwear. She said nothing. I looked down at my siblings who were also looking at the mirror in shock, just as I was. Paul spread her legs and then got on top of her. He put his penis in her and started to slam his body onto hers.

I was so close to the edge of the bed that I was able to surreptitiously slide off and sit behind Rani and Todd. We exchanged looks, and then Rani pointed to the TV; she didn't have to say any more. We tried our best to avoid looking and listening to their bodies slapping together, but the fact that we were sitting in front of the mirrored wall made it unavoidable.

We sat frozen in place until they were done. At that point, we got out of there, bumping into one another in the doorway in our haste to leave.

———

Paul told us bits and pieces about himself. He and I had a Ping-Pong-like conversation one afternoon. He told me he liked boxing and had a great left hook. I told him I liked Captain Hook, but liked Captain Crunch better. He told me he used to be a fashion photographer and was now a realtor. I told him I thought pictures were cool. He said he would like to take pictures of me one day. I said that would be fun. He told me that his family was from Germany. I told him my family was from Philadelphia. He told me that he didn't like the Jews. I didn't know what "the Jews" were, so instead of asking, I turned away and retreated into the den to finish a one hundred-piece puzzle I was working on.

Shortly after my get-to-know-you discussion with Paul, he called Rani into the formal living room. He said he had spent special time with me and now wanted to share some time with her. He sat with her on the white, plush sofa and asked her about her interests. She said she didn't have any, so he instead told her he wanted to share an interest of his with her—"something I've not even shared with your mother."

He fished in his front pocket and produced an old-fashioned key. He looked at it affectionately and then got up to unlock the large white armoire that stood against the wall across from them. Rani sat curiously on the edge of the sofa. He pulled out a small tattered brown pouch and sat down next to her. He placed the pouch in the palm of his left hand and with a mischievous smile, tossed it to his right hand. He stared at it for a moment, then untied the strings and pulled out a red patch with a white circle in the middle of it, and in the circle was a strange, black, crisscross symbol. He looked from it to Rani and said it was his prize possession from one of his ancestors in Germany. He called it a Swastika.

Rani had never seen anything like it, but the crisscross symbol looked angry—hateful. She instantly knew it was something that she didn't want to see again, especially because of the weird look on Paul's face while he was holding it. He ran his fingers over it, gloating about how it was an important part of his history. He asked her if she wanted to hold it, and she said no. Paul looked insulted. The interaction made her uncomfortable, and she just wanted to get away from him and the house as quickly as possible. She kept eyeing the front door. When Paul again asked her if she would like to hold it, stretching his open palm toward her, she leapt up, ran to the front door, jumped on her bike and peddled away from the house as fast as she could.

———

Paul made it evident that he wanted Mom to quit the show. During family dinners, he said he could not stand the thought of other men watching her. Mom would just smile and continue to eat as if he were just offering his opinion on current events. Shortly after dinner, she would pick up her bag, kiss us goodnight and leave for the Tropicana.

No one knew, but she had secretly been thinking about quitting the show. The Tropicana sold Les Folies Bergere to a group of mobster investors. The word backstage was that they wanted to change the show to a completely nude program by the end of the month. But, in order to quit, she needed a job—a backup plan. She absolutely had to have some sort of refuge from Paul on a daily basis.

———

During her last weeks in the show, Mom came home from work past one in the morning. Paul would wait for her by the door, draining drink after drink. Mom would walk in and find Paul sitting idle, like a dog waiting for his owner. She would smile at him and immediately pour herself a drink. Paul would then drill her about the evening—"Who did you see?" "Who did you speak to?" "Why?" No matter how she answered, he struck her. She hit back. Slap for slap, they would finally wear themselves out sometime after two, and the fight would culminate in angry sex. From my room, I'd first hear the screaming, then the moaning that provoked me to get out of bed and peek downstairs. Inevitably, I'd see them having sex on the carpeted steps, the tile floor, the living room sofa, or against the front door.

After two weeks of his late-night verbal and physical abuse, Mom came home even later. If by chance she came home earlier, she made sure she had consumed enough alcohol beforehand to be able to endure whatever mood he was in.

————

Paul told Mom he was determined to find a business venture that would lure her away from the show. She said if he found the right opportunity, she would consider leaving—never mentioning that she had made the decision to resign anyway. Paul buried himself in research to find a lucrative, local business to invest in. He came up with an entrepreneurial idea in just two days and made it his mission to bring it to fruition as swiftly as possible. He created a business plan and got the ball rolling within a week by purchasing a storefront property. Once he had everything in place, all he needed was a CEO. He presented the plan to Mom, and she was pleasantly intrigued. Paul was elated.

One day before Les Folies Bergere was to go all nude, she resigned. For Paul's benefit, and consequently her own, she made it seem as though it were his decision for her to leave the show.

————

Slendermaker opened to much hubbub in the spring of 1974. It was a new genre of quickie weight-loss centers. Clients would lie between heated mats for thirty minutes and burn off water weight. There were four weight-loss treatment rooms, a bathroom, and a generously stocked bar.

After preschool each afternoon, I was picked up and taken to Slendermaker. I'd help check in women in all sizes and shapes.

They'd disrobe to their underwear in a private treatment room, Mom would weigh them, and then they'd lie between heated mats for thirty minutes. Once the treatment was complete, Mom would weigh them once again. Not one woman was ever disappointed. They usually hugged Mom, because they miraculously lost three to five pounds in just thirty minutes.

Slendermaker became the "go to" destination to burn off just enough water weight for a special evening.

———

Now that mom was working at a place where Paul had control over her daily activities, he backed off from his iron-fisted tactics for a while. He knew she was working with women all day and that seemed to pacify him.

However, he took up behavior that was even more reprehensible.

———

The first time Paul came to our room, Rani was nine years old. She woke when his body blocked the hallway light. As he moved closer to her bed, she pretended she was asleep. She felt him sit on her narrow bed, and then gently tap her arm.

She looked at him with sleep-filled eyes and said quietly, "What?"

"Do you like cherries?"

This got her attention, and she opened her eyes wider. "Yes, I love cherries. Especially since they're in Shirley Temples."

He got off the bed and stood next to her pillow. She looked up at him, about to ask if he had cherries with him, when he opened the sarong he was wearing. He placed his hands under his genitals and said, "These are my cherries, and I want you to suck on them."

She looked at him with a confused expression, and he said,

"These are my cherries, and they are for you." She rolled over and put one of them in her mouth and then the other.

He said, "That's a good girl."

When she pulled away, he leaned down to her face, making sure they had eye contact in the darkness. "This is between you and me. You cannot tell anybody what you just did. My cherries are only for you, and this is very special. If you tell anyone, you will get in lots and lots of trouble."

Rani nodded her head, acknowledging that she understood— and now that they had an understanding, his visits came weekly.

Some nights he spared Rani and came directly to my side of the room. I was always in deep slumber when he came to my bedside and tapped my arm. I would open my eyes and see a big, dark figure. My stomach would lurch until he'd crouch down, and I realized it was Paul. He would run his fingers up and down my face. I would giggle, figuring this was his way of saying goodnight. He'd whisper, "You know, I love your mother so much it makes me crazy" or "I love your mother so much and that is why she makes me want to punish her sometimes."

Other times he would whisper in my ear and tell me how sweet I was, which I understood a whole lot better than the reason he gave for beating my mom.

————

I began wetting my bed at night. Sometimes I would accidentally wet my bed; other times I did it while I was wide awake. I was terrified that the bogeyman would pop out of the nighttime shadows, and I didn't want to leave the safety of my bed.

After two months of my bed-wetting, Paul and Mom decided something had to be done. I was playing with dolls in my room when Mom called me downstairs. From the top of the stairs I saw a strange man in an ill-fitting brown suit standing next to Paul.

I came down the stairs slowly. The man stuck out his hand, introducing himself as "Tom McCoy, TBWE: The Bed Wetting Expert."

Without smiling, I put my cold, tiny hand out to shake his long, skinny, sweaty palm. We all moved into the living room, and Tom McCoy sat uncomfortably erect on the edge of the white sofa. While he tightly gripped the handle of his briefcase between his knees he asked, "Do you pee in bed?"

I looked at my mom, and she nodded, so I said, "Yup."

"Do you know why?"

"Nope." I didn't have the courage to tell him that most of the time I peed in bed while I was awake.

He asked me more questions about peeing, which made me chuckle. I was four years old, and Tom McCoy the bed-wetting expert in an ugly brown suit was talking to me about peeing while we all sat in our formal living room trying to be earnest about it. I had had enough and stood up to leave.

Tom frantically fished in his bag and produced a bottle of little red pills. He addressed my mom: "She needs to go to the bathroom right before bedtime, and she should not drink water after six p.m. She should take one of the red pills each afternoon and that should stop the bed wetting." He then looked at me, "Will you make sure to take one pill each day?"

I nodded, but if the little red pill did not make the bogeyman go away, I would continue to pee in bed.

Mom, Paul, Rani and me.

Halloween picture in our yard.
Todd is a rock star, 8 years old.
I am a mariachi, 4 years old.
Rani is a gypsy, 9 years old.

CHAPTER NINETEEN

Summer 1974

We flew back to Philadelphia for the summer. We spent our ritual week at Grandmom and Grandpop's sorting coupons, swimming and fending off small talk from the building's elderly occupants.

After a week, we were off to Aunt Betty's house. We spent a fun-filled three days with our cousins, playing in and out of their kid-friendly home.

Our grandparents picked us up on day four, in time to drop us at our new overnight camp.

The seemingly interminable drive felt like we were heading across the country, but in reality it was only forty-five minutes away in Perkiomen Valley, Pennsylvania.

At five years old I was once again the youngest camper, but so excited to be placed in a real bunk with other kids. I was going to be in the junior division, which was for campers seven through ten years old.

Upon arrival we were informed that I was going to be in bunk number one with ten older girls, ages six and mostly seven. While Grandpop took Todd to the boy's camp across the water, Rani and I were directed to our age-appropriate divisions. Rani went uphill to the older division as Grandmom and I were directed down the dusty path, past five A-frame wood bunks until we reached my bunk. We were greeted on the small porch by two overeager, over-jubilant, college-aged counselors. My no-nonsense Grandmom barely smiled as she handed them an envelope and my bottle of little red pills. "This is Suzanne, and this note is from her mother. Make sure you read it." She then gave me a big hug, told me to have fun and walked back up the dusty path, sashaying in her big polyester dress and plastic summer sandals.

My counselors' smiles turned weary as they looked from me to my departing grandmother. A note from a mother who was not available to drop her five-year-old daughter off for eight weeks of overnight camp was not a good sign.

The note from my mother asked them to take me to the bathroom at eleven o'clock every night and to give me one of the pills daily to prevent me from peeing in bed. My counselors rolled their eyes and had their first summer dispute in front of me—*which one was going to lug me to the bathroom?*

Every evening I overheard my harebrained counselors argue over who would take me to the toilet and then wipe me. Sometimes I listened to them bicker and then peed in the bed to spite them. The poor girl who lost the argument would freak out when she discovered my pee-soaked nightgown. Then they would go into a fit of laughter while deciding if they should wake me to change my sheets.

At five years old I was not socially perceptive, but I was quite certain I was not popular. One didn't have to be an overly nosey camper to learn that I had a bed-wetting issue, especially from the way my counselors debated my nightly bathroom trip in front of us each night. It was also possible that I smelled like urine until after our 10 o'clock swim class each morning.

I did make an effort to engage with the resident nose-picker. I figured since no one wanted to come close to her because she picked her boogers and then ate them, we could form an alliance. However, she became somewhat popular when she rebuffed my offer of friendship. I should have cared, but I didn't because I was the only one in the bunk who had a big brother *and* sister visit me every day. That older-sibling status empowered me enough to go happily about my day.

About three weeks in, I made my first camp friend. Her name was Ruby. She had a full face, short hair and a spunky attitude. She said it didn't matter that I peed in bed; I was just another girl to play with. She found a spider outside our bunk and decided to share it exclusively with me. She declared that it was "our summer pet." We put it in a covered shoebox outside and periodically watched it climb up the walls and try to get out. We spent the rest of the summer torturing slugs on our bunk porch, de-legging daddy longlegs, playing with our spider, laughing our way through daily activities, and trying to ditch Saturday morning Shabbat services.

Me at summer camp.
One of the youngest campers.

CHAPTER TWENTY

Fall 1974–Spring 1975

After just five months, Slendermaker became a huge success. Mom had a new career under her belt and had taken up tennis as a hobby at the Southern Nevada Tennis Association (SNTA). Paul did not like this. He couldn't account for her whereabouts if she was playing tennis sporadically during the day. His fuse became short . . . again. He was drinking before she walked in the door, and if she came home late, he got furious. If she didn't call to say she was on her way home or she was playing tennis, he got even angrier. He spat out mean words when she walked in the door, and after dinner, there would be verbal fighting.

The more he raged at her, the more impatient she became with us kids. If my brother or sister misbehaved on any level, she undid her belt and whipped them in the hallway. I would sit on the stairs, cover my eyes and cringe each time I heard the belt crack on their backs and legs as they whimpered on the floor beneath her.

We were having dinner at the beautiful kitchen table Paul had constructed with his own two hands. All of us chimed in at some point, revealing something special about our day. Mom said something humorous about a male customer who came into Slender-maker. Paul had not anticipated that a male would ever come into the place, and it ticked him off.

His mood changed from light to dark in a nanosecond. He stood up so quickly it toppled the glasses over. We fell quiet, waiting to see what he was going to do next—we knew there was more to come. He placed both of his hands under his beloved table and flipped it over. We pushed back in our chairs to avoid the crush of plates, silverware and food. The tabletop cracked and coins spilled out. The only sound in the room was the rattling of change spinning and settling onto the kitchen floor.

He turned to Mom, struck her across the face with the palm of his left hand and walked out. She followed him, screaming that he was crazy.

Rani, Todd and I all dispersed in different directions. They went to their rooms, and I took refuge under the dining room table, hugging my knees to my chest. I could not understand why Paul destroyed and hit things that he loved so much.

I didn't come out from under the table until it was quiet throughout the house. I decided right then that underneath the dining room table would become my safe place. From this vantage point, I could see the most heavily trafficked areas of the house, but felt that no one could see me.

———————

Either my parents let our nanny go or she quit at some point that winter. There was so much screaming, drinking, fighting and smoking, it was amazing that she stayed as long as she did. Rani was now in charge of Todd and me after school. The days went like this: I'd go to Slendermaker from school at one o'clock. Mom would drop me at home to meet my siblings at three, we'd have a snack together, Rani and Todd would run out the door to play with their friends, and I'd sit under the dining room table waiting for someone to come home.

———

It was early spring when I began asking for a dog. My persistence finally paid off in April, just before my fifth birthday. Paul came home with a beautiful auburn Afghan hound named Sheika. I claimed her as my own.

I spent every second out of school with Sheika. She was not bright, which frustrated everyone but me. She ran out of the house every time the front door opened and consistently peed on the white carpet.

Paul said he was so frustrated with her stupidity that he was going to hire a dog trainer. This was a good thing because whenever I got home from Slendermaker, I gladly watched my siblings run off to be with their friends while I learned how to train Sheika. I watched the trainer command Sheika to do certain things with treats as rewards. He told me it was all Pavlov: rewards and punishments.

After the trainer left, I would practice the commands with her until dinnertime.

After four weeks, it was clear there was no improvement in Sheika because every time that front door opened, Sheika ran out and/or peed on the carpet. Paul blamed it on her stupidity and said she was un-trainable. He fired the trainer and said Sheika would be good for only one thing—breeding.

With the trainer gone, I realized I didn't like being alone in the house after school, even with Sheika's company. One afternoon I asked Rani to let me go with her to her friend's house. She ignored me as she walked out the door with Todd close behind her. The next day I tried to follow her out the door, but Rani held me back with an outstretched arm.

"You know that little red pill you take?" I nodded yes. "Well, if you come into the afternoon sun, it will make you blow up."

I cried inside the doorway, inching away from the blazing sun and watched her leave. Now I had something else to add to the list of things that frightened me:

1. bogeyman

2. leaving my room at night

3. faces popping out of the dark

4. being alone in the house

5. exploding in the afternoon sun

That night, my mom found me crying in my room. She sat on the floor beside me and asked what was wrong.

"I don't want to blow up in the sun or take the red pill anymore."

"What are you talking about? Where did you hear such nonsense?"

I told her what Rani told me. She pounded her fist on my bed before she stormed out of my room. Her mood lately, like Paul's, could flip like a switch. I was super sorry I had said anything. I sat under the dining table hugging my knees as I listened to the belt slapping Rani's backside again and again.

———

Your list of fears stemmed from Paul. He was your "bogeyman." He is no longer in your life and no one is hiding in your closet, under your bed or coming out of the dark now. Do some items on this list still exist for you?

Well, I don't think I'm going to blow up in the sun. I wisecracked at my attempt to make the mood lighter. Even though she grinned at me, I could tell that she wasn't pleased with my joke. I straightened up in the loveseat and tried again.

I've grown out of most of the others.

You are a smart young woman and you will come to realize, over our sessions that this list should no longer exist for you. It is all part of your childhood fears, which was understandable at the time, but not rational today.

She jotted in her journal, and I leaned on the leather armrest.

Let's continue.

———

The week after Rani was punished for the red pill lie, she reluctantly allowed me to follow her to her friend's house. I was so excited; I skipped behind her all the way around the block to her friend Patty's house. When we got there, Patty gave me two Barbie dolls to play with. I happily sank into their ultra-plush white carpet and played while Rani and her friend laughed over photos in *Tiger Beat* magazine.

After an hour, Patty's mom said it was time for us to head home. Her mom smiled at me and remarked how nice and quietly I played. When I got up, the mother shrieked and pointed to a yellow spot on her plush carpet. I had been so consumed in my doll-play that I had ignored my need to pee. The mother's voice started to rise as she grabbed a roll of paper towels and complained about how she would never be able to get the stain out.

As Rani, embarrassed, tugged me by the arm toward the front door, Patty's mother looked up and pointed to a red ring mark on my arm.

"Look at that! That is ringworm, Rani!" In a disgusted huff, she told her that I should go to the doctor. Rani didn't know if she meant for the ringworm or the peeing, but she could not drag me out of there fast enough.

I was never allowed back in Patty's house again. Neither was Rani.

———————

Rani brought a new friend home from school. I had never seen her before and thought I would chance hanging around them until Rani told me to get lost.

They were standing in the driveway after they got off the school bus, and I went out to join them. The girl's name was Marci, and she was new in town. She had short black hair, golden skin and I liked her because she smiled at me. None of my sister's friends ever even looked at me, so I was immediately smitten with her. After a couple of minutes, a bunch of my sister's friends joined us in the driveway. They were talking about going for a walk in the wooded area far behind our home. Rani ran into the house, yelling back at us, "I'll be right back! I have to get something."

A few minutes later, she came out holding an armful of rope and said, "Let's go." I looked at her, questioning if I could come, and she nodded that I could. My heart leapt with excitement as I followed them all into the secluded area.

The girls thought it would be funny to tie Marci up to a tree. Marci was reluctant, but went along with the game half-heartedly. Once her hands were tied behind her back and her torso and legs bound to the tree, everyone stood back and looked at her. Rani and her friends held hands and started to dance in a circle around her. They sang Ring-Around-the-Rosie and threw dirt at her feet. Marci started crying. I didn't understand why my sister and her friends were playing this mean game, but I just wanted to be included so I joined the circle and danced around with them.

After thirty minutes of this, we left the wooded area together

—with Marci still tied to the tree. I looked back at her, and she was hysterically crying, pleading for someone to let her loose. After an hour, Rani ran back, untied her and then ran into the house, slamming the door behind her. She was panting with her hands on her knees, as though she had just finished a marathon.

Hours later, the police showed up at our door with Marci's parents in tow.

Paul answered the door. There was a lot of loud arguing and pointing from Marci's angry father. Once they left, Paul and Mom took Rani to Marci's home to apologize. They told her she was lucky that Marci's parents didn't press charges.

Rani got in big trouble that night. Out came the belt, and I heard the relentless blows strike her over and over.

———

This seems out of character for Rani. Why do you think she did this and why do you think you went along with it?
I guess it was her way to take charge of a situation? To have some control because of her out-of-control home life? As for me, I was just happy to be included in anything my sister did.

I agree. This was her way of having some control. I am not validating what she did, because we can both agree it was not right, but I can understand why she felt like she needed to take control of a situation . . . any situation.

———

Grandmom and Grandpop came to visit that spring. We were so happy to see them and show off our home. Paul was different in their presence. During their weeklong stay, he barely drank, he didn't get angry or use verbal profanity, have impromptu sex in front of us, or visit our room. He was kind, considerate, and calm all day. Instead of taking to the bottle as he usually did at night, he just had one glass of wine. Rani noticed the change and tried to figure out why he was so different in front of our grandparents. She wanted to keep him this way, so she silently hoped our grandparents would stay. When they were due to leave, she tried to encourage them to stay a bit longer, but to her dismay, Grandpop had to get back to work.

———

Why did your siblings not mention anything about his behavior to your grandparents while they were there?
Rani was the only one of us who thought the things going on in the house didn't seem right, but she was too scared to say anything. When you think about it, back then, who would have believed a child who said, "My parents are having sex in front of me" or "My stepdad beats my mom" or "He comes in my room at night and makes me suck his cherries"? It would have seemed absurd.

Paul was on such good behavior—even charming when my grandparents were around. Everyone outside of my family unit thought he was a gentleman. If my grandmother knew he was an anti-Semite, far beyond all the other shenanigans, she would have dragged us out of there without looking back.

Were they the only family visitors that you remember?
Our twelve-year-old cousin Tori came to visit the second year we lived with Paul. One afternoon she and I were running around the house and ended up outside my parents' room. We looked in the doorway, and my mom's legs were in the air with Paul on top of her . . . they were naked, of course. Tori started laughing. My mom, yelled, "Stop laughing!" and we ran off.

Tori knew right away that this was not normal. This sort of thing didn't go on in her house. I recently asked her if she ever said anything to her parents about that incident, and she said, "I darn well did! The very second I got back." Her mom, Aunt Betty, told her she was full of it and to stop making up stories, so she dropped it.

Does anyone in your family now know what happened to you guys over the years?
Well, my mom obviously knows that we saw Paul beating her. Rani and I just recently shared with each other what he did to us. No one else knows that part of it. Not even my mom.

More jotting in the journal, then she looked up and nodded at me to continue.

Grandmom and Grandpop during their Las Vegas
visit in front of our home with Rani and me.

Mom and her tennis friends at SNTA.

Rani, Sheika and me.

CHAPTER TWENTY-ONE

Summer 1975

My third summer at overnight camp (my second one with bunkmates) was highly successful. I miraculously managed not to pee in bed at night and made many friends. My siblings didn't have to visit me as much, because I had what was called "camper-confidence." I became a counselors' favorite and had the ability to make my fellow campers laugh . . . a lot. I was bold enough to try out for the camp play, *Joseph and the Amazing Technicolor Dreamcoat*. I was gunning for the part of Joseph, but was assigned to "a green leafy tree/chorus." The play was mostly set in a dry desert of Egypt, so I was perplexed at how a green leafy tree fit in, but I got to sing and was in almost every scene. I loved every minute of it.

After camp, we spent a week alternating our stay between my aunt's home and our grandparent's apartment. As always, we spent our last two days uneventfully at our father's home. He and his wife stayed in their bedroom watching sports, while we either swam unsupervised or watched TV. We could have run a crack whorehouse in his den and he would have never known. The only attention he paid that weekend was to Rani's ragged nails. He offered her money if she stopped biting them. He said if she came back the next summer with nail growth, he would give her two dollars per nail.

———

Interesting that he took notice of that. Did the incentive work?
Not at all. I guess we each had our own unbreakable habits. I peed in bed, and she chewed on her nails.

You understand that these were habits brought on by nerves? Your body's way of dealing with your home life. None of which was your fault.
Looking at my own hands, remembering Rani's chewed nail beds, I said quietly, *Yes. I get that now.*

CHAPTER TWENTY-TWO

Fall 1975

Mom and Paul picked us up on the tarmac in Vegas with big smiles and hugs. We left the airport like one big happy family. It was a new year, and what had happened last year was a forgotten memory.

I was starting kindergarten and was excited to be old enough to go to school with one of my siblings. Todd and I could bike to school together, while my sister began middle school.

Paul told Rani that she was enrolled in and would be attending "Nigger County." He said it was located next to a high school in a bad part of town. The following day Mom drove her by her new school to check out the environment. The school looked peaceful, pleasant and, indeed, it shared a driveway with a neighboring high school.

Entering sixth grade at six feet tall, Rani had no choice but to carry herself with confidence. She knew she was going to be one of the tallest students and did not want to seem intimidating. She wanted to present herself as friendly and welcoming. She got on the bus standing up straight and smiling on her first day. When she got into the school, she noticed that not only was she the tallest one in her classroom, but in the entire school—and she was definitely a minority. Unlike Paul, she didn't care about skin color; she was just excited to make new friends and to be out of elementary school. People looked at her that first day, but no one spoke to her.

On day two, she was met by a group of black high school girls as she got off the bus. They were pointing and laughing about how tall she was for a middle-school kid. They said loud enough for her to hear, "She must be stupid and failed ten times." They laughed and teased her as she walked into school, hunched over, "Hey Big Bird, fail a grade or two?"

By the end of the week, a larger group of black high-school girls had gathered in front of her school to "check her out." They called her Big Bird again, but added "white freak" and threw food at her. She tried to ignore them and get into the confines of the building as quickly as possible.

The girls in her own school began tormenting her between classes. No one wanted to be associated with the Big Bird, white freak. The boys laughed and grabbed at her body when she walked by them asking if they could "get a piece of her big, white ass." She walked as fast as her long legs would carry her, but the boys got in her face even if she diverted in another direction.

By the second week of school, Rani sprinted from the bus to the school entrance. She could limit the harassment if she made it through the door quickly enough.

By mid-October, the high-school girls learned of Rani's first name. They began teasing her for having a funny name. A week later, word leaked out that her last name was Dushon and the name-calling became relentless. Not only did they taunt her because she was freakishly tall and white, but she also had two funny names.

Rani held back the tears at school, but as soon as she got off the school bus and walked into the house, she'd fall apart.

Mom comforted her at night and told her it was just this one year—she promised her she would be able to attend a different school the next year, and it would be much better. Rani insisted on changing her name no matter what school she attended. She could not change her height, but she had the ability to change her name. She said she would use her middle name, Lyn, and Paul's last name, Wagner.

As Mom witnessed what Rani was going through, she considered what Todd would encounter the following year. He was taller than Rani by two inches, and had the Dushon name. If her daughter was tormented for her height and name, she knew he would be as well. She had to come up with a strategic plan that did not involve his going to that school.

———

While Rani hated her school, I rather enjoyed mine. I liked my peers and the fact that I got to ride my bike to school alongside my brother. Since I got out of school an hour earlier than Todd did, I rode home alone. After my first week of biking home alone, I constantly had a nagging feeling that someone was following me. As I rode along the busy street toward my house, I thought someone could pull up at any time and throw me into their car.

By week two, I pedaled home twice as fast so no one could snatch me. Several times I got my pants caught in my bicycle chain. Whenever that happened, I would hop off my bike in a panic and drag it behind me with one hand on the handlebar. Once I got to the corner of our street, I'd dart up the driveway with my heart pounding, untangle my pants from the chain, grab the newspaper and run into the house. I'd quickly slam the door behind me and double lock it, checking through the side window to make sure no one was there. Sheika would greet me with a lick to my face and then pee on the white carpet.

Once my breathing became steady, I would grab a cup of water from the kitchen and sit under the dining table. I'd calm down with the newspaper on my lap and read the headlines—like my Grandmom told me to do.

Late that fall, Paul introduced us to the MGM hotel. This was the first time we had ventured to the Vegas strip since Mom's show. We were going to see a movie in the elaborate theater.

Before we entered the theater, we met the MGM lion in the lobby. It was the pre-movie showpiece, and we gawked at it like good tourists before we entered the grand theater. There were red velvet couches instead of single movie theater seats, and waitresses dressed in extremely short, low-cut dresses took our beverage orders.

We saw a very inappropriate-for-me James Bond flick that night. During the sex or violent scenes, Mom halfway covered my left eye as I watched between her fingers. I never understood why she attempted to shield me from such things when I had seen much worse at home. (However, about three years later Mom and Rani took me to see *Halloween*. I finally saw things in a movie that were far worse than what was going on in our house. Mom tried, as she always did, to cover my eyes during the bad scenes—but I knew the moment I came face-to-face with Michael Myers on the movie screen that night, there was great potential that I would pee in bed for the rest of my life.)

Just after the Thanksgiving holiday, Todd and Rani spent a long afternoon teaching me curse words. They said, "shit" and I would repeat it four times. They said, "dick" and I would repeat it four times. They then added words that they called compounds, like "mother-fucker," "asshole" and "shithead." We practiced until they felt I had each word memorized. They were in hysterics as they told me that I should say my new words to Mom when she got home.

When we heard her car pull into the garage, they hid behind the stairs, muffling their laughter, and told me to greet her with my new vocabulary. When Mom walked in, I ran up to her and announced, "Hi mother-fucker, shithead, dick, asshole." I smiled proudly, knowing that I had remembered every word perfectly.

Mom looked at me, and I felt the wind of her approaching hand before it reached my face. I let out a shriek that didn't even sound familiar to my own ears. I put my hand to my hot, throbbing cheek, fearing it would slide off if I didn't hold it in place. Mom yelled for Todd and Rani. I had flipped her mood switch, and they were in big trouble. They sheepishly came around the corner of the stairs, daring not to make eye contact. They were rewarded for their vocabulary lessons with a relentless whipping right there in the foyer.

It was unclear if Mom had most recently begun to wear belts as a fashion statement or as weaponry.

––––––––

Late fall, Paul said it was time to mate Sheika. She was bleeding on a monthly basis and had successfully ruined the white carpets with yellow and red stains. He said, "We might as well make use of her and make some money on her pups."

The next week Paul introduced us to a man and his male afghan stud that he called Droy.

The man left Droy with us and said he would come back for him in three days. He and Paul shared a private laugh about the dogs mating.

Paul grabbed Droy by his collar and led him out to the yard where Sheika was busy drinking our heavily chlorine-infused pool water. He called for us to join him, saying it was important for us to watch them mate—which happened almost immediately. The stud took one sniff of Sheika's behind and mounted her like a horse.

I was dumbfounded by their behavior and looked at Paul who turned to Rani. "It is your responsibility to make sure Droy doesn't fall off Sheika while he's humping her. Hold the dogs together if necessary to be sure that Droy gets his seed into her."

If Rani's eyes could have popped out of her head, they would have. "There is NO WAY I am going near those dogs while they are doing *THAT!* No way!" She then abruptly turned around and stormed into the house.

Turned out, the dogs had no problem effectively humping on their own. I found it fascinating and watched them go at it for so long. Just as I became uninterested, they simultaneously lay down to rest. Before bed, I peeked outside and Droy had mounted her again.

Sheika got pregnant. We eagerly waited for her litter of puppies to arrive. Paul said that we could keep one of her puppies, but he had to sell the rest of them and share the profits with Droy's owner.

After eight weeks of anticipation, Sheika went into labor. We made a makeshift labor unit for her out of a large box and a blue comforter. It sat in a shady area of our yard. It seemed like forever for her to squeeze the first adorable puppy out. We were captivated as we watched it snuggle up to its mom's belly. We left the puppy alone and waited all day for the others to come out. None came. Her entire *litter* consisted of one puppy, and we named her Starsky.

We hired a new trainer when Starsky was one month old. Fortunately, Starsky was smarter than her mom. Sheika continued to pee on the carpet and run out the door at every opportunity, while Starsky waited obediently to be walked. One day Sheika ran out, and no one went to look for her. That was the last time any of us saw her.

Paul had the white carpets replaced, and there were no more reminders of Sheika.

Sheika and her puppy Starsky.

CHAPTER TWENTY-THREE

Spring 1976

Paul decided I should get my ears pierced. He said, "Now that you are turning seven, it's time." I said I didn't want to, but he was not interested in negotiating. He swept me under his arm and carried me into his bathroom. He sat me on the counter like an inanimate object and said, "Don't move."

To my misfortune, he had premeditated the whole ordeal. The piercing materials were laid out on the counter: a sewing needle, an ice-cube tray, rubbing alcohol, a cotton ball and a pair of small gold earrings. A bolt of fear shot through me. I slid off the counter, and he grabbed my torso and put me in a headlock. I struggled to break free as he abruptly put the ice cube behind my left ear and poked the needle through the front of it—then he did the same to the other ear. He wiped each ear with a damp cotton ball, put the earrings in and said, "You're free to go."

The weather warmed up quickly, and my siblings chose to go swimming after school instead of running to their friends' houses. I was very happy to have their company. I loved spending time at the pool with them—even though I had not yet learned to swim during the summer months back east. While Rani and Todd played in the middle of the pool, I splashed around on the hot tub steps.

One afternoon I dared myself to swim to the other side of the hot tub. As I leapt forward, I went directly underwater as though there were blocks tied to my feet. I bobbed up and down for air, splashing my hands about. I couldn't find the sides or feel the bottom of the tub, which at that point seemed bottomless. In one of my gulps for air, someone grabbed my arm and pulled me to the side. I clung to the hot pavement for dear life and watched Rani swim back to the middle of the pool.

I added "pools" to my list of fears and hid all my bathing suits in the far corner of my closet. I was confident of never swimming again, and no matter how deathly hot it got, I was not going to chance even sitting near the pool. I was happy to observe my siblings from the cement patio, a safe distance from the pool.

That weekend Paul learned of my near-drowning experience, which he found to be preposterous.

He confronted me in the den and said he wanted to take me out for a swim. I said I was never swimming again and, in fact, had gotten rid of all my bathing suits. Paul's face got red, making it clear he would have none of this. He tossed me over his shoulder like a rag doll and headed for the glass sliders. I grabbed onto his sarong, which he wore every weekend, and hoped this would prevent him from throwing me in. He opened the sliding doors, walked to the edge of the pool and jumped into the deep end, pulling me down with him.

He held me underwater for an eternity. When he propelled us to the surface, I grabbed onto the side of the pool and clumsily climbed out, gasping for air in my soaked clothes. I was never-ever-ever going in that pool, or any pool, ever again.

———

Paul surprised us by bringing home a Chinook RV. He said this would be a great way for us to travel together. The Chinook was very interesting. It was virtually a home on wheels with a bathroom, kitchen, living area and room for four to sleep comfortably.

He told us we would be taking trips to the Grand Canyon to hike and to Utah to ski. The RV took up our entire driveway and became the new hangout for my siblings and their friends.

Paul wanted to get a trip in before we headed back east that summer. He decided that our first RV destination was going to be to Brian Head, Utah, for spring skiing. None of us had ever been skiing or to Utah, so we were excited about our pending adventure.

I was assigned the copilot position by Mom and had the important duty of reading road signs to Paul while he drove. Todd and Rani tortured each other in the back by fighting or playing cards. Mom was in constant motion cleaning, dishing out snacks or relieving me for an hour or two from my position in the front passenger seat.

When I read the sign that we had arrived in Brian Head, Rani and Todd cheered loud enough to startle Paul. Being that I was the copilot, I quickly sensed that this pissed him off. He was on edge from a long day of driving and was now furious due to the loud intrusion in our small space. He abruptly swung the RV to the side of the road and turned back to Rani and Todd who stood looking at him expressionless. He opened the door, jumped down the steps and told them to come outside. Mom was in the back fast asleep. They knew they were in trouble and didn't know if waking Mom would help with what they anticipated was coming their way. They quietly went out the RV doorway, down the stairs, and stood next to Paul. He took them by the neck, one hand on each, and smashed their faces into the snow, similar to what a child would do with a bucket of sand on the beach. When he let them up for air, their faces were red, raw and dripping wet. I feared I was next, but he just pushed Todd and Rani back into the RV, got in the driver's seat and continued onward. We all looked at each other, stunned, as Paul flatly announced that we had arrived at our final destination.

————

I never *became one* with skiing, even with daily lessons. Rani and Todd were old enough to receive instruction with their peers on the slopes, but there was not an appropriate age group for me. My parents were able to get me into a program with a handful of beginner adults. I stood in a parallel line with ten people who were as challenged as I was. We fell like dominos all over a small bunny hill through the morning and then limped our way to lunch.

One afternoon, toward the end of the week, Mom and Paul picked me up. They were windswept and chipper as they told me they were taking me on the chairlift to the top of the mountain. I started to whine halfway up the mountain that I was too scared to go down. I told them I hadn't learned how to ski yet. The only thing I had mastered was how to get up when I fell. They said that this would be the best way to get the hang of it. When we got off the chairlift at the tippy top of Brian Head, they started their descent and hollered back to me to join them. When I said I was too scared, Paul bellowed, "Meet you at the bottom!"

Abandoned at the top of this mammoth mountain was almost worse than my swim episode with Paul weeks earlier. I stood rigid as I watched them disappear into little dots. A kind instructor found me minutes later crying by myself and asked me where my parents were. I pointed down the mountain. He took me down between his legs, so that our skis paralleled. He tried to lift my spirits by telling me how good I was doing. When we got to the bottom, he escorted me to a bench and asked me if I was okay. Now that I was on flat earth, I assured him I was just perfect.

————

When we returned home from Brian Head, I was pretty sure I did not want to go skiing again. While I added that to my list of things I didn't like, Rani was happily approaching the near-end of her middle-school year. She would soon be turning twelve and was old enough to know that 1) she never again wanted to see the people she went to school with that year . . . and 2) she didn't like Paul's weekly visits.

She voiced her thoughts on the latter to Paul the night after we got back from vacation. When he came to her bedside, she said she didn't want to suck on his cherries anymore. He told her she had to, and if she protested or said anything, he would kill her mother. There was nothing more she could say. He had made the threat of all threats, and she knew he was not kidding. She continued to do as he asked.

When school ended, we celebrated at home. Rani announced that she officially changed her name, effective immediately. She did not want to be associated with the name Rani or Dushon. She wanted to be known as Lyn Wagner from now on. She certainly didn't have any love for Paul or his name—it was just practical. Not only was it ordinary, but since he was married to our mom, it was also convenient. She said we could still call her Rani at home, but any new friends would only know her as Lyn.

————

Mom's concern for Todd's attending middle school escalated when school ended. When she brought up the matter with Paul, he said, "He can tough it out at 'Nigger County' like Rani did." She knew Todd could probably hold his ground, but he was quieter and more vulnerable to being pushed around. She knew he could not live through a year like the one Rani experienced, nor did she want him to. Asking Paul to move just to be in a different school district was not an option, and she knew he would not pay for private school.

To avoid a fight at home, Mom called Dad. This was the only good option for Todd—to live on the East Coast with our father his sixth-grade year.

She told Dad that Rani was teased, groped and bullied daily, and she could not stand to see Todd go through the same. She suggested that Todd live with him through the sixth grade, and then come back to Vegas for the rest of his schooling. She also asked him to start Todd's Jewish education toward a Bar Mitzvah.

Dad finally agreed, but with much hesitation. With his second wife and her two children, Todd would be another responsibility, but he couldn't say no.

———

Interesting . . . actually disturbing. Your mother was so concerned about Todd's religious experience, but married an anti-Semite?

Dr. Tanner looked at me for a reaction, but I had nothing to say. She had made a statement, and I had no answer for her. It was foolish, we could both agree on that, but I was not giving it to her. Todd did have his Bar Mitzvah the following summer, and my mom was so proud of him. I didn't give her that either. It was bad enough that I didn't know what Paul meant by "the Jews." When my grandmother told me to be proud of my Jewish roots, I was too young to put two and two together, but I presently felt ashamed that I hadn't.

———

The week before we headed back east, Paul said to me, "I am going to miss your little face" and suggested we take a "bubbly bath" together. We were sitting in their large Jacuzzi playing with a mass of bubbles when he jumped up, naked, dripping in suds, declaring it was a perfect opportunity to take photos of me. He pulled me out of the tub, towel-dried himself, dried me, put on his red sarong and went into mom's closet. He came out holding one of her black, feather boas. He put the boa around my bare shoulders and took a series of photos of me next to the glass sliders in their room. After a while, I asked if he wanted me to put my clothes on, but he said he just wanted me in feathers.

———

Did he often have you take baths with him?
This was the first time. After I got back from camp that summer, it became monthly. It happened only when no one else was home. He would wash me, taking extra time with my private parts.

    I hesitated for a moment to catch my breath as I recalled the memories.
The baths became showers when we moved to our second home a year later. It was then that he would ask me to clean his private parts.

You were a victim at such a young age. You were not responsible for his actions.
Uh huh. That was all I could get out as I felt the water works coming on. I was becoming an Oprah show special. I hastily grabbed a tissue from the industrial-sized, floral box on the side table and dabbed my eyes. Dr. Tanner remained quiet while I uncomfortably and silently cried into the one, now soggy, tissue.

Softly she said, I know you understand that this was not your fault. It is okay and safe to get it all out in here. You had no

one to defend you. You were all alone and had no idea this was wrong.

I just don't get how I didn't know this was totally wrong. It was just all just so . . . wrong. How could I be so ignorant? Furthermore, I am annoyed that I am crying about it now. I am not a crier. Is that even a word? It . . . is just . . . that I am stronger than this.

Crying is part of your healing and understanding. It would be almost unnatural if someone under these circumstances didn't have an outlet. You have all the right in the world to cry.

She hesitated while I continued to sniffle.

You were a child and there was no way you would know any different. That little girl had no idea that what was happening was utterly and completely wrong.

I didn't want to make the effort to respond. I dried my face with my tattered tissue and continued.

———

After the photo session with the boa, we got dressed, and Paul asked me to watch a program with him in the den. He poured himself a drink and we sat side by side on the large L-shaped sofa.

The program was about the Holocaust. Paul told me it was an important piece of history about the Jews. I didn't understand what the Jews were the first time he had mentioned it, so I asked, "What are the Jews?"

"They were the rotten people who went to jail for being dirty and bad. They were properly exterminated as you will see in this program."

I couldn't understand what I was watching at first, but after a couple of minutes, I was too scared to watch. There were two mean men with guns shouting at these poor dirty, skinny people in a desert-like, caged-in camp. I crouched into a ball and half covered my eyes as I watched the men repeatedly hit the people until they fell to the ground; then shot them. I flinched at each gunshot.

Paul paid no attention to me. He was glued to the screen as if he were watching the epic conclusion of *Gone with the Wind*. I started to fidget with my hands and kicked my legs back and forth over the side of the sofa. I just wanted him to see that I was uncomfortable, but to no avail.

I eyed the TV remote, contemplating changing the channel when Paul said, "Those were the ovens." He laughed out loud and said, "They were so stupid. They thought they were going in for showers! Are you watching this? Stupid Jew bastards."

I was way too frightened to watch anymore. He looked at me, finally noticing that I was uneasy. "Sit still. Stay quiet and learn some history."

I was all for learning something, but this was too scary. The people in the movie were sinister and awful; I grabbed the clicker and pretended I was going to turn the program off. He glared at me, got in my face and said, "Don't you dare."

I thought, *How bad could it be if I turned it off?* No one had ever hit me, other than a slap in the face, and I was determined to watch something else. I hit the off button, and the screen turned black. Paul looked at me, his eyes unwavering. His entire head turned a shade of red I had never seen before. I instinctively hopped over the sofa and ran for my life. In an instant he was in front of me, grabbing my arms tightly at my side. His face turned purple. He spat as he growled, "Never test me. I could fucking kill you!"

He walked back into the den, grabbed his drink, turned the TV back on and sat back on the sofa.

I stood frozen in place until my siblings walked in the door an hour later. I didn't want to test him by moving an inch.

Me wearing my mom's feather boa during Paul's photo shoot.

Mom skiing down slopes. I own this coat today and consider it vintage.

Todd and Rani playing in the snow in Brian Head.

Rani and me in the bathroom of a motel during one of our road trips. Took a night off from sleeping in the RV.

CHAPTER TWENTY-FOUR

Summer 1976

We boarded the plane back to Philadelphia early in June. We were excited to see our extended family and go to overnight camp.

After a fun-filled eight weeks at camp, we had our ritual weeks with our grandparents, then at our aunt's house, and finally went to our father's home.

We helped Todd settle in his new room for the school year. He would be sleeping on a pullout sofa in our stepmother's small, hot office. She had removed piles of manila files from her metal file cabinet for him to use as drawers. We watched Todd unpack his camp trunk of clothes into the two drawers that were allotted to him. The room was the only one in the house without air conditioning. It was sweltering, and I opened his door to let some cool air in. A second later, I heard our stepmother's stern voice, "Keep that door closed! It will let the cool air out of the rest of the house." Rani and I looked at each other, feeling sorry that our brother had to live in this hot little office for an entire year.

We said goodbye to Todd at the house, and our father drove us to the airport. We wouldn't see Todd until the following summer.

Ironic that you were feeling badly for your brother, when your circumstances at home were not optimal either?

I sat back for a second.

I guess I just didn't think about my home life being bad. I agree, very ironic.

I caught Dr. Tanner glancing at my hand.

Oh. Umm, I got engaged this weekend.

I noticed the ring. Congratulations.

Thanks.

How are you feeling about it?

Excited. Nervous, I guess.

What are you nervous about?

I feel like I'm ready. I've anticipated this moment happening for months. I mean, I told Bradley to get a ring or move out. We've been together for four years, and I know he's a good man . . . "

Are you "nervous" about losing your independence or feeling trapped?

I laughed.

No, he might be though!

I paused, knowing she was not amused.

I don't know what it stems from. I just have all this heightened emotion of excitement mixed with a hint of reserve. I love him, which I guess is all that matters here.

Suzanne, you are not your mother . . .

My face contorted, because I did not want to go down this path again. She quickly said:

Let me stress that I am not here to judge her, or provide opinions on such matters, but, frankly, the choices she made, albeit not good ones, were based around her children. That was quite noble for the time, but she did abandon you during critical times in your childhood.

One of her many problems was that she feared her independence, where you, a young adult, embrace it. Even if you are not aware of it, you decided what kind of person you were going to be a long time ago. You went to high school and college—successfully completing both. You moved to New York City with a wad of cash in your pocket, motivated to do something big on your own. Do you see what you accomplished already? Not many people coming from where you did could have accomplished so much.

I stared at her blankly. She had not gone on such a verbal tangent since we met seven weeks prior. I didn't know if I was more shocked by all her words, or her revelation about me. At twenty-six, I was not aware that I had accomplished anything significant with my life.

You have a successful career that you love, and you are in a mutual, consenting, happy relationship. With this already accomplished, your past caught up with you and you were smart enough to seek help.

You are just discovering who you are, and what you are going to find is that you are remarkable. You are a young woman with good, strong values and have great drive to be independent—yet you have found an opening to share your life with someone who loves you and you love back. Given your background and the fact that all of this happened even before you sought therapy is incredible.

I see a young woman ready to take the next steps and share her life. You are going to be a wonderful partner and mother someday.

It was a lot to digest. I had been living as this person, but never took a moment to look at me as a whole, from the outside. I was someone who did make good choices that were based on what I felt were best for me. I could share my life without giving up who I was; I would just be me, plus a great other half. A partner. An equal partner who treated me with respect, kindness and love. I sat quietly. I was on the brink of tears, but fought to keep them back. Therapy had turned me into a wussy.

What are you feeling?
I choked the words out. *I feel overwhelmed. I don't know if I can explain what it is. I don't know why I feel like I am going to cry.*
I paused to swallow the annoying lump in my throat.
I think those may have been the nicest words an adult has ever said to me or about me. Or maybe because I am realizing I am not that little girl anymore? I don't know.

We are just are getting there.
She said nothing more and exhaled as she leaned back in her seat. I thought she was as shocked as I was that she had actually spoken more than one hundred words in one session. After sixty seconds of tick, tick, tick, from the wall clock, I shook my head as if I had finally comprehended a physics problem, and continued my story.

CHAPTER TWENTY-FIVE

Fall 1976

When Rani and I arrived back in Vegas, Mom and Paul said they found a new home. They called it a "three-bedroom-three-bath, five-thousand-square-foot dream-house with lots of potential." I was suspect of any home that took one-long-string-of-words to sell us on it. Mom told us they had made an offer and hoped it would be accepted. She said when Todd moved back the following year, we'd convert the sunroom into a room for him.

To Rani's relief, Mom let her know that she would be in a new school district, in a wonderful, affluent area. Paul chimed in, "This home is in an exclusive, private community where lots of white, famous people live."

Rani and I looked at each other with similar looks of anticipation, "Famous people?"

While Rani looked out the window and daydreamed of Leif Garrett, I envisioned Sean Cassidy and me singing duets of "Da Doo Ron Ron" in our new backyard.

Their offer was accepted the next day, and Paul managed to sell our home the following week. We packed up with the assistance of two burly-man movers and had three days to get settled into our new home before school started.

The house was located on the other side of town in a quiet, gated community named Sierra Vista. An extensive wood horse fence surrounded the entire community. It was the defining line from the outside world and our new one. I could tell this was going to be a nice, safe place to live.

We drove through the front entrance, which was located off a quiet road. We slowly drove by beautiful homes with well-kept lawns and elaborate landscaping. I loved that there were no stop signs or yellow lines—just clean, paved roads that led into one another. Paul and Mom said they would drive past some of the famous homes. Rani and I could hardly contain our excitement as we eagerly waited to hear the names of our teen crushes.

"Jerry Vale lives right there and across from him, Orson Wells."

"Who are they?" I asked, and was ignored.

"This is where Pat Cooper lives and Bobbie Gentry lives over this way."

"We don't know who these people are," Rani said deflated. "Can we just go to the house?"

Mom pointed her finger out the window, "Sergio Frankie lives right there! Our home is behind his."

Rani and I let out a "Humph" in unison. This was just another no-name person who had no impact on our lives.

We turned a corner and entered a small cul-de-sac with two homes. One was an A-frame that Mom said was built for Frank Sinatra, but he never lived there. That was exciting, since we actually knew the name, but he didn't live there, so it was irrelevant.

Our new home was on the left. We pulled into the driveway and saw a sprawling, brown, ranch-style home. Paul pulled into a carriage garage, and we got out of the car. Standing on the driveway, all we could see was a six-foot-tall brown wood fence that enclosed the backyard.

Paul led us down a path to the front door. He said he wanted us to see the backyard first. We followed him into the house and down a terra cotta-tiled hallway, like the one in our former home. We passed a spacious sunken living room with a floor-to-ceiling stone fireplace and went out a wall of sliding glass doors. He eyed us, anticipating our reaction as we saw our new five-acre yard. Starsky was happily running and jumping around the yard like a newly released caged animal.

There was a pool made entirely of stone. It had a waterfall and a diving board! If that weren't earth shattering enough, I spotted a tire swing hanging from the tallest tree I had ever seen. I skipped my way over to it as Paul touched my shoulder directing me back into the house. He said it was time to see my new room. Disgruntled, I followed him and Rani back toward the house.

Paul took us back into the large corridor between the sunken living room and the glass sliders. He eagerly walked ahead of us, blurting out features of the home as if we were prospective buyers. He pointed in the direction of our bedrooms, saying that our home was conveniently spread out on one level. Rani's steps slowed and her body went rigid. I was right on her heels and wanted to see my new room, so I impatiently scurried around her.

Our bedrooms were off a private hallway with a large bathroom between. The rooms seemed equal in size, but hers had a king-size bed and mine had twin beds. Mom had already put my large Raggedy Ann doll in my room, so there was no mistaking which one was mine. We were sitting in our individual rooms when Mom called from the hall, "Come, girls, I want to show you the rest of the house."

We followed Mom and Paul to their bedroom on the other side of the house. We entered from the front hall into their dressing room, which felt like an amusement park funhouse. Every square inch of the room was mirrored with the exception of the cream-colored carpeting. The dressing room connected to a mirrored hallway that led to a mirrored bathroom and mirrored bedroom. In every direction, I saw a million of me . . . up, down and across.

We exited their room through a doorway directly connecting to another room. Mom hit the light switch, illuminating an office.

It was a dark, rectangular room with heavy red velvet curtains that covered more glass sliders to the yard. It was furnished with a masculine wood desk, sofa, armchairs, TV, and a fully stocked bar.

From the office, we entered the hallway that led back to the sunken living room. Paul pointed to where the television would go and announced that the room was "officially the family hangout." They then took us into the dining room and through a swinging door that led to the kitchen. The tight space was mostly filled by a large island with a butcher-block cutting board built into it. Paul nonchalantly pointed out a stereo system built into the wall that would allow us to hear the same music throughout the house. Rani and I rolled our eyes at each other, hoping we wouldn't have to listen to his favorite showtunes every day. Off the kitchen was an enclosed porch with dizzying palm-tree-design wallpaper, which led into the hallway where my room was.

Once the tour was complete, I retreated to my spacious room. I was smitten with our new home. I jumped on my bed, testing it for bounce-ability, and then rolled around on my carpeted floor. I knew I would no longer fear being outside of our new home—the community seemed so safe and isolated.

While I was rejoicing in my room, Rani was feeling uneasy in hers. She should have relished having her own bedroom, but instead, she anticipated the worst. All she could think about was how we were all living on the same floor. There were no longer stairs separating her room from Paul's. She feared he was going to visit her more often because she was easily accessible *and* alone.

———

On the first day of school, Mom drove me to the bus stop. She told me I would normally ride my bike and leave it at the bus stop, but she wanted us to map out the route. When we pulled up, there were already four girls waiting. Seconds later, the bus arrived, I kissed Mom goodbye, jumped out of the car and followed the other girls into the bus.

When I entered my classroom, the teacher had just begun calling roll. I sat in my seat and listened to her call my classmate's names. When she said, "Suzanne Wagner," no one responded. I was the only one who had not said, "Here," but kept looking around dumbfounded like everyone else. Finally the teacher asked, "Which one of you is Suzanne?" and I responded, "My name is Suzanne."

Later that week, I was sent home with a school letter that had the name "Suzanne Wagner" on it. It was strange to see the name in writing. I was staring at the letter in the kitchen when my mom came home that afternoon. She put her arms around me and explained that since she and Rani were using the last name Wagner, she didn't want me to be the only one with a different last name.

––––––––

What are you thinking about? Was it upsetting to you to have a different last name?
No, I didn't care about the name change. I was just thinking . . . whether to tell you that I had an incident this weekend.

She said nothing, waiting for more.
Bradley and I went skiing. We got in the chairlift line and my body gave out. It was like I was a marionette whose strings were cut; I just collapsed. My head and brain were functioning, but my body failed me. It was a total mind-body disconnect.

Hmm. Then what happened?
A circle of spectators tried to help with my poles and skis, but I couldn't move anything other than my head. Bradley carried me to the first-aid clinic. Everyone there had broken arms and legs, and I was the freak show whose body collapsed for no reason.

Nothing freakish about it, Suzanne. Did you see a doctor?
There was a homeopathic doctor on duty and after a vitals check, he asked me if I had ever had an anxiety attack. I nodded yes, and he said that was what he thought it was. He told me to go home and rest. Then I called my mom and bawled. I was pretty shaken up.

Did you go home and rest?
Yes, and I was okay for the rest of the weekend.

Why were you hesitant to tell me this?
I don't want to take a higher dose of Paxil. I only want to get off of it.

We don't have to increase your dose. You are going through a lot mentally. You've only been on Paxil for four months now, and I think it's been helping. This incident may be a result of what we are getting into. Go to your general practitioner for a blood workup just in case. But I agree with the doctor, it seems typical of anxiety. I would keep your physical activity to a minimum over the next few weeks, and I will wean you off Paxil when I feel you are ready.
I exhaled with relief. *I will. I promise.*

Rani started seventh grade and quickly made a lot of new friends. Starting a new school as Lyn Wagner gave her renewed confidence. She began inviting girlfriends to the house, but quickly learned it was not a good idea. Paul was often at home, and once she and her friends were in the door, he wasted no time hitting on them.

One day when Rani and her new friend Shari were hunting for snacks in the kitchen, Paul casually sauntered in. He said hi to Rani and then stood intimidatingly close to Shari. Rani stepped in the middle, put her hands on his chest and pushed him back. This was the first time she ever laid hands on him defensively. Paul grinned at her as though they were playing a game, pushed *her* aside and stood back in front of Shari. Rani then grabbed her friend by the hand and ran out the front door. She swore never to bring anyone around the house again.

Rani feared Shari would tell her parents or other kids in school about how strange her stepfather behaved, but she never mentioned it. She figured Shari didn't realize what Paul was doing, but it was now clearer than ever to Rani that something was wrong with him.

————

There was an incredible sense of freedom riding my bike in our new neighborhood, knowing I didn't have to worry about people in random cars abducting me. I rode around each curved road of our gated community, absorbing every inch of my new territory. There were at least two miles of roadway leading in and out of private streets just like ours. I sped past magnificent homes with perfectly manicured lawns and ornate metal gates. I targeted pomegranate trees that I was certain to pilfer from and small grassy hills I wanted to roll down.

After just three weeks, I had acquaintances in the neighborhood and made a best friend. Her name was Sharon, and she lived right around the corner from me. She had tan-colored skin, was super tough, and started fistfights at the bus stop every morning. I liked her instantly. Their home was as large as ours, but they had a gated driveway that held at least a dozen fancy sports cars. She said she was Indian and her father worked in the tobacco industry. She told me we could smoke cigarettes for free anytime we wanted. She was a good protector, had cool cars and offered free gifts . . . what more could a seven-year-old ask for in a friendship?

Sharon's four-car garage was lined with enormous iceboxes. Each one was loaded with over a hundred cartons of cigarettes. When we were seeking an adventure, we'd take a carton, hide it under Sharon's shirt and ride our bikes to the top of my street where several large cactus bushes concealed us while we smoked. We'd light one cigarette after another, inhale, choke, cough and laugh before we'd fire up another.

When we weren't polluting our little lungs, we danced to Top 40 on the radio or rode our bikes around the neighborhood like juvenile delinquents, scouting homes with pomegranate trees. Once we found a property of our liking, we parked our bikes on the lawn and picked as many pomegranates as we could hold in our arms. We'd then sit on the hot curb, break open the fruit's skin, and tear the little juicy pits out of the delicate flesh. We'd giggle as the juice ran down our arms, staining our faces and clothes, and we delighted in the fact that we scored the best free treat on a hot Vegas day.

———

True to Rani's fears, Paul visited her room a few weeks after we moved in. It was after midnight when he opened her bedroom door. The bright hallway light woke her instantly. He put his finger to his lips, reminding her to keep quiet and that this was their secret. She could smell the unmistakable scent of liquor on his breath before he even reached her bedside. Rani averted her eyes as she anticipated his untying his red sarong, making her suck on his cherries. She waited for him to put them in her face, but to her surprise he just stood above her. She felt his eyes on her, so she continued to avert hers by facing the far wall, hoping he would just go away.

It surprised her when he pulled down her sheets. She protectively grabbed them up and tucked the hem under her chin, exposing only her hands and face. He grinned, then yanked the sheets down forcefully. Rani trembled, unable to control her emotions and feared what he was going to do next. He pulled up her nightgown and tugged at her low-rise, child-like, briefs. She pressed down on the bed, stiffening her entire body so he would not be able to pull them off, but to no avail. He grabbed both sides of her briefs, tugged them down and tossed them to the floor. She stared wide-eyed at his chest, still avoiding his eyes, as he pulled off his sarong, exposing his erection. Rani tightened her entire body and closed her eyes and lips . . . anything to keep him from penetrating any part of her.

He got on the bed and Rani winced. She fought rolling toward him from the weight of his body on the mattress. He pried her stiffened legs apart, pushed himself between them and tried to put his penis in her. He pushed and pushed, while she tightened and tightened. He finally let out an exaggerated, "Humph" and got off the bed without replacing her underwear or pulling up the covers.

He stood over her, drilling his eyes into her. Rani felt exposed, angry, sick, and wanted to crawl under her blankets and cry. He moved to the side of her bed, thrust his penis toward her face and said, "Suck."

Too frightened to defy him and wanting him to leave her room, she did as he asked.

As he turned to leave he said, "You tell anyone about this, I will kill your family." Rani felt her stomach turn at his familiar words, but she didn't cry. She was too angry to cry.

Paul continued to visit Rani several times a month. She developed a defense by exercising her vaginal muscles. She wanted to make sure he could never penetrate her. As simple as her strategy was, it seemed to be effective. Paul ended up frustrated at her bedside, but never left her room until she placated him with oral sex. She knew she had to do this to satisfy his sick desire to have sex with her.

Rani began overeating. She was aware that she had to do more than Kegel exercises. She thought if she gained enough weight, Paul would lose interest in her. She was determined to get to a place where he no longer wanted to touch her. She began hoarding small bags of chips and candy bars from the concession stand at school and stashing them under her bed. If she went to a friend's house, she came back with at least one snack to hide under her bed.

————

In speaking with her most recently, did you ask her why she never said anything to your mother?
She said she didn't like what was going on, but was too scared to say anything. Paul told her that if she ever said anything to her mother or anyone else, he would kill her family. He seemed quite serious when he told her this. She actually did think that he would kill us. Paul also told her that this was something people didn't talk about, so she didn't. He started messing with her when she was so young that of course she was going to believe everything he said. She did eventually tell my mom. We're just not there yet.

Do you really think your mother had no idea what was happening to your sister?
She was consumed with her own issues—Paul's jealous rages and beatings, his constant demand for sex, their drinking into oblivion and just plain survival. She would have never thought he would be sneaking into our rooms in the middle of the night. By the time we moved to our new home, they were both intoxicated 90 percent of the time, so she was long passed out by the time he ventured to our side of the house.

In high school, I wrote an end-of-year paper on alcoholism. Not because of my childhood—or maybe it was, I don't know. Anyway, I attended AA meetings. I had permission to sit in the back of the room and no one ever said anything to me. I listened to the addicts. It was very sad.

Sad because it was personal?
I didn't think it was personal at the time. I just learned about addiction and how someone's life, and the lives of those around them, can spiral out

of control so quickly. I learned about "alcoholic blackouts," where a person can function with no memory of events. That hit close to home for me. I truly believe that my mom experienced self-inflicted blackouts for the latter part of our years in Vegas with Paul. I didn't and don't look back thinking, "My gosh, if she didn't drink none of this would have happened to us." I just think she was going through her own hell and drinking was her escape.

Do you bring this up as an excuse for the bad decisions she made, because there are no excuses, Suzanne. She put you and your sister in the hands of a monster. Even if she didn't know you were being abused, the fact that he was verbally and physically abusing her *in front of you* was bad enough.

As I said during our first session, I don't blame her. I know that doesn't sit well with you, but I just don't find it prudent to blame. I have the decision to live in love or live in hate—like my mom's therapist said to her years ago. I choose to live in love. Blame, anger and all that comes with it . . . it's just so mentally exhausting. I don't have it in me to fight history that can't be changed. Why bother? It happened already. I am alive today and am here to talk about it. I am just trying to move forward and be the best person I can be. I want to deal with my own mishigas.

Mishigas?
Yiddish for craziness.

Dr. Tanner laughed. Not a hearty laugh, just a quick outburst. I thought, *This is what it took to get this lady to giggle? A little Yiddish?* She wrote something in her notebook, and with her head down she motioned for me to continue.

————

As it was with Rani, Paul behaved differently the first time he came to visit me in my room in the new house. He appeared out of the darkness, startling me just as he did in our old house. I looked over at the twin bed next to me, half-expecting to see my sister, but quickly remembered that we no longer shared a room.

Paul stroked my cheek, as always, and mumbled things under his reeking alcohol breath that I couldn't understand. After he stroked my cheek, he slowly pulled down my covers and slithered like a python into my tiny bed with me. His hand moved from my face and traveled south. My eyes followed his hand, because this was not something he usually did. I assumed he was checking to see if I had peed in bed yet, which I had not. He gently pulled my nightgown up to my neck and slid his fingers down around my torso. I fought the urge to giggle, because it tickled. He then bent his head over my chest to kiss my non-existent boobies. After that, he moved his head down my body, gently spreading my legs apart. At this point, my covers had fallen to the floor, and he was on his knees with his face and forearms at my thighs. He put his head between my legs and began to lick my private area.

"What are you doing?" I said meekly.

He ignored me, pushing my legs farther apart. I didn't like what he was doing, and I struggled to close my legs. I stared at the ceiling, counting to ten a dozen times, waiting for his sandpaper tongue to stop. When he finally finished, he put his finger to his lips and told me that this was our secret. I looked at him without any emotion. He stood up, pulled down my nightgown, pulled the covers to my chin and kissed my forehead, as if it were the most normal thing to do, and left.

I then peed in bed.

———

Hmm, Dr. Tanner said, as she feverishly penned in her journal. Was this an isolated incident or did he come to your room more than once?

That was just the first incident in our new home. After that, he came in a couple of times a week.

And that was for how long . . . ?
About three years.

You were still peeing in bed at this time?
I no longer peed in bed when I was at camp but, pathetically, I did when I was at home. I was now changing my own sheets and using a rubber mat to protect my mattress. I didn't stop peeing in bed at home until I was ten years old . . . the week we left Vegas.

So you stopped taking the red pills before or after you moved into the new house?
I stopped taking them after my first summer at sleep-away camp. Turned out that my camp counselor's father was a doctor, and he told her they were just sugar pills. I overheard her tell the co-counselor. I was supposed to be fixed just by thinking they were working. You know, the placebo effect . . . sort of like me and the Paxil. I was expecting her at least to smile, but she just looked at me with a straight face. *Anyhow, I was still scared to go to the bathroom at night, so I just peed in bed.*

She looked at her notes, flipped some pages over and looked up.

You said you felt safe in your new home.
I did feel safe at home during the day; it was just after bedtime when I got scared. I was always nervous of things, or people, popping out of the dark.

Do you get scared now? Of the dark?
Not really. I do check under my bed and in the closets when I get home from work—even though I have a doorman and no one could get up to my floor, let alone my apartment, without a key.

This is not rational behavior, Suzanne. It was Paul you feared all those years. He is no longer here to hurt you or come to you at night. You are okay—safe and in an environment you *choose* to live in. You are an adult who is able to protect herself. He can't get to you anymore, nor can any man against your will.

I get that. I know it's ridiculous that I look; I mean, what would I do if there was someone under the bed? I laughed.

Suzanne, there is no humor in this; you should know this by now. I know your instinct is to laugh, but please, I want you to try to stay focused.

––––––––

In the late fall, Paul announced we were taking the RV to the Grand Canyon. It was only a half day of driving, so that meant there was a good chance Paul would not get road rage.

Arriving drama-free in the early afternoon, we parked the RV and went on a nice, invigorating hike. Even though we could sleep in the RV, Paul got us rooms at a local motel. Mom and Paul stayed in one room; Rani and I in another.

After our first full day, we had a pleasant dinner and headed to our rooms for the night. Just outside the door to our room, Paul handed us four quarters and said we could use them for the beds. There seemed to be no correlation between a quarter and a bed, but Rani and I dashed into our room to find out. By sticking a quarter in the slot over the bed, it would vibrate for ten minutes. Rani and I lay on our backs laughing as we spoke in vibrate-language until we passed out.

During the Grand Canyon trip, Mom and Paul didn't fight; we were too busy for him to focus on her. We hiked, rode donkeys, took pictures, ate leisurely meals and got back to our rooms after dark. We looked like your average, happy, tourist family.

––––––––

In early December, we took what would become our yearly RV trip to Brian Head, Utah. The drive only took part of the day, so after lunch we set off on our four-hour journey.

The first leg of the trip was easy, though boring, as we set off through the familiar, dry desert. Once we got out of Nevada, nature came to life with scatterings of green plant life. As we got close to the mountains, white dominated the ground cover. As dusk approached, heavy snow began to fall. Paul suggested we put the chains on the tires before we started up the mountain, but Mom, Rani and I voted to keep moving. He relented and pressed onward.

When we hit the steep incline toward Brian Head, the RV began to slip. Night had fallen and the snow left him with low visibility. Paul announced, to no one in particular, that he was very pissed that we didn't put the chains on earlier. My mom, Rani and I looked at each other like, *"Oh shit."* He cursed under his breath as the RV slowly crawled up the mountain.

A snowdrift made it impossible to see and the back tires of the RV were swerving badly. Paul said, "We have to stop and put the goddam chains on our tires now or we are going to fall off this fucking mountain." He put on the hazard lights as I moved from my usual copilot position to the back of the RV. I didn't want to be in close proximity to his pissed-off self.

Paul slowly pulled over and instructed Mom to take the wheel. He told her she would have to move it back and forth when he told her to, so he could get the chains on. As he pulled the chains out of the inside closet, the RV began to slip. I ran to the sofa, next to Rani, and we looked out the side window. The red blinkers provided quick second-long views of the snow-covered road—and how frighteningly close we were to the edge of it. If we kept sliding, we would fall over into the darkness, which at that time seemed to have no visual bottom.

Paul ran out the RV door, dropped the chains and stuck his face in the open door a second later. He told Mom he needed her help outside and instructed Rani to put on the emergency break. He told her to push it down as hard as possible, even keep her foot on it, while holding the steering wheel to the left side. He and Mom ran out the door, and I watched as we inched closer to the edge of the road.

The front tire chains were on in less than five minutes. Mom came and turned the wheel so Paul could put the chain on the left back tire that was still on the road. The right rear tire was half on the road and half in the air. Mom listened to Paul yell, "Turn the wheel left; turn it right." He came in a moment later saying he got the chain on the left tire and that would be enough to get us up the hill. Mom and Paul were dripping with cold sweat and snow, as they both took the front seats and the RV started climbing up the hill again.

———

The weekend before Christmas, we shopped for a tree. Paul selected the biggest tree on the lot, reasoning that we had a lot more room in our new home. Paul, Mom, Rani and I spent several evenings leading up to Christmas Day decorating it with lights, ornaments and tinsel.

On Christmas Eve, presents were loaded under the tree. The next morning I woke before everyone else and sat impatiently in the den as everyone sauntered in, rubbing their sleepy eyes. I tore open board games, toys and saved the biggest gift for last. It was heavy, so I had to keep it on the floor as I ripped off the paper. To my delight, it was a pair of white roller skates with pink wheels. I put them on and skated out the front door. I mastered skating in one day and fell in love with my first sport.

The week after Christmas, my sister made plans to meet her friends at a roller skating rink. With much urging from Mom (and begging from me), Rani agreed I could go with her—only to hear her mumble the entire car ride there about how I better not pee anywhere.

When we entered the arena, I was mesmerized. It was the most incredible place I had ever seen. The entire room was sparkling from a bright light hitting one massive disco ball. Appropriately, the song "Disco Inferno" was streaming out from six oversized speakers affixed to the walls. I trailed closely behind Rani, as I tried to absorb the magic taking place before me. To her annoyance, I was so distracted I kept stepping on the back of her sneakers, forcing her to fall forward twice.

Rani sat me on a bench near her friends while she went to get her rental skates. I proudly laced up my new skates and could not wait to try them out on a real skating surface. When I was done, I looked up and caught one of Rani's friends eyeing my skates.

"Your skates are far-out."

I beamed. She might as well have nominated me prom queen! She hadn't mentioned my tragically hip outfit, but I was certain she admired that also; dark blue shorts with white piping, my baby blue Sean Cassidy T-shirt, and white tube socks pulled tightly to my knees.

While we waited for Rani to put her skates on, the friend that complimented my skates began kissing the boy next to her. Boz Scaggs's "Lido Shuffle" was playing. I was suddenly transfixed by the song and their kissing. Everything else faded, and I imagined the bright spotlight moving from the disco ball to them. I was fascinated by their mashing faces and hair-sprayed, feathered-hairstyle heads moving like a solid unit.

My sister looked at me and said under her breath, "Close your mouth, dummy. Big deal! They are just making out. Stop staring!"

It was the first time I had seen people make out and from what I could tell, this was a serious make-out session. "Lido" continued to play as my heart ached with so much lust that I was practically drooling. There was something tender about their lips touching and tongues intertwining. I had to hold myself back from puckering up and moving toward them. I was experiencing my sexual awakening.

The song ended and, as if on cue, so did their kiss. I watched them get up, hold hands and enter the rink. I followed them around and around, fascinated with the hot boy who far surpassed my crush on Sean Cassidy. I held my breath as I watched his brown corduroy vest fly open as he skated, revealing his tight blue button-down shirt and the top of his tan cut-off OP, corduroy shorts. My body yearned for him, and I would have given up my new skates to trade places with his girl. I wanted my chance to make out with him to "Lido."

I skated closely behind my crush, hoping he would notice me, but lost him when the song "YMCA" came booming out of the speakers. The floor got too crowded for me to keep up.

The night came to an end at nine o'clock. Rani, her friends and I followed my crush to the front door. Unfortunately, he was sucking face with his girl every time I tried to catch his eye. As Mom pulled up, Rani waved goodbye to her friends. I looked over at my crush one last time and to my utter supernovae happiness, he winked at me. Whether that was his flirty good-bye or a little tease, no matter—I was madly in love.

———

Do you understand why you were so fascinated with this boy? *Only at this very moment. Wow, to think I have thought about that boy and this song for so many years. It was the only tenderness I had ever seen between opposite sexes that fascinated me. I was totally absorbed by that boy that night; I remember it like it was yesterday. To this day, when I hear "Lido" I smile, thinking of that boy. Thankfully it wasn't Jethro Tull!*

I unexpectedly laughed. She disregarded my joke.

The front of our new home on Mira Monte Circle.

The den, wall of glass sliding doors to the outside and our dining room.

Grand Canyon pit stop. Mom sitting on rock, Rani standing with sunglasses, and I have an ice cream cone.

Us at the Grand Canyon.

CHAPTER TWENTY-SIX

Winter 1976–Spring 1977

Somehow, our dog, Starsky, was capable of jumping the six-foot fence around our yard and disappeared. We drove around and looked for her for one week straight. The following week, Paul found her after she had been struck by a car. He took her straight to the vet to be cremated. I never knew if the story he told was exactly true, but it was supposed to provide what he said was "closure."

I wanted another dog and found myself desperate enough to beg for any form of a pet. I had spent so much time with Starsky that I needed something to fill that void. One day after school in January, Paul told me there was a surprise in my room. I dashed in to find a large, glass aquarium. It was filled four inches deep with sawdust. I peered in and saw a little rodent darting in and out of the sawdust. I had hoped for a bunny or a dog, but I did say I would take anything. I got what most people hire an exterminator for—a mouse.

Paul thought it was a boy, so I named him Mickey. I took him out for an hour a day to run around my room, and then put him back in the tank. Our home was so big, he would get lost if I gave him full freedom.

I only had Mickey for two weeks before he doubled in size. When I got back from school one day, I looked in the tank, and there were ten baby mice. Paul was wrong; Mickey was a girl and having lots of babies.

Within hours, there were forty or more baby mice piling up on the side of the tank. By nighttime, there were too many to count. I was very upset, because I knew there was no way Mickey could feed all of them. They each looked like little, pink jelly-beans that kept multiplying. Paul said they would be fine, and we would figure out what to do the next day. When I got home the next afternoon, the babies started dying, and I got frantic waiting for Paul to come home. I ran from the front door, to my room, to the tank over ten times waiting for anyone to come home and help me.

When Paul finally arrived, he looked at the tank from my doorway and said there was nothing we could do. He said more than half of them were already dead. I asked if we could pour a gal-lon of milk in there to help feed them. He laughed and said they would drown. He carried the tank out of my room, and I never saw it again.

Paul said that maybe we would get another dog soon.

Paul and Mom bought a sailboat and docked it at Lake Mead. Paul saw this as a mutual hobby they could share outside of the house. Paul knew this would prevent her from spending time at SNTA playing tennis and more time with him. The boat was equipped with two sleeping cabins, a galley kitchen across from a laminate dining table with vinyl seating, a bathroom and an 8-track tape player.

From the very start, I could tell I would not have sea legs. I didn't like the way the boat rocked back and forth while it sat in its tight boat slip. I got dizzy looking at the height of the sails. I got sick to my stomach thinking about being confined on the vessel, isolated in the middle of nowhere with my drunken parents listening to *Cabaret,* Paul's favorite 8-track tape.

And so, the sailing weekends began. The first few weekends we went out on the water as a family and learned the tricks of the trade. Rani and I learned how to pull the lines, draw the sails and most important, I learned "starboard." This was the right side of the boat where I would dry heave or vomit when I became seasick.

After our first couple of excursions, Rani managed to dodge every other weekend by going to Lucy's house. I, unfortunately, got to go out on our family boat with Paul and Mom all by myself.

Then the parties began. Paul, Mom and I would arrive on deck Friday afternoons. Paul would open the cabin door and immediately pop in the *Cabaret* tape. Mom and I would lug bags of groceries and bottles of liquor from the car, to the dock, to the boat that was constantly teetering back and forth. I'd literally feel the bile creep up my throat just looking at it sway in the dock. Once we were aboard and settled, we would pass out for the night and await their friends' arrival in the morning.

At seven a.m., Paul reset the 8-track tape to "Life Is a Cabaret." He'd hum along as he got the boat ready for a day of sailing. By ten o'clock their friends would arrive, usually two to three couples a weekend. Everyone would do their best to help get us out of the dock, but no one knew what the hell they were doing. Mom and Paul would overcompensate by bouncing around the boat making sure the lines were pulled and would yell "duck" when the mast came swinging from side to side.

Once we were out of the marina and safely in the middle of nowhere, the drinking commenced. Everyone drank the day away and sang along to the redundant, awful, *Cabaret* tape as the sun moved from east to west. I sat uneasily inside the cabin, cursing the bad music and trying to avoid my pending nausea. I would eventually work my way out of the cabin and head starboard. I would end up hanging over the railing like a wet rag by nightfall. From time to time, some intoxicated friend of my parents' would come my way and patronize me. "You okay?" or "Isn't this invigorating and amazing!" I would reply how fine I was and how wonderful the boat trip was. The only "amazing" thing to me was that I hated being on the boat more than the actual act of throwing up.

By the end of the long, tortuous evening, and the tenth continuous loop of *Cabaret,* we'd return to our slip at the dock for the night. Everyone was usually too drunk to drive home, so slept wherever they could find a spot on the boat. I would lie on the top deck staring at the only thing not moving—the starlit sky.

For me, the highlight of the weekend was when we headed home. We drove Sunday evening through the high, dark Nevada Mountains. Since there were no streetlights, the only thing we could see outside was illuminated by our own headlights. Once we got through the mountains, I was always struck by the sight of Las Vegas. The heart of the city sat in a sunken valley of glowing lights. It was the most captivating display of colors, beckoning one to come and play, a sight I enjoyed recreating on my Lite-Brite. Once I saw those lights, I knew we were close to home and safely off the water for another week.

———

Rani joined in my campaign effort for a pet and began to plead with my mom for a dog. She begged so much that I no longer had to. Mom finally took us to the ASPCA. We adopted a terrier-Chihuahua mix and named her Daisy.

Rani put Daisy in her coat pocket with her cute little puppy face sticking out, and we got into the car. I heard Rani whisper to her in the parking lot that she would be able to tell her all her secrets. She said that it would be okay, because a dog could never tell anyone.

Instead of taking Daisy right home, Mom took us food shopping. Rani kept Daisy in her coat pocket as we shopped. When I put my face down close to her, she would lick my nose. I adored her. At the checkout counter, the woman packing our groceries said, "What an adorable puppy!"

My sister said thanks, as I stood by with a shit-splitting grin on my face. The woman said, "She looks like her name should be Daisy."

My sister and I were amazed. "That is what we named her!" We all giggled and left the market knowing we had a very special new addition to our family.

Daisy was a precious, caramel-colored, happy puppy. As soon as we got home, I claimed her as mine. I loved her and slept with her every night. I walked her and fed her. When I got home from school, she was there to greet me with kisses and unconditional love.

Unfortunately, Paul was not as fond of Daisy as Rani and I were, and took his frustrations out on her if she got in his way. One afternoon, after we had had Daisy about four weeks, he got so mad at her for following him that he opened the door, picked her up and dropkicked her down the walkway. She yelped in pain as I ran to her aid.

Another day, Daisy accidentally peed on the floor. I was late getting home from school, and she couldn't hold it in anymore. Paul and I arrived home (and saw the pee) at the same time. He flashed me a look, and I ran to the kitchen to get paper towels. By the time I got back, he had her in his hands like a football and punted her out the front door as he had done a couple of days before. I held my breath so I wouldn't cry. Daisy yelped so loudly, it physically made my stomach hurt. I just knew that he had to have broken every bone in her innocent little body. I ran to her and held her. She licked my tears while I cried. Two kicks like that in one week and she survived—she was definitely one of us.

Sharon and I entered the school talent show. We spent an afternoon tucked away in our hideout behind the cactus bushes, planning our performance, while we smoked her father's cigarettes. We agreed on dancing, because it was something we both agreed we did well. I suggested we choreograph something to my favorite song, "Boogie Oogie Oogie."

I asked Paul to pick up the 45 vinyl single for me, and he brought it home the next day. Sharon and I practiced in my bedroom that night. For hours, days and weeks we practiced two steps to the left, two steps to the right, and twist downward when the lyrics said, "Get down, boogie oogie oogie." We picked out matching red-and-white checked shirts, jeans rolled up to our knees and black-and-white saddle shoes.

Our performance was flawless, and we had parents on their feet applauding us. Sharon and I looked at each other, pleased that we were a sensation. Mom sat in the second row while Paul stood close to the stage and snapped photos. They were just like any other proud set of parents in the audience.

It was only when we got home that the evening turned dark. Paul was furious that Mom spoke to someone's father at the show. Paul was convinced the man was hitting on her. Mom told him he was being ridiculous, that the guy was not only standing with his children, she was having a conversation with him *and* his wife. Paul stormed off to get heavily liquored up and came back to punish her an hour later. They had a slapping match that looked a lot like two girls might have at my bus stop.

————

It was on a Saturday night, weeks before I was to leave for summer camp back east, when Paul first called me into his bedroom. He invited me to watch TV with him and Mom. Rani was at a sleepover, so I was thrilled for the company. I liked watching TV in their room because you could see the program in every direction via the reflections in the mirrors.

The problem was, if Paul initiated sex with my mom, I could also see that from all angles.

I was lying on the bed, stomach down, watching *The Love Boat* when I saw Paul pull mom from her dressing room to the bed. I anticipated what was going to happen, so I inched to the farthest side of the bed. I figured I could easily slide to the floor without their noticing. When the bed started to rock due to his rough thrusting, I grabbed onto the side, preventing myself from falling, and began my quiet descent. As I was sideways between the bed and the floor, I felt someone grab my arm. My head shot back to see Paul's outstretched arm and hand holding me with a vise-like grip. I froze and counted to ten a dozen times with my eyes closed, waiting for the sex to end. When the heavy moans erupted, he let go of me. I slid down the side of the bed and crawled on all fours out of their room.

The marks on my arm from his grip lasted through the entire next day. I took that as his silent reminder that I should never defy him.

Sharon and me in the school talent show dancing to "Boogie Oogie Oogie"

Paul's photo of us in a
secluded area off of Lake Mead.

Mom during one of our
weekend sailboat parties
on Lake Mead.

I am posing while the boat is safely docked.

CHAPTER TWENTY-SEVEN

Summer 1977

Rani and I were off to Philadelphia for the summer—eight weeks of summer camp and the usual visits split among our family members.

The week before we headed back to Vegas, we stayed with our father. We thought Todd was flying back with us, but learned that he enjoyed school and his friends in Philadelphia so much that he wanted to stay. Reluctantly, our father and stepmother decided that he would live with them throughout high school, until he left for college.

At the end of the week, Rani and I headed back to Vegas, without our brother.

CHAPTER TWENTY-EIGHT

Fall 1977

As Rani continued to gain weight, I got skinnier. Where food was her coping mechanism, in more ways than one, I had an aversion to it. I simply never paid attention to food, eating only when my stomach growled for it. Between the ages of eleven through thirteen, Rani gained more than sixty-five pounds. I never thought of her as heavy, but her weight gain started to piss Paul off. In fact, it infuriated him.

My bedroom was closest to the kitchen, so I overheard the many arguments Paul and Mom had about Rani's weight. School had just begun, and Paul yelled at Mom for letting Rani buy school lunches. He said she needed to be monitored and should eat prepacked food from home. He complained about how fat she had gotten. I could hear him banging cabinet doors shut while searching for food, blaming Rani for eating everything.

"Where are the Goddamn cookies? Where are the crackers that used to be in here? Who ate all the cheese . . . ?" He continued to scream, condemning Rani for the disappearance of any morsel of food. "Here are the fucking cookies! I folded the bag a certain way, and this is not how I left it! She ate most of these fucking cookies!"

Mom tried to defend Rani by taking the blame for eating the cookies, but this just further pissed him off.

"Liar! Bitch! Whore!" I heard more cabinet doors slam shut and the sound of his hand slapping Mom's face. "Fucking liar!" he screamed repeatedly.

I heard scuffling and was sure that Mom was fighting back. Then, silence. After a few minutes, I was so worried—I just wanted to hear someone say something and thankfully, he did.

Paul said calmly, "I am going to hide food from now on. If you give Rani any food that is not monitored, I will beat the shit out of you." Mom didn't reply. I heard her stomp out of the kitchen. I knew she would probably drink enough that evening to block out anything else he had to say.

When I heard Paul leave the kitchen, I got up and knelt by the side of my bed. I put my palms together and prayed in a whispery voice like Laura Ingalls did that week on *Little House on the Prairie,* "Please make my sister skinny. I will take all her fat on my body if you can do it. Please!"

When I got home from school the following day, I couldn't find anything to eat in the kitchen. My tummy was grumbling. I looked in the cabinets and found nothing but neatly aligned boxes of tea, sugar, flour and spices. The refrigerator held condiments, radishes and dinner waiting to be cooked that night—raw hamburger meat. I fortified my hunger with several spoonsful of raw hamburger meat and a handful of radishes.

The radishes burned my tongue and the raw meat caused worms in my stool days later. I decided that I would stick to eating pomegranates from neighbors' trees or snacks at a friend's home from then on.

―――――――

Rani wanted to start making money of her own. The opportunity came when our neighbors, the Franks, asked her to babysit. Mr. Frank was a tall, gray-haired, attractive sixty-two-year-old. Mrs.

Frank was a beautiful blonde with fair skin, big blue eyes and in her late twenties. Together they had a chubby, brown-haired, blue-eyed, three-year-old daughter who, according to Rani, was spoiled rotten. They paid five dollars an hour, so she ran when they called.

One evening, the Franks said they were going out to dinner and needed Rani to sit for three hours. When they left the house, Rani put the girl right to bed and raided their stocked pantry. She tossed small bags of chips and cookies in her bag for home, and then took out everything she could possibly eat in under three hours. She put the goods on the coffee table and camped out in front of the television.

An hour earlier than expected, Mrs. Frank burst through the front door. She limped into the TV room, and Rani saw blood dripping from her fur cape. "Rani, I need you to go home, now!" she said hunched over and completely out of breath. "Mr. Frank will be back soon and he is very angry with me. You need to leave."

Rani asked her if she was okay, as she saw blood on her arms and legs start to drip onto the floor. Mrs. Frank quickly explained that she and her husband got into a fight. She said she was bleeding because she jumped out of the moving car and ran home. Rani insisted that she should stay because Mr. Frank would certainly not hurt her in front of the sitter. Mrs. Frank dug her five-carat ringed hand into her Gucci handbag and tossed a $100 bill at Rani. "Please, I beg of you. Go home. Now!"

Rani took the money and hurried out the Franks' front door. When she got to our driveway, she peaked over our shared fence to see if everything was okay, but Mrs. Frank had drawn the shades. She came home feeling helpless. She lay on her bed and ate the cookies she took from their pantry, storing the rest of the snacks under her bed.

Later that week Mrs. Frank and her daughter moved into a townhouse ten miles away. We learned she was having an affair with Wayne Newton and her husband had found out.

Do you think Rani thought spousal beatings were the norm, since it was happening next door?
I don't know. I think that was a crazy exception and she was upset by it. I don't know why, because much worse was going on in our home. But when I look back, in most of the homes I went to the parents were usually yelling at each other. The violence had begun to seem normal to me. We didn't have assemblies in grade school informing us "If this is happening at home, it is not right." At least not where we went to school.

Dr. Tanner flipped through some pages in her notebook and looked up at me.

You've not mentioned your mother in a while. Was she around the house less?
It's just that Paul's presence became larger than life and that's what I remember most. My mom was working, then home for family dinner and by nighttime, in an aloof, zombie-like state, drinking and smoking cigarettes to deal with her domineering husband. Paul would not let her out of his sight once she got home from work. She was there though; Paul made sure of it.

Paul went through phases of wanting to be a photographer again, constantly wearing a camera around his neck. He often called me into his room to bathe with him, and then he would turn it into a photo session. He would lather me up, leave me in the shower while he loaded a roll of film and then clicked the shutter button like a madman.

One afternoon he had me in a frothy bubble bath and exclaimed, "You look adorable. This is the ideal time to take some photos of you." He ran out and came back, loading film in his camera. He shut the door and locked it. He took one picture before I heard Mom banging on the door, screaming for him to open it. He paused for a second, smiling at me as if no one was there and continued to take pictures. My mom screamed, "Let her out, you bastard!"

I tried not to cry or seem concerned. I pretended that it was absolutely typical for my mom to be beating on the door, screaming at him to let me out. I had no idea what her panic was about, but it led me to believe that Paul was doing something wrong.

After several minutes, the banging stopped. He seemed pleased with himself. He helped me out of the tub, dried me off and opened the door. I was hoping Mom was still there, but she had gone.

———

My first real adrenaline release was riding a moped. Lisa, a sixth grader who lived right next to the bus stop, had gotten one for her birthday—an awesome canary yellow Honda that everyone in the neighborhood envied.

Every afternoon when a group of us got off the elementary school bus, we saw her riding it around her circular driveway. One day after school, I got up the nerve to ask if I could ride it. She said she may let me one day, but I would have to be very careful. I told her in a saccharine-sweet voice, "I am the most careful person in the entire world. Anyhow, I know how to ride a moped, it's easy." I thought, *How much harder is it to ride a moped than my own bicycle?* I continued to ask her every day after school that week, and she'd reply with an enthusiastic "maybe."

In my thinking, this meant YES. I would be tenacious until I was the first one in the neighborhood to ride it. I knew I could break her by the next week. Eight days later, she relented.

Four girls from the bus stop, impressed by my determination, followed me to watch. We all traipsed behind Lisa toward her garage. When she got to the door, she put out her hand like a school crossing guard stopping traffic, and told us to wait at the far side of her circular driveway.

She disappeared into the house and minutes later one of her two-car garage doors opened. And there it was—the canary yellow Honda moped! She rolled it out with her two hands holding the handlebars. She pulled it past a row of metal trashcans that still awaited the garbage collector.

She pulled the bike up next to me and reviewed the operating instructions several times: "Just pull the handle toward you to go, and turn it back to go slower. Pull this metal bar back to stop alto-gether; it's the brake. Go slow. Don't go in the street. Just around my driveway. Go slowwww."

We practiced five times with the engine off before she finally made me take an oath to go slow. I impatiently agreed, "Okay, okay, I get it. Go slow, turn handle to go, pull handle back to slow down, brake with metal bar, around driveway."

I sat on the bike seat feeling fully empowered by the magni-tude of the engine and the envious neighborhood girls watching me. I turned on the ignition and listened to it purr before I kicked up the bike stand and turned the handle. I zipped around her driveway, my hair whipping behind me as I went faster and faster. I forgot where the brakes were and panicked. I needed something to stop me or I would never stop; I flew at warp speed into her per-fectly aligned metal trashcans and directly through the *closed* garage door. I heard Lisa shrieking from behind me.

I was scratched up, as was her bike. Trash littered the driveway. She was furious. Not only had I damaged her new bike, I dented all three of their metal trashcans *and* created a substantial hole in their garage door. I didn't know what to do and my scratches started to bleed.

I said I was really sorry and limped down her driveway, past the awestruck crowd of kids who bore witness to my unintentional Evel Knievel stunt. I limped down the street toward my house, feeling defeated and embarrassed.

Later that night, Lisa's parents called. Paul answered the phone. I hid in the far corner of my room, humiliated by my inability to ride a stupid moped and scared of Paul's reaction. I figured we would have to pay for the bike and garage repair, plus replace the metal trashcans. When I heard him hang up, he didn't come looking for me.

An hour passed before I came out of hiding, and it was only because Mom yelled that it was dinnertime. I sheepishly walked into the kitchen with my head down. Mom took one look at my scratched-up legs and the twelve Band-Aids I haphazardly put over them and said, "You're lucky you weren't badly hurt. Let's clean these cuts up properly."

And that was all I ever heard about the moped incident.

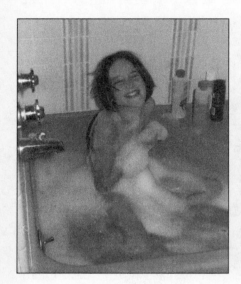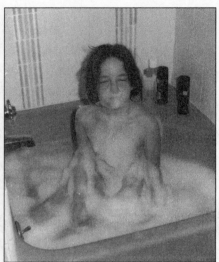

Paul's photo session with me when my mom began banging on the door.
He tossed bubbles in my face to distract me.

Daisy and me in my bed.

CHAPTER TWENTY-NINE

Winter 1977–Spring 1978

By December, the boat on Lake Mead proved to be too much of a burden, and much to my delight, they sold it. I celebrated the end of the boat-era by dancing around my room to the Bee Gees.

———

It was my first significant Vegas snowfall. I gazed out my bedroom window as white flakes dropped from the sky and put me to sleep.

The next morning there was a decent amount of accumulation. The sky was a crisp, clear blue. I couldn't wait to get out and play. I dug in my closet to find my bag of ski clothes. Once I was all geared up, I grabbed Daisy under my arm and ran out the front door.

The only evidence of life on my entire street was the tracks of my shoes in the snow. When I put Daisy down, her legs disappeared into the white powder. We ran around for hours, with her disappearing underground several times, only to send me into a fit of laughter when her cute, furry face appeared out of nowhere. It was the most exhilarating and peaceful day I had had in a while. I loved the feeling of the soft snow under my feet and the sight of my breath in a cloud of cold smoke.

Very late that night, I woke to Mom and Paul fighting in the front hall. The fight concluded with a door slam and, inevitably, I knew that my mom was outside, most likely shoeless, in the snow. I sneaked into the kitchen after I thought I heard Paul stomp down the hall to his room. I peeked out the sliders, and Mom was in a T-shirt and jeans, dancing from one bare foot to the other, trying to pry the doors open. I felt sad that I didn't have the guts to run and open the doors, but I heard Paul coming down the hall and ran back to my room. I sat up in bed and hoped he had felt some remorse and would let her back in. I eventually fell asleep.

The next morning was quiet in the house. I took Daisy into the backyard through the sliders in the den. The night was so frigid that the snow had hardened and created a flawless glass covering of white. Daisy walked on the top of the *faux porcelain* while my shoes cracked their way through it. We walked past the kitchen sliders and from a slight distance, I could see the impressions in the snow where my mom was tossed outside and tried to get back in. As we walked closer, my heart began to race as I saw that the white snow was blemished by a few spots of red. I wrapped my arms around my body, trying to warm both the physical and the mental chill. I then grabbed Daisy and went inside to make sure that Mom was home *and* no longer bleeding. I walked from the den into the kitchen and saw her sitting at the counter with an ice pack on her lip. She grinned at me with her eyes half-mast. I half-smiled back, happy that she was okay, but feeling guilty for not helping her.

———

Paul cornered Rani one afternoon and said he wanted to take "beautiful birthday photos" of her before her fourteenth birthday. He said the photo session would also be a favor to him, as he needed to break in a new camera lens. Rani chewed on her nails, looked at him and reluctantly agreed.

I trailed them outside and hid, watching him position her next to a willow tree in the far corner of our yard. He took a series of photos and then asked her to take her clothes off. Rani looked at him in disbelief, fighting back tears of frustration. Paul came to her side and assured her it was "just between them" (and me, hiding behind a tree near the pool). He said he would provide her with a translucent scarf to cover her privates, which he conveniently had handy in his camera bag.

Rani slowly undressed, clearly hating every second. She had put on a lot of weight, and I could not tell if it was modesty, shame or total embarrassment she was radiating, but I felt it. I held Daisy to my side, petting her head nervously. With every snap of the shutter, it was obvious that she was getting more and more uncomfortable. She kept looking over her shoulder, convinced that people were watching. Paul tossed the scarf her way, and she tried her best to conceal her body.

He finished a roll of film and knelt down to put in another roll. Rani began shaking and asked if they were done.

He ignored her and requested more poses, while he snapped on different lenses. Once they were finished, she looked completely humiliated. She quickly put on her clothes and ran in the house. Paul methodically put all of his lens equipment away and walked out the back gate of the yard. I heard his car engine start and he was gone.

I went into the house to see where Rani went. Her door was closed and Elton John's version of "Pinball Wizard" was blaring from her stereo.

———

Paul's nightly visits to Rani's room became so frequent that she tried to avoid coming home at night altogether, even on school nights. She slept at various friends' homes whenever she could.

Paul confronted her one morning when she came home before going to school.

"Where have you been?"

Rani steadied herself, having prepared for the moment he would address her absence. "I slept at my friend's house. We had to study for a test and I just fell asleep there."

He stared at her for a long moment and then told her he got her a gift. "I came to your room last night to give it to you."

Rani knew he was trying to make her feel apologetic for not sleeping at home, but it was not going to work. She said nothing while they stood awkwardly in the front hall.

"Are you not curious about what it is?"

"What is it?"

"I got you your own phone and phone line."

Rani genuinely smiled. "Thank you so much! That is great!" She gave him a quick hug and ran to her room.

She left the house for school that day feeling that she had just gained a sense of privacy. She could talk on the phone without feeling like someone was listening, someone like her intrusive stepfather.

That night Rani stayed at home for the first time in four nights, blasting Ted Nugent and talking nonstop on her new phone. At ten-thirty, she shut off her light and went to sleep.

Paul came in at eleven-thirty. He sat on the bed and shook Rani awake.

"What?" she said in a pissed-off voice.

"How is your new phone?"

"Great. I like having privacy. Thank you."

"I expect that this will keep you quiet about me coming in your room at night?"

She then realized that the phone was a bribe. She knew he figured that she slept out more because she didn't want him touching her. He was concerned that she was gaining confidence and might be bold enough to tell Mom about "their secret."

"I just want to make sure we understand each other. I care about you, but you know what I will do to your family if you ever say anything." He began caressing her arm, sending a wave of chills down her spine.

Rani's body got rigid as he untied his sarong and slid next to her in the bed. Like all the times before, he unsuccessfully tried to push himself into her.

Rani was fuming with anger. She vowed to sleep out the next couple of nights, phone or no phone.

With Rani's bedroom empty for days, Paul walked the additional ten feet to my room. He came in late at night. He caressed my cheek, pulled down my covers and kissed me from the neck on down to my privates. Once he was done, he pulled up my covers and I rolled over to go to sleep . . . like I always did.

But on that spring night, he was frustrated and didn't leave.

I had already closed my eyes and rolled over, when I felt the tap on the side of my cheek. I looked over, thinking he was going to say goodnight again, but came face-to-face with his erection. He held his penis in his hand and tapped my face with it, again and again.

I just stared at it and felt Paul's eyes on me. He said, "I want you to put this in your mouth. Lick it with your tongue."

I didn't look up at his face, because I didn't want to question him—but I didn't want to put that thing anywhere near my mouth. He said more forcefully, "Put it in your mouth or lick it."

I began to lick the top with my tongue. He sighed with frustration, forcefully grabbed the back of my head, plunging it forward, sticking his entirety in my mouth. I pulled back, releasing it from my mouth, gagging and choking. He stood at the side of my bed, not moving as I continued to gag. Once I settled down, he pulled up my nightgown and stood over my torso, tugging at his penis for a ridiculously long time. I focused on the far wall. Finally he exhaled with an "ahhh!" and all of this white gook squirted onto my stomach. I stared at it. It was the most revolting substance I had ever laid eyes on. He told me to sit still and left the room. I stared at it, not breathing, petrified it was going to slide into my belly button and infect me, or worse, grow into a big blob and swallow me up. Seconds later, Paul was back with a wet washcloth. He cleaned it up, kissed my forehead and whispered in my ear that this was our secret. I nodded and he walked out.

———

You think he came to you because your sister wasn't there?
This, I will never know. Rani would have never left at night if she thought for one second that her eight-year-old sister would become his nightly prey.

It really didn't matter if your sister was there or not; he was already violating you. He was a sick man. You did not deserve this and it was not your fault.
I felt the water works coming on and grabbed a tissue. She wrote in her notebook for a moment, flipped a page back, and then looked up at me.

It sounds like his molestations were more frequent as you got older?
He came in at least three times a week. I just think that when Rani was no longer around, he pushed the envelope with me. Instead of just going down on my privates, he forced oral sex, ending with ejaculating someplace . . .
I stopped, disgusted with the memory, and my nose started to run

before the tears this time. I mumbled, *I'm just grateful he never tried to have sex with me.*

————

Rani was spending so much time at her friend Lucy's house, that when Lucy suggested they go to Rani's, she felt she had to oblige. Lucy didn't have a pool, and it was so hot, they wanted to swim. Rani just hoped Paul would be working.

Luckily, his Mercedes wasn't in the driveway. Shortly after they were settled into their lounge chairs, Paul came outside to greet them. Rani was derailed. She didn't know if she should grab Lucy and run for her life.

Before she could process her thoughts, Paul looked from Rani in her purple one-piece Speedo, to Lucy in her pink string bikini and said, "I have a great idea! I would love to take some photos of you both. I'm testing out a new brand of film and could use some subjects."

Rani tensed up, released her fingertip from her mouth and sucked in her breath—too overwhelmed to say anything.

Lucy's face flushed, and Rani feared what she was thinking. Then Lucy exclaimed, "Sure! I'm flattered!"

Paul responded directly to Lucy, "That's great. The photos would be much better if you got undressed. That is just the kind of photography I'm used to doing."

Rani choked out the words, "Absolutely frickin' not!" She was mortified that he had the audacity to ask a friend to do this, when she had recently been so humiliated by having to do it herself.

Paul laughed and said, "I'm just kidding. I just want to take a few photos of you guys just as you are."

Lucy giggled at his humor and adjusted the top of her bikini. She then quickly got up from the lounge chair and walked toward Paul.

Paul took Lucy's arm, grazing his eyes over her bosom as Rani followed slowly behind. He escorted her to the big willow tree where he took Rani's photos weeks ago. He was in the middle of telling Lucy how he used to be a professional photographer when Rani caught up with them, grabbed Lucy by the arm and said, "We have to go." She wanted to get away from the house before things got even weirder.

From that afternoon onward, she began hanging out at Lucy's house as much as possible. Lucy's parents were divorced and she lived with her father who was a casino dealer. Rani loved passing the time there for many reasons. Lucy's dad was never home, there was a sense of freedom at her house, and she had a crush on Lucy's brother, Greg.

Greg was a good-looking seventeen-year-old who was responsible for introducing Rani to pot. Lucy and Rani cut out of school early several times a week to smoke and laugh the afternoons away in Greg's room.

———

Your sister had an escape? Did you have a mental escape or realize that you even needed an escape?
I didn't think about an escape, so to speak. This was my home, where we lived as a family, and there was no place I would have rather been. But when things got hairy, I listened to music. The radio was always playing and filtered through every room in the house. To this day, I have a reservoir of songs in my head that dig up the happiest or saddest of memories. I mean, I still think about that guy at the roller rink when I hear "Lido."
I stopped and smiled at the memory.
Music is this amazing universal language that can unify and uplift people. It was something I could always count on during the hardest of times.

Paul's verbal and physical attacks on Mom continued to escalate. Perhaps they just seemed more violent because she had lost the conviction to fight back. Early evenings he would verbally attack her when she got home from tennis. Intoxicated, he would start the same way every night, making an effort to enunciate each word.

"Where. Have. You. Been?" Even before she could utter a word, his voice intensified; "I-know-you-were-out-fucking-some-one-you-BITCH!" This was followed by the sound of his slapping her or shoving her against a wall and then more name-calling: "Bitch! Fucking whore! Slut!"

Mom only put her hands up to protect her face. She had succumbed to the abuse. When Rani was home, she and I would slowly inch our way into the front hall—the beating zone. Helpless, we would stand silently and witness the beatings. He would straddle her on the floor, slapping her face from side to side . . . spitting ugly, obscene words at her. When he wore himself out, he would get up and leave the room—then with much effort, Mom would stand up, walk to the kitchen and dial 9-1-1.

The police always came in pairs. They would usually be greeted at the door by a cheerful Paul. He was kind and well-mannered as they questioned him about the 9-1-1 call. Mom would come from behind him and say he was beating her. They would stare at her for an exaggerated moment, taking in the sight of her. One of the officers would eventually speak up and say, "Are you okay now?"

Mom would reply, "Right now, yes, but he was hitting me moments ago."

"Well, ma'am, it seems that everyone is okay. So, we have no further business here," and the two policemen would trail each other out the door with their heads down, speaking into their walkie-talkie radios, "All good here on Mira Monte Circle. Woman looks unharmed."

One time I was sitting outside when the police arrived. I heard one of the guys complain about the weekly calls "from the hot broad" on Mira Monte. Both men began laughing and stopped when they saw Daisy and me sitting on the walkway to the front door.

By late spring, days and nights ran together with a pattern of school, home, play, dinner, screaming and fighting.

One evening Paul hit Mom so hard that her nose bled. Rani and I were aghast. We knew that Paul had made her bleed before, but never when we were watching. Rani lost it and fearlessly screamed, "Get off of her or I am going to call the police!"

I was paralyzed. I couldn't believe she had spoken up. She was becoming so brave. Paul jumped off Mom, and I was afraid he was going to slam Rani into the wall. He looked at her for a brief moment. She was as big and tall as he was now, and she would've probably given him a good fight, but he darted out of the front hall. We helped Mom get up and stood on either side of her so she could steady herself. She said she was okay and unsteadily walked to her room, waving her hand behind her and said, "Leave me be."

Rani and I didn't have a moment to think before we heard loud, strange sounds coming from the office, the den and then the kitchen.

I followed Rani like a shadow as she peeked into the kitchen. Paul had pulled the phone out of the wall and left the bare wires hanging out. I followed her into the den, and we saw the phone wires hanging out of that wall also. We then saw him, from inside the glass sliders, pulling the outdoor phone out of the stone wall.

Rani said, "Oh shit." She knew this was his way of guaranteeing that we could never call the cops on him again. She ran directly to her room and grabbed her phone from her bedside table. She crawled under her bed, pulled the cord out of the socket and safely concealed it beneath the bed, under a shirt with her secret stash of food. She then sat on her bed and hoped Paul would forget about her phone and private line.

He tore every phone in the house out of the walls that night, except the one he had forgotten about in Rani's room.

———

The morning after the phone raid, Rani met up with Mom in the kitchen. Mom was dressed for work, looking composed, as always. She was holding a cup of coffee and smiling as though the horror of the night before had never happened.

Rani was still in her pajamas and spoke with conviction, "We have to get out of the house and away from Paul. He is so dangerous, Mom! If he won't let us call the police, he can just kill us at any time."

Mom's smile faded, she looked down at her cup of coffee, "Don't worry. I'm going to take care of things."

Rani walked out of the kitchen mumbling to herself, "Yeah, you're doing a great job of taking care of things."

———

Was your mom always like this after these abusive evenings?
What do you mean? Like what?

As though the prior night had never happened.
Yes. She was always fresh, bright and beautiful in the morning, no matter what. Paul also acted as if nothing had happened. He would come into the kitchen in the morning looking unfazed—and sober. The only one who

began bringing up the bad nights was Rani. She was losing her patience with what was going on in the house and began vocalizing it to our mom.

How did you feel about that, seeing your mom get up as though nothing had ever happened?

Well, I was happy there was no more screaming and that my mom was okay. I never thought about it further than that. I was independently dealing with a magnitude of mental and physical stuff from four to ten years old. Yet despite what was going on in my house, I was still a regular kid—I was going to school, playing with friends and running around the neighborhood. My mom, ironically, led by example. I guess that just seeing her pick up the next day and go about her normal business . . . well, that was my example. I don't know how else to explain it.

Look where that *example* got you. You put all of that behind you and you are standing at your apartment window, fifteen years later, deciding whether to jump or not. You built emotional walls to protect yourself, which thankfully helped you as a child, but these walls have also been preventing you from dealing with the issues of your childhood. We are going to work at taking these walls down brick by brick. On another note, you continue to glamorize your mother. A part of me finds it sweet that you only see the positive, but she did anything *but* set a good example for you.

I get what you are saying—I understand. Following her lead may have come back to haunt me, but I still can't blame her. We can argue this for the rest of the session or continue onward.

Dr. Tanner jotted in her notebook, and I continued where I left off.

———

After a night of abusive fighting, Paul surprised Mom with two tickets to the Caribbean Islands. During breakfast, he told her that he wanted to prove their passion was still alive and that he was a good man. It was his attempt to erase a turbulent and violent week.

Rani was not pleased when she learned about the trip. She had already urged Mom several times that week to leave Paul. Mom said she had the determination to leave him, but just had to find out the right way out and the right time to do it.

Mom concocted a plan that would allow her to spend time apart from him that summer while we were away. She figured it would at least be a start, so she could figure out how to leave him and where we would go thereafter.

After four days in the Caribbean, carrying on the charade that she was blissfully married, Mom encouraged Paul to spend one night in Florida. She wanted him to see a boat she saw advertised for sale. Paul was thrilled with her spontaneity and agreed.

The boat was a fifty-four-foot, teak sailboat that slept six. She had discreetly spoken to the owners a week earlier and negotiated a deal. They owned a slip in San Diego that she could rent for a year for a fixed low rate and they would even deliver it to San Diego.

Upon seeing the boat, Paul fell in love. Acting as though my mother hadn't spoken with them, the owners told him that they could transport it to an inlet in San Diego. This was a quick flight from Vegas or a straight five-hour drive.

Paul and Mom stepped aside and discussed the possibility of vacationing in San Diego on the weekends. The boat needed a lot of work, and she told him it was just the kind of project that could use his TLC. She said it would be a great summer project for them while we kids were at camp. Mom convinced him that when he was done with it, they could sell it for a great profit.

Mom's hope was that Paul would get so busy at work, he wouldn't have time for the boat and she would use it as her summer escape. If he ended up having the time to go to San Diego, she would find excuses for why she had to stay back in Vegas.

In late May, we took the RV to San Diego to see the new sailboat. While Mom and Paul reminisced about the great times on their former boat, I had a pain in the pit of my stomach from recalling the ear-wrenching lyrics of *Cabaret* paired with debilitating seasickness.

When we arrived at the marina, we were taken aboard the new boat, which was substantially larger than our former one. It was docked in a fancy, all-inclusive community with restaurants, bars and a nice bathhouse. Mom told us that when we got back from camp in August, we would "spend the rest of the summer here." The mere thought of going from a five-hour plane ride to a rocking boat for the remainder of the summer was appalling.

The beginning of Rani's photo shoot before Paul asked her to disrobe.

Daisy and me playing in our front yard after the big Vegas snow.

The boat in San Diego named *The Hessvicking*, which I interpreted as "The Heaves-sickening."

CHAPTER THIRTY

Summer 1978

Summer came and Rani and I were off to Philadelphia. The day after we left, Mom had plans to head to the boat as a potential escape, but she could not bear the thought of Paul coming after her. Rani's words had gotten to her, and she finally took the first step to end her marriage. She discreetly reached out to a lawyer whose name she scribbled down from a highway billboard: James Vanderbilt, Jr., Esq.

She met James that week. She told him about the abuse she was suffering and that Paul was monitoring her coming and going, whom she spoke to, and was even supervising every morsel that was eaten in the kitchen. She broke down as she said she could no longer take living under his iron fist. Everything she did was restricted, and she needed to get out.

James told her she didn't have to live this way and agreed that she needed to get out—not only for her own safety, but for her children's safety as well. He said she should get enough money out of the divorce to live comfortably with her daughters.

"I will be serving Paul with papers, which are basically his divorce notification. Take measures to protect your family, because by the sound of things, he may get violent or upset when he receives them."

She left his office feeling empowered. She was finally going to end the madness.

———

Paul briefly looked over the first page of the divorce papers and tossed them aside. They sat on the kitchen counter until the day they met in court the following week.

Mom entered the courtroom with her lawyer by her side. Paul was already there. When he saw Mom walk toward her seat, he sobbed like a baby. Just as she sat down, he knelt beside her and begged her to stay with him. He promised to change and be a better man. He pleaded with her to give him a second chance.

Mom was sympathetic. When Paul was good, he was very good, even charming. She saw the pain she was inflicting on him and thought that maybe there was kindness in him after all. She tossed caution to the wind, looked at James and whispered, "Sorry."

Paul stood up, took her in his arms and cried, "Thank you, Olivia. I will not let you down. I love you. I will be better, I promise."

They left as a married couple from the courthouse, hand in hand. He enthusiastically told her, through his now hopeful, dry eyes, that he was going to change and things would be better than ever.

———

When we returned ten weeks later, I was ecstatic to learn that the boat had been sold. Mom told Rani she served Paul with divorce papers just after we left mid-June, but he was so broken that she couldn't go through with it. She said when they got home from court, she told him she needed some time alone and exiled to San

Diego. She was gone for one, independent, glorious week before Paul surprised her on the dock. He saw her socializing with other boat owners and didn't like it. She didn't like his arriving unannounced. They got into a screaming match on the deck of the boat. He pulled her into the cabin and the argument escalated into a fistfight.

The boat was sold a month later.

What she refrained from telling Rani was, the day after the boat sold, Mom went to see her lawyer—again. She told James she could not take being married to Paul any longer and had to get a divorce. She said she wanted him out of the house before the kids came back from camp. He asked her if she would stick to her guns and follow through this time. She swore she would. She said she was at a point where she hated him so much that she couldn't stand the sight of him.

Once again, the divorce papers sat on the kitchen counter. Paul had only taken a quick glance when he received them and, once again, made no mention of them for the remainder of the week. The following Monday, Mom dressed in a black pant suit and walked stoically into the courtroom with her lawyer by her side. She was determined to wash her hands of Paul.

Paul entered the courtroom looking defeated. He had tears rolling down his face even before he looked Mom's way. She started to second-guess herself. *Am I actually going to do this? I'm going to be all on my own in Vegas with my children. Can I do this on my own? Isn't it better to just stay with him and have someone to take care of us?* Her self-doubt overruled her hatred for him. She slowly stepped away from her attorney's side. He looked at her and vehemently shook his head. She apologized, grabbed her bag and walked out of the courtroom with Paul close on her heels.

CHAPTER THIRTY-ONE

Fall 1978–Early Spring 1979

Paul surprised Rani with a yellow Honda moped shortly after our school year started. It looked exactly like the one I had crashed into Lisa's garage. She eyed Mom and then Paul, who had a triumphant smile on his face. She quickly surmised that it was some kind of bribe, but didn't care. She hopped on and drove down the street out of sight.

———

I met a sweet, redheaded, freckle-faced girl at school named Joanie. Her house was a fifteen-minute car ride from ours. She lived on a grassless, dusty farm where chickens and roosters roamed aimlessly. It was not as nice as where I lived, but it felt like a happy place. Everything was free and untamed. This was a nice change from our home, where Paul's abuse reared its ugly head the week we returned from camp.

Joanie's parents were extremely friendly, pleasant and calm. They welcomed me for dinner every Saturday night, which turned into sleepovers. Joanie and I would stay up late listening to the chickens settling in and woke to the rooster's cock-a-doodle-doo.

The first time I slept over, they invited me to go to church on Sunday morning. Joanie encouraged me to come so we could spend more time together. I thought it had to be fun. Everything Joanie and I did was fun, so how was this going to be any different? I had never been to a church, so had no idea what to expect.

When we arrived in the parking lot, my eyes fixated on a massive cross with the figure of a man on it. He had nails in his hands and feet. Joanie grabbed me out of my trance and weaved us into the nicely dressed crowd of smiling people entering the church.

Inside, a man in a black robe walked on stage, and Joanie told me we had to be quiet, fold our hands on our laps and listen closely.

The man in the black robe spoke loud and forcefully. I kept hearing the words God, Jesus, Mary, the Lord and prayer. When boredom got the best of me, I took to picking the dirt out from the bottom of my shoes. Once I completed that task, I counted how many stained glass windows there were; then the different colors of cut glass in those windows. Joanie looked at me, taking pity on my restlessness and said I could go out in the hall if I wanted.

I jumped off the bench and quietly walked into the hall. The hallway ended with another cross with the same man nailed to it. Looking at him freaked me out, so I went to find the bathroom. Finding the correct door, I pushed it open and shut the door behind me, exhaling with my eyes shut. I opened them to find a row of women sitting on a bench, each with a baby sucking on their breast. Church had officially become the most awful place I had ever been. I stood there uneasily looking at them, looking at me, with their sets of breasts exposed. I had to do something, but I didn't have to pee, so I went to the sink, where I found a cool paper soap dispenser. After two minutes of soap play, I sheepishly walked past the breast feeders and into the hall. The man on the cross was intimidating me now, so I returned to my seat and Joanie.

As the sermon ended, the priest invited all the children down the aisle. I followed Joanie, knelt down on my knees like she did, opened my mouth like she did and he placed a white wafer on my tongue.

After church, they dropped me off at home.

Did you go to church with them often?
I must have gone at least seven or eight times.

Why did you continue to go to church with them if you didn't like it? Did you know you were Jewish at this point?
I had no religious identity. We celebrated everything from Easter to Passover. If there was something to celebrate, we had a dinner and my parents had another excuse to get loaded. I continued to go to church with them because I liked being included with her family.

I frowned and continued. *My grandmother would have been horrified if she knew I was on my knees praying to Jesus and taking communion. As I told you, she tried to instill in me to be proud of my Jewish roots.*

It was not your fault that you didn't have a religious understanding. You went to a Jewish summer camp, celebrated every holiday, and had Nazi beliefs thrust on you. It's important for you to erase the tarnish that Paul left on you about religion.
I didn't comprehend any of the Nazi stuff he spoke about. He wasn't a religious man, just an ignorant one. I also didn't digest the stuff I learned at summer camp. I just accepted my reality, day to day. I guess that was my religion—survival.

Rani continued to stay away from the house on most nights, but made a habit of telling Mom or Paul when she was leaving. I would hear her quickly blurt, "Going out, see you later," then run out the door and hop on her moped before any questions could be asked.

One evening she went into their bedroom to let them know she was leaving. She heard voices coming from the office next to their room. She opened the door quietly and peeked in. The room was dark with the exception of a film projector light glowing. She looked on the sofa to see several faces watching the screen. Rani didn't even know they had company over, so decided to leave without bothering them. As she closed the door, she glanced at the screen and her jaw dropped. A man had his forearm up another man's anus. She couldn't stop watching as the man pounded his fist in and out of the other man. She looked back at the viewers and caught Paul's eyes on her. She shut the door, her heart pounding and ran out of the house grumbling, "That was the grossest thing I have ever seen!"

She came home to sleep that night, figuring their guests would stay too late for Paul to come to her room. Before bed, she stopped into the kitchen for a glass of water. Paul appeared at the doorway and said with sarcasm, "Did you like what you saw?"

She glared at him, as she walked past him in the tight doorway.

———

As the Christmas holiday season approached, Paul seemed in good spirits. There were several days without his explosive anger or the nightly visits. We were busy creating and buying ornaments for our six-foot tree. Mom and Paul were out into the late afternoons buying gifts.

I woke early on Christmas morning and ran to our present-packed tree. I turned on the television to make sure everyone knew I was up. Rani, Paul and Mom followed shortly. It seemed that they dragged themselves out of bed for my sole amusement. I was especially curious about a massive mound covered by a king-sized sheet. As if he read my mind, Paul said, "That is for you."

All at once he pulled off the sheet, exposing the most shocking of gifts—a black Corvette go-cart. My eyes popped out of their sockets. I guess they knew better than to get me a moped, but this was way cooler! I ran my fingers along the Corvette logo on the side and asked if we could take it outside for a test drive. Paul insisted we open our other gifts first, but I knew everything else would pale in comparison to my new car.

With much urging from me, we all went outside. I sat in the perfectly formed little seat just made for my little self and waited for instructions. Paul said it could go about ten miles per hour, and I simply had to push a button to get the engine running. It held one gallon of gas, which was enough to get me around the neighborhood for a couple of days. I was told I could drive anywhere in our community, but not outside the main entrance.

With my instructions noted, I took a right out of our driveway. My bike was a forgotten memory; I had upgraded to four wheels. I sang, "Hot Child in the City" at the top of my lungs as I drove out of my cul-de-sac. Just a block from my house, I saw a boy I knew from the bus stop who also got a go-cart for Christmas. His name was Trip, and he had a yellow Volkswagen Bug. Truth be told, he was driving a chick mobile, and I knew he envied my wheels. He asked if he could try it out, and I told him he would have to wait until I broke it in.

Trip and I met a couple of times a week and raced around the community. It was a blast. When I wasn't cruising around with Trip, I had Sharon ride next to me on her bike.

I was driving solo after school one day and saw a lot of commotion coming from the community horse stables. If you lived in Sierra Vista and owned a horse, this is where it was kept. I drove the long dirt road that led to the stables and was met by a man holding a walkie-talkie. He said he liked my wheels. I beamed, proud of my wheels and asked what was going on. He told me they were filming an episode of *Vega$* and, if I wanted to watch, I could park alongside a line of buses that the actors sat in between filming.

I pulled over to the first bus and sat in my car to observe. There were two men talking to each other in front of an empty horse stable. They seemed pleased to see each other, shook hands, one guy said, "Hello, Dan Tanna," and then someone yelled, "CUT!" The men then walked away from each other, turned around, walked

back, and did their greeting all over again. After seeing this interaction four times, I started my engine to venture elsewhere. I
looked up and saw Dan Tanna standing in front of my Corvette.

"Fine car you have here."

"Thank you."

He asked if I liked the scene he just filmed. I told him it was
pretty boring. "You keep doing the same thing over and over. I
don't get how you get anything done."

He laughed heartily, put out his hand and introduced himself.
"I'm Robert Urich. Pleased to meet you."

I shook his hand and smiled back at him, not getting the joke.
He engaged me in conversation about my Corvette. I told him
everything I knew about my very cool car. He said I could stay and
watch the rest of the shoot if I wanted. I thanked him, but said I
had to be on my way. I hit the gas, leaving Mr. Urich in my dust.

———————

Rani, Mom and I were in the kitchen discussing school projects
when Paul came in and announced he was taking Mom to Tahiti as
a belated holiday gift. This was a surprise, since they had recently
been to the Caribbean and San Diego. Rani shot Mom a look but
knew that Mom had already relented. Enraged, Rani walked out of
the kitchen.

Later that night, Mom went to Rani's room and told her that
the trip was Paul's olive branch to make things right with her. "I
have to go and appease him for now. I am so full of hate and fear
of him, I can't say no. I also agreed so I could buy some time and
figure out how to get us away from him."

Rani stressed to her that we had to get out. "He senses things
are starting to come undone and I believe he thinks I am at the
root of it—which is pretty scary."

Mom said she would think of a way to get us out.

No matter how Mom presented the situation, this vacation was not going to sit well with Rani. She knew Mom would fall right back under his Svengali-like spell, forgiving and forgetting all the bad things he had done. Our escape was not happening quickly enough for her.

Paul went into Rani's room that afternoon and asked her to speak to Mom. He said he felt her slipping away and wanted Rani's help to bring her back.

"I will buy you a Mercedes. Just help her see that she should stay with me."

He was pleading with her and Rani was disgusted with the bribe and the closeness of him. "I'm fourteen. What am I going to do with a car?"

"Anything you want, I will get it for you."

She wanted him out of her room. "Okay, whatever, I will talk to her."

Rani was going to speak to her, but it wasn't going to be to his liking.

———

While in Tahiti, Mom met an optometrist from California. He was vacationing with his wife. She and Paul had drinks with them the first two nights. The second night, Paul excused himself to go to the restroom while Mom continued to talk with the couple. The doctor's eyes lingered on Mom's and without saying a word, he made it clear that he was interested in her.

All Mom could think about was how to get out of her marriage, and here was this nice, married man, making a pass at her, filling her with hope. Meeting a potential suitor on vacation worked for her once before—it just might possibly work again.

Mom saw the doctor poolside the next day and felt a spark between them. They made excuses to their spouses and met up at a private area of the resort for a quick drink. They discreetly connected several times during the week. He was enamored with her, and she was desperate for her next escape. The last time they met up, they passionately kissed and planned to be in touch when they got back home.

The night they returned from vacation, Mom couldn't wait to pull Rani aside and tell her the good news. She was bursting at the seams as she told Rani that she met a nice man in Tahiti. She said he was an eye doctor, that they had had several chance encounters at the resort and had even shared a kiss. She said she would show her photos of him when she got her film developed that week. She acknowledged that she didn't know what would come of it, but she had high hopes that this could be their ticket out.

A few days later, Mom came into Rani's room and showed her the photos of her and Paul with the optometrist. Rani was indifferent, not understanding how this man was the solution to our gigantic problem. She only wanted to know when we were getting out of the house and away from Paul. Mom told her it would just be a matter of time.

———

The following weeks, Rani's frustrations grew by the day. Mom was doing nothing to get Paul out of the house and the abuse continued. He yelled and beat her while they were both stupidly drunk. He continued to find Rani in her room on the rare nights she regretfully slept at home. Her patience was wearing thin and she continued to corner Mom to find out when she planned to get us out of the house for good. Mom continued to assure her that we would be leaving soon.

Paul came into Rani's room that night. She had come to her wit's end.

————

For my tenth birthday, I invited friends over for a swim party. Rani was in charge of overseeing us and making sure that no one drowned. We were playing in the yard when Paul interrupted us. He rallied us around him saying he had a fun party game for us to play. Because we were nine years old, we were still open to the idea of an organized activity.

Wearing his red sarong, thankfully tied tightly around his waist, he gathered us around him on the patio. "We are going to play Spoon Tangle." I immediately knew I would not be psyched about this game without even knowing the rules. I gave him a thin-lipped look, hoping he could read that I did not want to play, but he ignored me.

Paul placed us shoulder to shoulder in a straight line. He then held out two spoons that were connected by ten feet of red string. He explained that he was going to put one spoon through each of our bathing suits and we would have to figure out how to get out of the tangled mess using only our mouths. I winced at the thought of his putting the spoons in my friends' suits, but the situation was already out of my control . . . he had begun putting the spoon through the top of one girl's suit. It was an impossible game with impossible odds, but my friends seemed thrilled by the challenge.

Paul took his time putting the spoon through the armhole of the girls' one-piece suits as he ran his hand across their flat chests and out the other armhole. My face flushed, but I pretended to giggle along with my friends. After twenty minutes of fussing in our suits, we couldn't untangle ourselves. Paul thought this was quite entertaining and took photos.

By this time, Rani had almost fallen asleep with boredom. She watched us struggle for several minutes before she came over with a pair of scissors and snipped the strings in several places.

Rani, Mom, and me on
Christmas morning.

Driving my Corvette
go-cart on Christmas.

Paul's spoon tangle game at
my birthday party in our
yard. I am in the black suit,
Paul is in his red sarong and
Rani is sitting down.

Rani and the girls after she cut
the strings out of our suits.

CHAPTER THIRTY-TWO

Late April 1979

Rani sat up on her bed, her long legs hanging over the side of her yellow, floral comforter. She stared in the oval mirror just above her bureau, biting her already chewed, raw fingernails. She spoke under her breath to her reflection: *I have to do this tonight.*

She ran her fingers through her thick, brown, shoulder-length hair. She frowned at the now bushy sides that were her attempt at feathered, 70s-chic hair. She then erratically moved her hands back and forth, doing her best to make a mess of it. The last thing she wanted to do was look attractive. Her cheeks flushed with hate-filled anger. *I am going to do this tonight!*

At fourteen, she was six-foot-two inches tall, and her weight had propelled to 175 pounds, but she knew that no matter how heavy she got, she would never be strong enough to fight Paul. More frustrated than ever, she grabbed a small bag of potato chips from the diminishing stash under her bed. Pensively she looked back at the mirror, while ripping open the bag. She finished the bag in seconds and reached under her bed for another. She cringed as she remembered Paul's visit to her room the night before. . . .

He was intoxicated, as usual, and Mom was passed out. She cursed herself for not sleeping out again that week, so she could have avoided him. She saw the door handle turn, and he was at the side of her bed in

*three swift steps. Rani's eyes were already open, anticipating his next cal-
culated move. Her entire body tensed, cussing him in her head. Even though
she was equal in size, she still feared fighting him off.*

*He wore the red sarong around his waist and nothing else. He untied
it, letting it drop to the floor. For years she would not meet his eyes, but
that night she did with hate and fury through narrowed slits. He put his
finger to his lips, reminding her that this was their secret. For just a
moment she closed her eyes tight, goose bumps crawling along her skin as
she thought about his promise to kill her family if she told anyone. She
could not believe he had asked her to convince Mom to stay with him; he
was completely and certifiably crazy.*

*Paul took no time in lifting her cotton nightgown, searching for the top
of her waist-high bloomers—although unsuccessful, it was one of her new
defense tactics to keep him away from her. She continued to stiffen and
tighten every muscle in her body. He tugged down her bloomers, tossing
them on the floor.*

*He pried her legs apart, fighting her usual stubbornness. He unsuc-
cessfully tried to enter her. By this point she had mastered how to close her
vaginal walls so tightly he would never gain access. It didn't take long
for him to get frustrated and he leapt off the bed.*

*He was red in the face, like a rotten boy who had not gotten his fair
share of candy. He walked to the side of her queen bed, just where her head
met the pillow and thrust his penis in her face. This was the only way to
get him out of her room. She did what she had to do to make him leave.*

"Arghh," she screamed, trying to erase last night's memory. She
had to take matters into her own hands to get her family out of the
house for good. She realized Mom wasn't capable of doing it,
because she had procrastinated for far too long. What Rani was
about to do was life threatening, but she had to take a big chance
to make a big change.

At around five p.m. she heard Paul opening and closing the
kitchen cabinets. He was singing his favorite show tune, which
sent chills down her spine. "'S Wonderful, 'S Marvelous . . ." She

whispered to herself, *I would love to shove that eight-track tape down your throat!* He was embarking on supper preparations. This was the moment to drop the bomb. She couldn't wait any longer, and her intense hate for him fueled her courage.

She walked gingerly from her room, down the short hallway that led to the side entrance of the kitchen. *Thump-thump, thump-thump* . . . the pounding of her heart was so loud that she feared he might hear. She peered around the corner of the kitchen to see what he was doing, and like a predator in heat, Paul instinctively turned his head. His red sarong flipped open as he turned, exposing himself to her.

She stood there for a moment, her skin hot from the shock of being caught earlier than expected. She took a deep breath and screamed at him, "Mom had an affair while you guys were in Tahiti!"

His face turned beet red faster than she could spew out her words. His almost bald head turned as red as his face. His breathing quickened as his tanned, hairless chest started to expand and contract. His evil blue eyes pierced her to the wall, forbidding her to move, but she kept screaming at him. "She did this right under your nose while you guys were away! He was a doctor and he was there with his wife!" She continued to blurt out any other details she could remember that Mom had told her a week earlier, "Snuck off . . . Intimate meetings . . . they kissed passionately . . . she showed me pictures . . ."

She stopped when Paul's head looked like a pressure cooker ready to explode. She knew this would be the last straw. He put his hands on the end of the built-in, butcher-block cutting board and stood still. Then in one swift move, he pulled it out of its perfectly aligned space with the counter and threw it against the refrigerator.

Rani backed out of the kitchen, then turned around and ran to her room. She shut the door and fought the urge to lock it. She knew he would be coming for her. She crouched down on the floor, double-checking that her phone, the only one remaining in our four-thousand-square-foot house, was safely hidden under her bed. She said "Thank you!" to the empty room that Paul had forgotten about it when he had torn all the phones out of the walls.

Once again, she sat on the edge of her bed in front of her oval mirror. And waited. Rani knew this was the beginning of our own personal World War III. She hoped this was enough to make him leave or kick our family out of the house.

Then she saw his bare feet under her door. She was tense as she sat on the edge of her bed. Her sweaty hands grasped the comforter as she prepared to face whatever he had in store for her. The door swung open. Paul stood there with a photo album in one hand and a gun in the other. *What the hell?* Before she could blink, he was by her side. He pressed the gun against her left temple, threw the album on her lap and screamed at her to look through it. Rani froze and began to sweat from the force of the gun against her temple. She could not comprehend why she was supposed to look at photos. He yelled even louder, spit coming out with each word. "Show me who the fucking guy is or I will blow your brains out!"

Rani trembled and her hand shook as she tried to turn the pages of the album.

"Show me! Who the fuck is he?"

The photos Mom had shown her last week had been perfectly placed upon each page with memorabilia from Tahiti: a card from a restaurant, a napkin from a bar, the cover of a matchbook, random confetti and so on. Rani pointed to the photos of the doctor. That was all he needed. Rani clenched her eyes, terrified of what he intended to do with the gun. Paul snatched the album from her lap, removed the gun from her head and dashed out of the room. Shaking with fear, Rani listened to him scream, "Olivia! Olivia! Where. The. Fuck. Are. You?"

It was happening. All hell was breaking loose. She had not anticipated a gun. Nervously, she did as she had planned; she pulled on the wire that led to the phone under her bed and dialed 9-1-1.

————

I was quietly playing in my bedroom with Daisy when the vicious screaming began. I picked her up and ran to the corner that was farthest from the door, then sat there and hugged my boney knees to my chest. My dark, straggly hair covered my face to protect me from whatever was happening outside my room. Daisy licked my hands, providing comfort as I tightened my body into a human ball.

At church that Sunday with Joanie, I had learned that God was always listening. I called on every holy name I could remember, "Jesus, Lord, God, Holy One," Then I called on the names I remembered from camp, "Adonai, Elohim, HaShem . . . whoever is listening, please don't let him hurt her anymore." I rocked back and forth, wondering if I confused the Gods by calling on them all at once. I listened to the familiar, hateful words echo off the hallway walls and make their way into my room. "You bitch! Whore! Bastard kike! I am going to kill you, Olivia!"

Each word felt like an assault. I had to see what was going on. I slowly got up and walked toward my doorway. Daisy followed, but I told her to sit and stay. I walked down the long, cream carpeted hallway that led to Rani's room. It was empty. She slept out most nights now, so it was wishful thinking that she would be around. I then tiptoed toward the screaming and entered the front hall. Thankfully, Rani was there. She was standing with her back to me, obstructing my view. I carefully came around to her side, staying as close to her as possible, and saw Paul, sitting on top of Mom, straddling her long, thin torso. I saw a gun and I gasped.

No one heard me or even turned to look. I could see Mom's long, athletic legs kicking to break loose from his hold, her white stilettos kicking on the red tile floor. I moved to the other side of Rani to get a better look. Paul had his large hands around her neck, "You cheating bitch! Mother-fucking-whore! I am going to kill you!"

I looked down at my beautiful mom. Her always-stylish red hair was damp from tears and sweat. Her impeccably tailored white suit was now wrinkled and pulled open, exposing her large, braless bosom. My breath hitched as our hazel eyes met—mine wide with fear, hers bulging and red. I saw the resignation etched in her face—she had finally been defeated. After six long years, we were going to have to witness her death by this monster.

I glanced at the large window adjacent from us and caught the reflection of Rani and me. It was the first time I had ever seen our reflection together. I was less than half her size—a five-years-younger miniature. I tried to gain her attention with my eyes. I desperately willed her to look at me but she was frozen, standing erect with her fists at her sides. I thought for sure Paul was going to kill Mom this time. My face contorted at the thought of the newspaper headline: "Vegas Showgirl Strangled to Death—Children by Her Side."

For the first time in a long time, the beating was as real to her as it was to us. She was sober.

The doorbell rang. Rani exhaled deeply, as if she had been holding her breath for hours.

Paul released his hands from Mom's throat, grabbed the gun and quickly stood up. He looked down at Mom, spat on her face and barked, "Whore!"

He then casually walked off toward his bedroom. Mom's color came back to her face as she rolled over and gasped for air. I stood frozen, afraid to help, afraid not to. If Paul saw us help her, I didn't know what he would do to us.

Someone was now pounding on the front door. Rani hesitated for a second, thinking that Paul would go for the door, but then dashed to open it herself. A police officer walked in and quickly stepped around her to assess the situation. The house was eerily quiet. Paul walked out into the front hall looking calm and cool. Mom stood up, wiped her face, buttoned her jacket and remarkably became her tall and poised self. She walked over to the officer while holding her neck and in a barely audible voice she said, "He tried to kill me."

The officer looked at Rani and me, then ushered Paul outside the front door. They spoke for a couple of minutes and then came back into the house. Paul walked off to his bedroom. The policeman turned to my mom, taking in her red neck and face. He hesitated, looked toward the ground, shamed and flushed, "Ma'am, we have been here many times. I just think that if you fear for your life, then you need to get out."

And like all the policemen before him, he walked out the front door and left.

CHAPTER THIRTY-THREE

Memorial Day Weekend 1979

Rani was on the cusp of turning fifteen, and I had recently turned ten when Mom informed us she was going to Philadelphia for Memorial Day weekend. Rani gritted her teeth, completely mortified that she was leaving us alone with Paul for any substantial amount of time—especially since he had recently threatened Rani's life with a gun to her head. She retreated to her room, slammed her door, blasted Elton John's "Grey Seal" and hoped we would survive the weekend.

Mom went into Rani's room. "I know you don't approve, but you have to trust me on this one." Rani glared at her. She had lost her faith in Mom's effort to leave Paul.

"Paul thinks I'm visiting family, but my real agenda is to find us a place to live. We have to move back east. It is the only way to get out of here."

Rani felt a glimmer of hope. "About time, Mom, but I'm scared at the thought of staying with Paul in the house for the weekend. What are you thinking, leaving us with him?"

"Don't worry about that. He's taking you and Suzanne to the mountains with our friends for the weekend. I had them promise to look after you guys."

This bit of information didn't comfort Rani. She doubted that another family was coming and feared what Paul could do to us even if we weren't in our own house.

———————

After Paul returned from dropping Mom at the airport, he came directly to our rooms to tell us how excited he was about taking us camping. He said his son, Junior, was joining us, as well as another family. Rani became somewhat relieved when she heard from Paul's lips that another family was coming; it provided a sense of security that he surely wouldn't kill us with others around.

———————

The camping area was located an hour and a half away from the house. At our campsite, Paul seemed surprised that we were joined by two groups of people that we didn't know. Rani was happy about it because she felt safer with a larger population of people around us. The other groups had already set up tents in a semicircle around a large, cement fire pit.

Paul set up three green tents, completing a circle of six tents in our small campsite clearing. One tent was for Rani and me, one for his friends, and one for him and Junior. Between our temporary, tent homes sat a five-gallon water tank that everyone had chipped in for at the campsite registration. It was supposed to last our tented "community" for the next seventy-two hours.

Once we unpacked our weekend provisions, Paul took us on a hike. As we walked through the woods, all we could hear were the sounds of small, skittering rodents and the shutter of Paul's camera. Just before dusk we had gathered enough sticks for the fire and a significant amount of perspiration on our bodies, so we headed back to the camp for dinner.

Paul went into his tent and began singing a tune from *Cabaret*.

Rani and I looked at each other and rolled our eyes. Someone had lit the fire pit and small bits of fire were popping in the air. Paul came out of the tent holding two bottles of liquor and became the life of the party, mixing drinks for everyone.

Once the adults in our camp were happily buzzed and laughing about nothing in particular, Paul purposefully walked over to Rani. She was wearing a sour look on her face as he handed her a vodka and orange juice. She was tempted to say, "No thanks," but instead she grabbed it. She had smoked weed, but never had drunk alcohol. She took a tentative sip, and then gulped down the entire contents of the plastic cup, letting it linger over her mouth to get every last drop.

In less than ten minutes, Rani was drunk. She got up and tripped over the bottom of her blue overalls, just missing the raging fire pit. She babbled some nonsense about being clumsy as some stranger pulled her up and directed her toward our tent. She staggered at the tent's entrance and fell, knocking over the five-gallon water jug. The water gurgled out so rapidly that by the time it was picked up there was less than a gallon left. This sobered the campsite quickly. Everyone began yelling at her to go to bed.

Paul and Junior came to Rani's aid and carried her into the darkness toward the parking lot. They pulled open their car's back door and gently slid her in. Paul scooted in next to her, as Junior came around the other side and scooted in on the other side of her. Without regard, both father and son had their mouths on Rani's face, neck and ears. The last thing she remembered was thanking God that she was wearing overalls, knowing it would be too difficult to get them off.

The next morning Rani woke up in the backseat of Paul's Mercedes sedan. She was alone, the windows were fogged up, and the doors were locked. One of the buttons on her overalls was down and the other was still connected. She had a hazy recollection of fighting multiple hands off her, like a horse's tail swatting flies. She felt sick to her stomach and wanted to get home as quickly as possible.

———

Mom came back from Philadelphia looking refreshed and appeared to be clear headed. Rani pulled her aside the first moment she could and told her about the camping trip.

"It was horrible! Paul got me drunk, and I slept in the car. I don't remember anything from the whole night. We have to leave Paul and Vegas now!"

Mom told her that she rented us a place at the Jersey Shore and promised we would be leaving soon.

———

The next day Mom called James, her lawyer. She said she needed to get the divorce and a restraining order, so her husband could not kill her and her children. She met James in his office that week, and they called Paul at home. He wanted to hear her tell him, point blank, that she would be divorcing him—for real, this time.

Paul hung up the phone and went barreling into Rani's room.

"I meant it when I said I would buy you a car. Any car you want if you can talk your mom into staying with me!" Rani was so taken off guard that she just looked at him, stunned. When his words sunk in, she knew he was finally getting a clear picture; Mom was gaining the strength to make her own decisions, and Rani had become her voice of reason.

A week went by and there was not one mention from Mom about leaving. Paul's moods were swinging radically, and Rani knew he was capable of killing all of us any day. Her telling Paul that Mom cheated on him didn't break up their marriage, so she had to go to Plan B.

————

I was in my room half asleep when I heard Paul hitting and yelling at Mom. I walked toward the yelling, slowing my steps as I got closer to the front hall. I looked in Rani's room, and, as expected, she wasn't there. I peeked out just as he pushed Mom out the front door and slammed it shut behind her screaming, "Cheater! Liar! Fucking whore!" Mom banged on the door to be let in.

Feeling helpless, I crept back into my room—conflicted about whether I should let her in, but what would Paul do to me if I did?

I heard pounding on the kitchen sliders. I knew Paul had gone to his room, so I felt I was safe and ran to kitchen. Mom was wearing a tennis shirt and shorts; tears were streaming down her face and she was banging on the door for me to let her in. I felt his presence like icky goo on my body. I didn't even look behind me as he said, "You don't want to know what I will do to you if you let her in." He turned on his heels and left.

I looked at Mom and started to whimper. He was right—I didn't want to know what he would do to me. It was a larger-than-life threat. Mom disappeared from the sliders, and I heard her try to open the living room sliders . . . then those to the office. I followed her from window to window, wanting to let her in, but too scared of the consequences. She finally stopped and disappeared into the blackness of the night. I went to my room, collapsed on my bed and passed out from sheer emotional exhaustion.

Rani came home the next morning and found Mom sleeping poolside on a lounge chair. She let her in the house and tucked her into her own bed, instead of the one Mom shared with Paul. She was gearing up for Plan B.

Rani outside
check-in at
campgrounds.

Me observing
the campsite.

Olivia visits with her parents during her trip back east Memorial Day weekend.
Olivia is on the bottom left, her father in the middle, her mother on the right.
Her sister and her sister's husband are sitting above them.

261

CHAPTER THIRTY-FOUR

First Week in June 1979— Plan B

Disoriented, Mom awoke that morning in Rani's room. Rani was lying next to her, waiting for her eyes to open. She hastily put down her *Tiger Beat* magazine, put her face inches away from Mom's and said, "I can't keep the secrets any longer. Paul has been touching me for years, making me suck on his penis and had several failed attempts at trying to have sex with me. It has been going on for so long I can't remember when it started."

Mom's mouth dropped open and her fists tightened into knots as she slowly sat up.

"I never told you before, because Paul threatened to kill me— well, all of us if I ever told." She took a breath, almost frightened of Mom's reaction, but her emotions were building. "I am telling you this, because I hope this will finally make you realize you have to leave him."

Mom sat still, as if frozen in a state of shock. Rani continued, "I confided in Dad, by phone, months ago, but he brushed it off and didn't believe me." Rani was in tears now. "I can't take this anymore. We have to leave! He is going to kill us!"

Mom sat still, opening and closing her fists, digesting what Rani had told her. All at once, she leapt to her feet. Rani pleaded with her not to tell Paul, "He will kill me, PLEASE do not say that I told you!"

Mom didn't look back. She walked on autopilot to her bedroom, found Paul there and the volcano erupted. She pounded on his chest. "You sick bastard! My daughter? You are fucking sick! You ever lay a hand on her again, I will kill YOU! You hear me? Yes, I WILL KILL YOU!"

They screamed back and forth for what seemed like hours. For once, Paul kept his hands to himself, probably trying to figure out how and when she found out. When Mom was exhausted from screaming and hitting, she went into her closet and started throwing her high-heeled shoes at him. Paul left the room, and she had a screaming, apocalyptic fit on the shoe-littered floor.

———

Rani listened to the raging madness and sat in her room, nervously noshing on a candy bar. Even though she pleaded with Mom not to say anything, Paul had to know it came from her lips. His voice resounded in her head, "If you tell anyone, I will kill you and your family." She took a quick look under her bed, double-checking that her phone was plugged into the socket.

Mom's screaming finally ceased. The house was quiet for a short spell before she started screaming, her voice now hoarse, "How dare you touch my daughter! You sick asshole!"

Then it got quiet. A nervous, uncomfortable kind of quiet.

Rani and I bumped into one another in our private hallway on our way to Mom's room. It was always safer to hear her screaming, because we knew she was alive. I trailed just behind Rani. We found Paul sitting on top of Mom, on the carpeted floor in her dressing room, repeatedly slapping her face. Rani yelled, "Get off of her!"

He turned to look at her with hate written all over his face.

With that one look, he had told her that she had disobeyed him and she was royally fucked. I peeked around Rani and he eyed me for a second. I held my breath. He jumped up as we aligned ourselves to the wall and he darted past us out of the room.

It was the first time Rani had spoken up to him in a long time; I thought the shock of that had stopped him in his tracks for the night. We ran to help Mom off the floor. She was weary and her body was limp from hours of battle.

We heard his heavy breathing at our backs just as we had gotten Mom to her bed. He had his gun pointed at us. Rani ran out of their room as I stood there dumbstruck. It was like someone pressed a pause button; no one moved or said anything. Minutes passed and still, nothing. The horrific silence was broken by the sound of the doorbell.

I heard Rani say in a rushed voice, "That way. That way . . . in the bedroom. He has a gun!" Rani had let two policemen in. Fortunately, they were on duty in the area when she called and they responded right away.

I saw Paul put the gun in the closet and with a pleasant face, greeted the police officers as they entered the bedroom.

"We need to see your gun, sir."

Paul reached into the closet and handed it to them. Mom, Rani and I were crying as officer number one, holding the gun, took it out of the room and began speaking into his handheld radio. I could hear him reading a series of numbers to someone from the hallway.

Officer number two asked Paul several questions that I couldn't hear over the loud thumping of my racing heartbeat. Officer number one returned to the room and handed Paul his gun. He said, "This revolver is properly registered and you are authorized to have it in the house."

Both officers eyed my mom on the bed, then looked back at Paul. "Well, sir, we have no more business here," and they left the bedroom. Rani and I stood still, not sure of what to do, as the police let themselves out. Paul was the first to leave the room, and then Rani and I departed to our rooms. There was nothing left to say or do.

Like so many times before, the violence was cooled down by the arrival and departure of the cops. It was certain that Paul and Mom would engage in intercourse shortly and everything would be fine for the rest of the night. It was the way he operated.

Just before midnight, Paul came to Rani's room. He stood over her bed, his voice monotone as he said, "I told you I would kill you if you told your mom."

She had her response ready. "I told her it was Junior who was doing those things to me. Mom must have been confused. You know how she is always drunk. She misunderstood me."

Paul backed out of the doorway, seemingly convinced and said, "Never forget what I said, Rani."

———

Just two days after the gun incident, Paul's jealous rages resumed. He began drinking in the early afternoons and interrogated Mom when she walked in the door. "Who were you with? Where were you when I called you? Who did you whore around with today, you slut?" He said he knew she only wanted to divorce him because she was fucking someone else. His anger and jealousy were now completely out of control.

By the end of the week, Rani was too angry to help or defend Mom anymore. She became numb to Paul's screaming and beating on Mom. She still joined me in the foyer to witness the abuse, but did nothing to stop it.

CHAPTER THIRTY-FIVE

June 1979—Escape

It was a hot, June afternoon. I was playing in the yard with Daisy when Rani came out of nowhere and grabbed me by the arm. I didn't fight her, because she looked so serious. I just called Daisy to follow us.

She held my hand in hers as she pulled me through our yard and out the tall brown gate that led to the driveway. We stood, hand in hand, where Mom would eventually pull up and park her car. Rani was breathing heavily, her chest heaving. Her grip was steady and tight on my hand. We stood for about fifteen minutes before Mom's car pulled up. She got out of the car, slowly put her purse on her arm and looked at us curiously. Rani inhaled deeply and said, like an adult scolding a child, "We are leaving! With or without you."

She looked from me to Rani and said, "We have to move fast!"

We hurried into the house and assembled in the kitchen. I had no idea what was going on, but they were very rushed and excitable. Mom thrust two large green garbage can liners into each of our hands. "Pack as much of your necessities in these as you can. Two bags each. Meet me in the front hall in five minutes. Go! Quickly!"

We dashed to our rooms, knocking into one another in our narrow hallway. I went directly to my necessary items, as Mom instructed, grabbing my stuffed animals one at a time and tossing them into one bag. I opened my drawers and put some clothes into the other bag.

We met in the hall four minutes later huffing and puffing with our adrenaline racing. Mom came from her bedroom dragging two stuffed garbage bags of her own.

We had never seen her in such a panic as she ushered us out the door to the car. She sped out of Mira Monte Circle and out the entrance of Sierra Vista, saying we would be spending the night across town at her friend Norm's house.

"I'm going to call your grandparents and get you on a flight to Philadelphia tomorrow!" she said in a rushed, breathless sentence, while her hands tightly grasped the steering wheel. "I will stay behind for a couple of days to iron everything else out."

Neither Rani nor I said a word. Our lives were changing as of that moment. Mom had made her move and knew she had to get us out of Vegas for our own safety. We had to get out of Paul's reach as soon as possible.

Once we were safely at Norm's, Mom went to the vet with Rani to get sleeping pills for Daisy's plane ride. She dropped Rani back at Norm's and said she was going back to the house to get more of her stuff. She was certain Paul wouldn't be back yet from appointments he had across town.

When she arrived at the house, she ran around trying to collect any money she could find. At one point she became overwhelmed with how desperate she was and shouted through the empty house, "I will NEVER let this happen to me again!"

————

We were eating Taco Tuesday take-out at Norm's when Paul drove up. Mom had been nervously looking out the window at the driveway, anticipating his arrival. She ran out the door, not wanting him to enter the house or see us.

She screamed at him, "Please go away. I will call the police! Leave here this instant."

Without a word, he got in his car and left.

———

The next day Rani, Daisy and I were on the ten a.m. flight to Philadelphia. Mom had hugged us at the airport and said she would follow us shortly. She told us to go to camp, have fun and we would have a home back east when camp was over.

We arrived at the airport in Philadelphia and were eagerly greeted by Grandmom and Grandpop. We walked with Grandmom, hand in hand, down the airport terminal as she told us that the complex pool had just opened and was waiting for us to break it in. We arrived at the baggage claim area and waited eagerly for the last remnants of our Vegas life to slide down the carousel. Suitcase after suitcase dropped out, but there was no sign of our bags. The carousel stopped turning. We looked at each other, thinking the bags must have been mistaken as trash. Then we cried out in unison when our large green trash bag liners were tossed up and out of the center carousel shoot. People eyed us as though we were lunatics when we ran up and hugged our plastic bags.

My Grandpop said nothing as he grabbed the four bags in his two strong hands and hauled them out of the airport, while Grandmom, Rani and I waited for an airline attendant to show up with Daisy. Once we had her safely in our hands, Rani released a loud sigh of relief.

We were finally free.

Part IV

CHAPTER THIRTY-SIX

Olivia Sandy Berger Wagner Dushon

Olivia was in court two days after the girls departed. She sat before the judge, sandwiched between her attorney and his associate. James wanted to be certain that when Paul showed up crying for forgiveness, she would not and could not change her mind.

As if on cue, Paul showed up with bloodshot eyes and looking weepy. Olivia's lawyer stood so suddenly, his chair fell over. He said to the judge, "This time, today, there will be a divorce!" He then looked at Olivia and said, "What name do you want to walk out of here with?"

"My children's name, Dushon."

She left court with a $125,000 divorce settlement and her freedom.

———

Olivia called her mother collect from the courthouse payphone. "I have divorced Paul. I can't get into the details, but I had to leave him. I got a one hundred twenty-five thousand dollar settlement."

Her mother replied, "Whatever the situation, Olivia, you need to get a job. You put that money right in the bank or I will tell you what stocks to invest in. You hear me? You need to get good interest on your money to live on. You also need a job to support those kids and to keep your mind stimulated."

Olivia knew she was right, but couldn't think past the week ahead of her. "Please see the kids off to camp. I'm going to stay here and sort things out. I will be at my friend Norm's for a while and let you know where I go from there. I'll return to Philadelphia when I can. I rented a place at the shore for the month of August, so the girls and I will meet up there after camp."

––––––––

With the kids settled back east for the summer, Olivia was free to figure out what to do with her life.

She spent the next several days tying up loose ends and playing tennis at the SNTA. She played with her weekly tennis group and took up games with several other members. For the entire week after her divorce, she immersed herself in this safe, social atmosphere while getting her affairs in order.

Two weeks post-divorce, she met a tall, dark, handsome Arabic man named Dhakir. She had just finished her tennis match when he quickly approached her from the neighboring court. He casually asked her to join him for lunch. She thought nothing of it, assuming he was also a tennis member. They continued to meet over the course of two days for tennis and lunch. He was an easy conversationalist, and she was enjoying his attention and company. They spoke about general topics until day three, when he asked if she was involved with someone. She shared that she was recently divorced and was at a crossroads in her life.

After knowing each other for only three days, Dhakir invited her to be a guest at his home in Los Angeles.

She had been crashing at Norm's home for over two weeks, and it was a good time for her to move on. She had nowhere else to go and a block of free time on her hands, so she accepted Dhakir's offer. She thought that perhaps her meeting him at this point in her life was kismet and maybe he could be the one to take care of her and her family.

CHAPTER THIRTY-SEVEN

Los Angeles, Last Week in June 1979—Dhakir

Dhakir was a millionaire and lived in Douglas Fairbanks, Jr.'s old estate in Beverly Hills. The road that led to his house was so steep and narrow, Olivia held on to the dashboard for dear life. Once they reached the top of the hill and were in front of his house, Dhakir said, "Welcome to my home."

Alarmed, Olivia looked outside the car window and said, "How on earth do you get the car back down the hill? There is no space to turn around without falling down the side of this mountain."

He laughed and then pushed a remote control button in the car. The car slowly turned around via a Lazy Susan device that was built into the ground. Olivia was simultaneously impressed and shocked.

"Let my servants take your bags." Two dark-skinned men wearing white robes and turbans on their heads ran out of the house, claimed their luggage and swiftly walked back in. Olivia figured his home had to be incredible inside and was eager to see it.

Anticipating polished marble floors and expensive art, she was astonished when she was faced with a dark and dirty mess. The house reeked of rancid spices and body odor. Heavy drapes covered all the windows. As her eyes adjusted to the dark room, she saw several male servants scurrying around. Olivia couldn't understand what they were assigned to do, because they certainly weren't cleaning.

She kept her composure as Dhakir led her up the stairs to her private room. The room was sparse, but noticeably cleaner than the rest of the house. It had a queen bed with fresh white linens, a dark wood antique-looking dresser with a matching mirror, and a small but clean bathroom. She assumed this was where all his women guests stayed, because it was the cleanest room she had seen thus far.

He told her they would be going to the racetrack that afternoon. "In the meantime, feel free to walk around the grounds and make yourself at home." He gave her a peck on the cheek and closed the door behind him.

———

Olivia was happy to be out of the dirty house and found the racetrack exciting. Dhakir handed her a wad of cash and said, "Have fun." If this was his way of dismissing her, she had no problem with that and went off to place her bets. She sat among the crowds of strangers and screamed along with the other spectators for her horse to win. She left the track that day having doubled her money.

She was exhausted by the time they got back to the house. There were several businessmen waiting for Dhakir, so Olivia excused herself for the night and went to her room. She expected that he would either visit or summon her later for sex, but she was happy to disappear for the time being.

Dhakir neither visited her nor summoned her that night, and she slept peacefully.

———

The next morning she went downstairs to find Dhakir sitting in his dusty, newspaper-strewn dining room. There were several servants placing platter after platter of breakfast treats on a long dining table before him. A woman in a silk robe was sitting next to him and got up as Olivia entered the room. He touched the woman's hand, dismissing her. He glanced up at Olivia and smiled when she walked toward him. "Tonight I am taking you to a party. You will need to get dressed up." He also informed her they would be attending the races again that day. They ate breakfast together and were on their way to the track an hour later.

The track was as thrilling as the day before, but even more so, because she had gotten the hang of it. Dhakir handed her a roll of fifty-dollar bills, and she went to place her bets.

———————

Back at the house that evening, Olivia looked for Dhakir to ask him how "dressed up" she needed to be for the party. She saw one of the male servants steaming Dhakir's suit and asked where she might find Dhakir.

He didn't look up as he asked in a heavy accent, "Do you know what kind of party you are going to tonight?"

"No."

"It is an S and M party."

"What do you mean?" she asked, intrigued, "What kind of party is that?"

He explained that people would most likely be wearing black leather with their sex exposed and having intercourse. "Some whipping one another, some chained up, some in handcuffs, ropes, sex games."

"Oh! Oh, right. I was just wondering what I should wear. I didn't prepare for that kind of—"

He said that a black dress and high heels would be suitable if she had them. He said he was sure Dhakir would not expect her, or allow her, to participate.

"Well, that's comforting, I suppose." She smiled at him weakly, even though he had not looked up at her once. She went back to her room and pulled on a short black dress and the highest heels she had packed.

———

As they approached the party, which was held at a mansion as large as his, Dhakir said, "Do not leave my side while we are here." It was not a request; it was an order. She held his hand tightly, assuring him that she had no intentions of leaving his side.

They were greeted by a tall, boxy man in a business suit that motioned for them to enter the foyer. They walked down a long stretch of sterile white walls and marble tile toward another massive man standing in front of a single doorway. Dhakir and he nodded at one another, the door opened and they walked through a smaller foyer that spilled into a large, sunken room.

The smell hit her immediately; it smelled of damp sweat and post-coital. The room was dimly lit, but she could see the mass of barely dressed bodies intertwined or tethered. Her eyes were drawn to the far wall where someone was wailing while being whipped with a leather whip. Olivia winced as it struck the target, and then diverted her eyes to the center of the room where a naked man, lying face down, was tied to a human-sized dial. It was slowly turning clockwise while two women took turns pushing a phallus into his rectum. Olivia recoiled. She had seen some crazy things in her time, but nothing as bizarre as this. She grasped Dhakir's arm with the hand that wasn't already holding his in a death grip.

He guided her upstairs, following the seedy trail of naked

sadism around the house. Once they circled back to the main room, he guided her toward the exit. She breathed a sigh of relief that he didn't want to participate or linger.

Once they were back in the car, she looked at Dhakir's finely structured profile. He was incredibly handsome and strong. He had financial security, but lived a strange life. His filthy home, the racetrack, concubines in and out of his bed, suspicious meetings and S&M parties were enough to convince her that this was no life for her family. She planned to use the next couple of days to figure out where to go after she left his house.

———

The next afternoon Olivia won big at the racetrack. As she waited on line to collect her winnings, she was approached by the most gorgeous man she had ever laid eyes on. He was a dead ringer for Roger Moore. He spoke with her briefly about the races, and by the time she was one person away from the cashier's window, he had asked her out to dinner. She looked at him, thinking about the possibility of ditching Dhakir for the evening.

"I'd love to go out tonight, but I'm staying at a friend's home."

"No problem. I can pick you up." His green-eyed gaze made her knees weak.

"The house is at the top of a very steep hill and much too dangerous a drive."

She thought it would not only be dangerous for him to drive up that hill, but Dhakir would certainly not approve of her going on a date.

She was at the window by this time and collected her winnings. She then turned to him and said, "How about this . . . I will meet you at the bottom of my friend's hill at eight." She wrote Dhakir's address on the back of a racetrack ticket, handed it to him and melted into the crowd as he said, "My name is Bradford!"

———————

At 7:40, Olivia told Dhakir that she was meeting an old friend for dinner. She promised that she would not be home late. She dressed in a sleeveless white sundress and low heels, purposely trying not to look too dressy for a night out with an "old friend." He didn't seem pleased that she had made plans of her own, but was too preoccupied with his strange group of colleagues streaming in and out of the room to argue.

She slipped out the front door unnoticed at 7:45. She carefully walked down the steep drive to meet gorgeous Bradford. He was waiting for her at the bottom of the hill in a beautiful red Corvette.

They had a perfect first date. She was not only taken by his striking, movie-star looks, but he was also funny and endearing. It was the most normal date she had ever had. The time flew by as they laughed and discovered that they enjoyed similar hobbies: tennis, sailing, traveling. She knew she should get back to Dhakir's by around eleven. She checked her watch and told Bradford that regretfully, she had to leave. They shared a romantic kiss as they said goodbye at the bottom of Dhakir's hill. Not wanting the night to end, they planned to meet the next afternoon.

———————

Over the next three days, Olivia made up every excuse in order to spend more time with Bradford. On their third afternoon together, Bradford said he wanted to take her to Palm Springs for a night. Only because she had gotten away with so much already, she figured she could easily convince Dhakir that she was going to an old friend's overnight. He was so busy with his business meetings, he nodded to her that it was fine.

She packed a skimpy black dress, a bathing suit and a toothbrush, fitting it all in her large purse. She wasn't about to lug a suitcase down the steep hill. Dhakir eyed her as she went for the door and asked her where her overnight bag was. She smiled and said she would just share clothes with her girlfriend. This made the overnight seem less suspicious.

Bradford and Olivia shared an idyllic twenty-four hours in Palm Springs. It was just what she needed—a passionate getaway with a gentle, handsome, normal man. On the drive back to Dhakir's, she knew it was time to leave his place. She planned to get a good night's sleep and figure it out the next morning.

When she walked into the foyer, Dhakir was sitting in the den with his business colleagues. He dismissed them all when he saw her. He raised his voice slightly,. "I know you have been sneaking around with another man. How stupid do you think I am?"

Her happy-getaway-glow faded. She didn't know whether he had followed her, but she did know this was not going to end well. At that second, she wanted to get out of his house and back east as soon as possible.

She looked beyond Dhakir to the dank and musty room and knew there was nothing left to say. His eyes followed her, as she turned and walked up the stairs. Once at the top, she rushed to her room, jammed her clothes in her bag and called a taxi to meet her at the bottom of the hill. She walked out the door and went down the hill without saying goodbye.

The taxi arrived just as she got there. She jumped in, perspiring from the trek downhill with her heavy bag, "L-A-X please."

When she got to the airport, she called her sister and said the words she thought she'd never say again. "Betty, it's Olivia. I'm coming home."

Olivia would be home for her first Fourth of July weekend in seven years.

CHAPTER THIRTY-EIGHT

Philadelphia, July 1979— Betty

Betty was working on a "Most Eligible Bachelors" feature for the *Philadelphia Jewish Expression* newspaper. She sat at her desk and smiled, thinking about assigning Olivia to the one-on-one interviews with the bachelors. It was a surefire way for her to meet some nice Jewish men.

While Betty was weeding out man after man for her story and feeling quite pleased with herself for thinking of such an ingenious scheme, she was interrupted by a man's voice.

"I'm looking for Lorn. You know where he is?"

Lorn was her boss. Betty looked up and was struck by this good-looking, tall, blond, blue-eyed, very well-dressed man. She thought, *If he's friendly with my boss, he must be some kind of successful businessman.*

"Unfortunately, I don't know where Lorn is at the moment, but do you have plans for July Fourth?"

"Why," he asked warily.

"My sister is coming back into town, and I forgot to get her a date."

He glanced at his watch, sending a message that he was a busy man with important things to do. "I would have to check my calendar. I'm not sure if I'm free."

Betty smiled. "Well, let me tell you a bit about her." She stood up, pencil in her hand, as if she were about to present the pitch of her life. "She is a tall, redheaded beauty who is moving back from Las Vegas. She was a showgirl."

"Hmmm," he said, mulling over that alluring nugget of information. "I think I can certainly find a way to free up my schedule. My name is Jon William by the way." He approached her desk to shake her hand. "Pleased to meet you."

———

Mom flew into Philadelphia International Airport on July 2 and went directly to the Jersey Shore to secure her August rental. She hoped that a home by the ocean would be therapeutic for her and for us.

She then returned to Philadelphia, spent time with her family and went out on the blind date Betty had lined up for her. Jon took her to a hoity-toity Fourth of July party. She had a nice time, but her heart wasn't into it. For once in her life, she didn't want or need the security of a man in her life. She wanted freedom. She had a summer home; she had the stability of her family around her, and looked forward to a stress-free August with Rani and me.

CHAPTER THIRTY-NINE

Ventnor, New Jersey, August 1979

Grandmom and Grandpop picked us up at camp. They told us we were moving to the Jersey Shore with Mom for the rest of the summer.

Grandpop pulled up to a red brick building, which was tightly fit in the middle of the block between similar-looking homes. Grandmom told us Mom had rented the entire second level of the three-floor duplex.

We got out of the car and were hit with the refreshing salt air. The street had beach sand scattered along the curb. I instinctively took off my sneakers and walked barefoot onto the white sidewalk. We followed Grandmom up a set of concrete steps that led to a second-floor porch. There was a set of narrow, wrought-iron stairs on the side of the porch that continued up to a third floor. Grandmom told us that was someone else's private entry.

Inside, we found a den, a small functional kitchen, two bedrooms, one bath, and a laundry room that led out to a fire escape. A portable radio in the den was quietly playing Dr. Hook's "Sharing the Night Together" when our sun-kissed mom walked through the front door with Daisy and a bag of groceries.

She welcomed us into her arms and then offered me a dollar to run down to the corner store and get candy. Eager for my little bit of independence, I took her offering and ran out the door. I could see the boardwalk and the Atlantic Ocean just blocks ahead.

After just a couple days, I felt at home and was so happy that our extended family was all around us. It was obvious that Rani was in heaven. She looked relaxed, carefree and happy. Our days were filled with good music, walks on the beach, family visits and lots of rest.

———————

During the end of our second week, Rani was sitting in the den with our cousin Tori, singing along with the radio. Something outside caught Rani's eye, and she leaned back on the sofa to peer out our perpetually open front door. A black sedan had pulled up in front of our walkway. These kinds of cars were not often seen on our middle-class street. Even though she was curious, she just resumed singing along with Tori.

When the car door slammed a moment later, she bent back again, curious to see who got out of the sedan. Paul was standing at the curb. He looked up and down the property, and then he looked up. Their eyes met.

The blood drained from Rani's face as he put his finger up to his lips, mouthing, "Shh, it's a surprise."

Rani fell sideways off the sofa and onto the floor.

Tori said, "What the hell, Rani? Sit up!" She sat her upright against the sofa and looked out the door. She saw Paul and screamed, "Paul's here!"

Paul slowly walked up the stairs as Rani regained consciousness. She could not stop shaking her head as she watched him approach the doorway. She couldn't believe he was here. He was going to beg Mom to go back to Vegas—he would lie to her and tell her that he was going to change. She could only hope that Mom was strong enough to send him on his way.

Mom walked out of her room and looked at Paul standing in the doorway. They walked toward each other and hugged like old friends. He told her he had called her mother to find us, telling her that he *had* to see Mom again. Rani mumbled under her breath with her teeth clenched, "Grandmom, if you only knew! Don't give in, Mom."

———

I was lazily walking back from the corner store with pink taffy hanging out of my mouth and swinging a bottle of laundry detergent in my right hand. I knew there were two loads of laundry wanting to be done, so instead of using the front door, I ran up the back fire escape stairs that were directly off the laundry room. I dumped soap into the washer and turned on the machine. I heard Donna Summer's "Hot Stuff" playing on the radio, which we now kept on twenty-four hours a day. I grabbed the taffy from my mouth and turned to enter the den. I took one step and froze.

Paul slowly walked toward me, crouched down to my eye level and said, "Hi, sweetheart." My eyes darted directly behind him to see my sister and Tori staring wide-eyed. I let him hug me, keeping my arms at my sides. I was frightened by the sight of him, and everything seemed to move in slow motion. We walked into the den, with his hand on my back. I heard him say something about visiting, but his words became muddled in my head. I felt like I was standing beside a ghost—the villain in a movie who is shot ten times and comes back to life.

After standing next to him for an awkward moment, I turned away from his hand, went back through the laundry room toward the fire escape. I crouched in the corner of the open stairwell, hugging my knees tightly to my chest. I thought if I could disappear, he would go away.

I didn't move until dusk, which was when my tummy began to growl. I cautiously tiptoed into the apartment. It was quiet with the exception of the radio. The den light was on, but no one was around. I wanted to get out quickly, so I grabbed money from the counter and ran out the front door. I did not stop running until I got to the pizza shop, three blocks from our place. I was out of breath as I ordered water and a slice of pizza.

I took my food and walked an additional four blocks to the boardwalk. I watched the ocean eat away at the sand. I took bite after bite, tasting nothing, but satisfying my hunger.

I came home after dark and saw that Mom's door was closed. I heard noises, so I peeked in. Paul was on top of my mom, both naked, having sex, with the blankets pushed to the floor. I was able to shut the door gently before my knees buckled. I felt pizza rise to my throat and crawled out the front door. I retched over the side of the porch.

I was not steady on my feet as I continued to crawl past the front door to find Rani. She would know what to do. Rani and Tori had become friendly with Kyle, the skinny twenty-one-year-old waiter who lived one level above us, and I was certain she would be there. I held on to the railing and climbed up the narrow iron stairs, my heart pounding. I peeked through the screen door and saw Rani and Kyle making out on his dirty, brown-checked sofa. Tori was nowhere in sight. My heart sank.

I slid down the narrow staircase and slumped against the front porch. My head fell against the railing. I started to cry, which graduated into heavy sobs. I screamed out loud to our deserted street, "I AM TOO YOUNG FOR THIS SHIT!" Things were spiraling out of control in our new world. I cried until there were no tears left. I fell asleep on the porch to the sounds of moths hitting the front porch light.

————

**It was not until you left Las Vegas that you realized Paul
was a bad man?**
*I guess so. When I saw him that day—it frightened me. It was like see-
ing Michael Myers in the movie Halloween without the mask and knife,
but just as scary.*

*I paused. When I was in the thick of it for six years, I accepted my
reality. Even when we were escaping to move back east with our garbage
bags, that was just the excitement of that particular day. I only knew that
I was experiencing a sense of stability at this beach house, and when he
showed up, it was just plain scary.*

**You no longer have anything to do with him. It has been
eighteen years and you have moved forward with your life.
You are getting married and your life is your own to make
of it what you want it to be. You are ready.**
Yes, I guess I am. I sighed with relief. A genuine smile formed on
my face and I felt good. Really good.

————

I woke to the sun stinging the side of my face, which was raw and
red. I was hot, tired and dehydrated. My brain pounded. I went
inside the den to put my face in front of the one electric fan we
owned. It was eerily quiet; even the radio that was never turned off
was off. I peeked in my room and found my sister asleep. I fearlessly swung Mom's door open, not sure of what to expect, and she
too was asleep—and more important, she was alone. I knew right
then that Paul had traipsed back to Vegas and we would never see
or hear from him again (and I was right!).

I turned on the radio and Bruce Springsteen sang, "The screen
door slams, Mary's dress waves, like a vision she dances across the
porch as the radio plays . . ."

I took the leftover change on the kitchen counter and left for the corner grocery.

The sun was penetrating, sunburn-hot now and hitting me from every angle. My face felt tight from the salty traces of my tears. I forced myself to take a deep breath in and out, as a car sped by blaring, "I need a lover who won't drive me crazy."

I laughed at the irony, and slowly, my walk turned into a skip as I made my way to the corner grocery.

CHAPTER FORTY

Connecticut, July 2011

My mom and I were sitting on the front steps of my house discussing this memoir. I was confident she had no idea how much, or how badly, Rani and I were molested all those years in Vegas, and I didn't intend to rehash it with her right then. We were simply talking about how crazy of a time it was—in the general sense.

All at once, she put her hand on my knee, gazed straight ahead at my neighbor's perfectly manicured lawn and said, "I am really sorry . . ."

Those simple, four words hit me in a way I never would have expected.

Acknowledgment

Validation

Compassion

Forgiveness

Closure

My heart seemed to swell in my chest. I could barely get out the words without choking on them. "It's okay, Mom, really. It was another life ago."

And it was.

The Aftermath

OLIVIA BERGER DUSHON WILLIAM

Mom and Jon tied the knot in June of 1980. Just after the nuptials, Mom found me sitting in an oversized chair holding my bridesmaid's bouquet (a single lily). She smiled and said, "You can call Jon 'Dad' now if you like. I'm sure he would love that."

"'Jon' will be just fine, Mom. I think I will just call him 'Jon.'" Although I was happy for her and liked Jon a lot, I was not interested in calling anyone "Dad" ever again.

Jon and Mom have been happily married for over thirty years. She enjoys life, her career as a real estate broker, traveling, spending time at the Jersey Shore, and visiting her grandchildren regularly. As a matter of fact, she is the most wonderful, energetic and loving grandmother my sister and I could have ever imagined. Rani, my mom and I visit my brother yearly in Las Vegas and spend nearly every minute of those visits laughing.

RANI LYN DUSHON

When we moved back to Philadelphia from Vegas, Rani was entering tenth grade. She switched her name back to Rani Dushon and began life as a conventional teenager. She graduated high school and then attended the University of Arizona, where my brother enrolled a year later. Rani and Todd reunited and became best friends at college.

While at U of A, a casting crew came to campus seeking extras for a movie titled *Revenge of the Nerds*. They were looking for heavy-set girls over six feet tall or girls under five-four with huge boobs. Rani tried out. She was called the following week and was told she had a "key role" as an Omega-Mu, the nerd sorority. When she got on set, she learned she would also play the girl-friend of one of the leads—Booger—(need I say more?), and they danced together in the first party scene. This was just one of the joyful events that helped Rani fulfill her childhood dreams during her college years; or better said, she was allowed to be a kid for the first time in her life.

When she was twenty-six, she went to Mom and Jon's home one afternoon to visit Daisy. Daisy had been diagnosed with epilepsy, due to the years of abuse Paul had inflicted upon her. Rani would check on her weekly. Jon told Rani that Daisy was hit by a car just an hour earlier. He said that Mom had gotten mad at her and let her out of the house. She was hit just 200 yards from their home.

Rani was horrified. Mom heard her crying and came into the kitchen. Rani pointed at her and blamed her for Daisy's death— and then all the horrendous memories of her childhood came rush-ing back. She screamed, "You killed my dog and you killed my childhood!"

Rani went to therapy and threw out all the mental baggage she had harbored for the past eleven years. Rani also cried off and on for weeks over Daisy's death. It was nearly a year before she could talk to Mom again.

Rani fell in love and got married in 1991. She had her first daughter in 1993 and her second in 1998; coincidently the same age difference as between Rani and me.

In March of 2001, Rani opted for weight-loss surgery. She had been married for a decade to a man who loved her unconditionally. She knew she could finally take the armor off, because she trusted him completely.

She and her family spend their time between Philadelphia and summers at the Jersey Shore.

TODD MARCUS DUSHON

Todd graduated from the University of Arizona with a law degree and moved to New York City to practice. After six years he wanted a change. Opportunity knocked for him in, of all places, Las Vegas.

Ironically, the day in 1994 when Todd moved to Las Vegas, Paul died of prostate cancer. My mother's friend in Vegas called to let her know.

Todd has practiced law there for over fifteen years. He is happily married with three children.

I phoned my brother several times while I was writing this memoir—sometimes to ask questions about specific dates, other times to rehash a memory. The following is from one of those conversations:

I said, "You know, Mom's pregnancy with Rani was a nice surprise, but she got pregnant with me as an excuse to hold their marriage together. Worse than that, I didn't even work."

Todd has always had a great sense of humor. In fact, he and my sister are two of the most hilarious people I know. Nevertheless, I was not prepared for this analysis.

"What the heck are you complaining about? Rani was a blissful surprise, you were a planned tactic, but I was a complete mistake."

We paused for brief moment, and then burst out laughing.

SUZANNE

After Mom married Jon, I adapted quickly to my happy, new environment.

I attended Arizona State University and studied at the Walter Cronkite School of Journalism. I graduated in 1992 with a Bachelor of Arts degree and was eager to move to New York City and do something incredible with my life.

During my first couple of years in NYC, I worked as a film publicist, then landed my dream job in magazine publishing, got engaged, completed an entire year of therapy, and married Bradley.

We had just returned from our honeymoon when my mom called with the news that she had ovarian cancer.

I asked one question: "Okay, how do we get rid of it?"

She told me of the treatments to come, and I knew she was going to make it through—my mom was indestructible, wasn't she? She had made it this far, and there was no way any higher power was going to take her from my sister and me now; there was so much more mothering she owed us. Lo and behold, she beat cancer.

After six years in publishing, I reached the pinnacle of my career, and Bradley and I decided to start a family.

My first child was born via C-section in October 2001. I had a brief face-to-face encounter with my beautiful son before I was rolled into a recovery room.

Two monumental things happened over the next twenty-four hours:

1. Around 1:30 a.m., in the dark recovery room, I woke up, instinctively feeling a pair of eyes on me. I looked to the hallway and saw a dark figure. The bright light behind the person made it impossible to make out a face. My entire body was restrained from the anesthesia, so I could barely move to ask

who it was. My heart began to race. The person walked slowly toward me, looking like an angel with rays of bright light streaking from behind. As the figure reached my bedside, I realized it was my mom. I cried for so many reasons.

If I had lost her to cancer, this was how she would have come for the arrival of my firstborn. She was my mom, and I was lucky to have her. She was *now* here for me, to love me and provide the tenderness only a mother can share with a daughter who had just given birth to her first child.

2. The day after my son's birth, a nurse brought him to my bedside from the nursery. She asked me if I would like to breastfeed. I took my son in my arms and thought about his first hours on this earth. I thought of his being forced to suck on my nipple, and the most awful chills ran up and down my body. The most natural and beautiful thing I could do with my new baby had been scarred by my childhood. I simply could not stand the thought of it. I turned to the nurse and chose the safety of humor: "We could both use a bottle. I'll have a Riesling, and this one, formula."

Today I feel complete with a family of my own. I am truly blessed to have a son and daughter that I find to be amazing on every level. They are smart, beautiful, confident and incredibly fun. Motherhood is the most gratifying and wondrous ride.

I know how fortunate I am to have the life I now have. I chose my path and I'm living it to the fullest.

A Message from the Author

I have always wanted to write a great story. The best one has been living inside of me, but until now, I couldn't write it.

Why now? We are living in an enlightened time of history. Although usually perceived as a good thing, with the overabundance of information we have become satiated, even jaded when it comes to stories of domestic and child abuse. One of my concerns in writing this book has been that people might think, "Oh boy, here's another victim." There is a continuum of victims daily, weekly, yearly; each of these victims has a story. I wanted to share mine because each time one of these stories is published, someone, somewhere realizes that he/she is not alone. Abuse crosses all lines—socio-economic, racial, religious, ethnic, gender. Perhaps the happy faces you see when you are out shopping, sitting in a PTA meeting, ordering Starbucks or eating a giant turkey leg at Disney have a story they don't feel they have the right, or the courage, to tell.

When I first pitched my story to an agent, she said, "Love it, but *that part* is not interesting. Unfortunately, it is *commonplace.*" I was floored. Where have we come as a society when we lack interest in or presume that stories about suffering atrocities are not interesting to the general public simply because it has become "commonplace"? And what does it say about a society where it *is* commonplace?

Besides the obvious (Showgirl/Vegas), what sets my story apart from others?

My past does not label or define me. It is part of who I am. It has been put in its proper perspective through the greatness of therapy and my determination to move forward. The message I wish to impart through this book is that bad things happen to good people, but a positive, even wonderful life can emerge nonetheless. Today I am a happy, healthy woman who followed a very different path from where I originated. I have a loving family of my own. I have children who love me, and I love them back.

This story revolved around my mother, my sister and me in the 1970s. It was a dark time, yet today we maintain a close relationship and speak several times a week. I share my day, a laugh, or debate insignificant things such as how best to roast a chicken or my inability to do my daughter's fourth-grade math. During the time I was writing this memoir, 2009–2013, I called each of them at least two or three times a day. I was relentless about getting my timeline and facts correct to the best of our collective memories; hence the term "memoir," and in this case, "collective memoir"— my mother's, my sister's, and mine.

I spent hours interviewing my mom for thorough, accurate, intimate details. (She may argue that "interrogating" was a more apt description of what I put her through.) On one of these occasions she belted out over the phone, "Do you have any idea how hard this is for me? The rehashing of all of this . . . "

I immediately apologized, yet felt crushed by her selfishness, or perhaps by my own—our emotions had become intertwined by this point. We said goodbye, and I then responded to the dead phone receiver, "Yes, Mom, I do have an idea of how hard it is. I was there."

Now that I am a parent, I can understand how complicated my mother's life was during that time and can better comprehend how we ended up in the hell we did.

As I said at the very beginning, if your story is like ours, or worse, I hope you will be encouraged to get the help you need to sort it out and leave it behind you—don't let the years that robbed you of your past rob you of your future.

Acknowledgments

I was told that once I found the right person to edit my book, I would just know. In early 2013, my dear friend Lora Krulak put me in touch with editor Shari Johnson; it was harmony from our first phone call. She understood me, my mother and family like she was one of us. She embraced me, and my story. She provided me with a unique friendship that will bond us forever. I thank her for all of her time, patience and love of words.

To my early-on readers, Sue Westphal, Marla Daniels and Pamela Davis, my thanks and love to you for not judging me and my story, but instead providing me with wisdom on how to make it better. I doubly thank Sue and Marla for their unwavering support and for making me a better parent each day with their motherly advice and zest for life. I am eternally grateful to *all* my friends and family who unselfishly discussed the book's progress with me, but respected that I was not ready to share all of its content. You all make my world that much better.

I thank my three Philly girls: Ilene, Bonnie and Kathy. By sharing your teen years with me, you gave me an enormous amount of childhood normalcy . . . only now will you realize how important that was to me.

Thank you to Jon, my stepfather, for coming into our lives, loving my mom the way she always deserved to be loved, and for taking us under his wing.

To my beloved Aunt B, thank you for your support and the heartfelt memories for my book. You are gone, but you will never, ever be forgotten. I miss you every day.

Thank you to my incredibly supportive brother who bore my random calls on specific childhood facts and provided, as always, much-needed hearty laughs.

Thank you to my mother. Unveiling the wounds in this book was difficult and painful for her, yet she supported my efforts 100 percent. She agreed that this was a hard story to share, but one that should be told. She is one of the most remarkable people I will ever know in this life, and she has been a positive, supportive, loving force since we moved back from Vegas.

I thank my sister—my unsung hero—in more ways than I could count. Without you, I would never have been able to pen this story. You gave me the daily fire to keep writing. You shared deep, dark, "sofa king" hideous secrets that documented some of the worst events of our story. You are brilliant, beautiful and amazing. You make me laugh every day, and you are a gift to everyone around you.

I thank my children, RBK and JSK, who patiently dealt with mommy as she wrote and wrote, every free second for the past few years. I thank them for showering me with happiness every day. They have allowed me to experience a childhood through their eyes, and it has been simply incredible.

A generous amount of gratitude goes to my husband for his patience and devotion. He experienced the highs and lows of my year in therapy . . . and we weren't even married yet! Where most men would have run, he stuck by my side. He has been my rock for over twenty years. He read the *many* final drafts of the book and suggested some structural changes that I was reluctant to make, but I did because in the end, he was right. Thank you for supporting me on this epic journey and for being the most caring husband and father.

And last, this is a shout out to all the naysayers . . . those whom I have heard over the years preach their unfounded scientific theories: "Children who come from abusive households cannot live a normal life." Without you, I would not have had the chutzpah to pen my story. You are right about one thing. My life is not normal. It is now extraordinary. It is filled with perspective, love, family and friends. Perhaps most important, it is filled with laughter.

About the Author

Suzanne R. Krauss began her career as a junior film publicist for The Samuel Goldwyn Company in New York City. She then moved into magazine publishing for some of the largest brand names in the U.S., including *YM* and *Cosmopolitan*. She invented the fashion accessory Zip'em in 2010 and is currently a marketing consultant. Suzanne lives in Fairfield County, CT, with her husband and two children. Visit her website: www.tovegasandback.com.